LANGUAGES AND CHILDREN— MAKING THE MATCH

Foreign Language Instruction in the Elementary School

HELENA ANDERSON CURTAIN
CAROL ANN PESOLA

SANDRA J. SAVIGNON
Consulting Editor

ADDISON-WESLEY PUBLISHING COMPANY

Reading, Massachusetts • Menlo Park, California • New York
Don Mills, Ontario • Wokingham, England • Amsterdam • Sydney • Bonn
Singapore • Tokyo • Madrid • San Juan

Illustrations by Grace Meyer

For the *Peanuts* and *Family Circus* cartoons used in this book, grateful acknowledgement is made to United Feature Syndicate, Inc., and Cowles Syndicate, Inc., respectively.

Library of Congress Cataloging-in-Publication Data
Curtain, Helena Anderson.
  Languages and children, making the match.

  Bibliography: p.
  Includes index.
  1. Languages, Modern—Study and teaching (Elementary)
—United States. I. Pesola, Carol Ann. II. Savignon,
Sandra J. III. Title.
LB1578.C87 1988   372.6′5   87-31885
ISBN 0-201-12290-1

Contents

Contents

Contents

Acknowledgements

It is impossible to list the many professional friends and colleagues who have encouraged, supported, and advised us during the progress of this book. Without your initial responses to our outline, your suggestions based on numerous drafts of each chapter, the ideas and insights you so generously shared, and especially the encouragement you provided when we needed it, this book could never have been written. We are deeply grateful, and we hope the book is worthy of you.

There are also special people in our personal lives who have made this all possible:

Tony Curtain—chief cook, copy editor, and encourager
Karen Weiss—detail chaser and steady helper "exceptionale"
Jacki Servi Margis—key wordsmith and designer
Sara Zaidins—artist, reader, and typist par excellence
        and
Kristin and Airi Pesola, who complained so little and gave up a lot
        and
Marta Muller and Christi Valek, who contributed in their own ways.

Thank you.

Preface

Languages and Children—Making the Match is designed both as a methods text and as a practical guide for school districts and teachers. It is intended for those preparing to teach languages at the elementary school level (grades K–8), for practitioners already involved with languages for children, and for teachers, parents, and administrators engaged in the planning or in the evaluation process.

The book has been written by practitioners primarily for practitioners. We have included the historical and theoretical elements that have been important to us in our own classroom practice and that we regularly share with our students and in workshop and in-service sessions. While we do not claim to have placed the teaching of elementary school foreign languages in a comprehensive theoretical or historical framework, we believe strongly that classroom practice must be built on a basic understanding of theoretical and historical issues. An understanding of theoretical issues can help teachers to know why certain strategies are successful; it can empower them to be effective planners of curricula and interpreters of the program and its methodology to fellow teachers, administrators, parents, and the public.

The primary concern of this book is with the acquisition of a new language by *majority-language speakers* who are not living in an environment in which their new language is commonly spoken. Students in bilingual and ESL programs, by contrast, are minority-language speakers in the process of learning the majority language, and they have complex needs in their adjustment to a different society—needs which we have not attempted to address. We believe, however, that the principles and strategies for language teaching offered in this book are also applicable or adaptable for teachers working with limited English proficient (LEP) students.

Many of the specific teaching suggestions presented here will be of special value to teachers who work in the first years of elementary school programs that provide foreign language instruction for less than half of the school day. Since so many programs across the country are new and are staffed with teachers who are relatively inexperienced at the elementary level, and because many teachers find it especially difficult to develop activities for meaningful communication in the early stages of second language acquisition, we believe that this emphasis will be the most helpful to the majority of readers. All of the activities can be extended and adapted to higher levels of language complexity and development and to other program models.

The term *elementary school foreign language* is used in this book to mean all types of non-native language programs for children. *FLES*, which in the past has sometimes had a broader interpretation, is used here to indicate a particular program, as described in chapter 3. The authors spent many hours discussing the issue. We considered such terms as *child L2*, *elementary foreign languages*, *elementary second languages*, *ELL (Elementary Language Learning)*, *world languages*, and use of the word *languages* alone.

No alternative is without its problems or potential for confusion. The term *foreign language*, while still widely used, has negative connotations of alienation for some parts of the community. *Second language* is used in some discussions to mean acquisition of the majority language by minority-language speakers. The term *second language* is sometimes inappropriate because a number of students in these programs may actually be acquiring a third or even a fourth language. *World language* can be interpreted to mean only the relatively few languages that are widely spoken outside of the residence countries of native speakers. The term *language*, when used alone, is easily confused with English language arts.

As so often happens in discussions among elementary school foreign language teachers, we have decided that the word "foreign," however problematic, is a useful one; thus we use *foreign* for most purposes when referring to the programs that are the focus of this book. Where they appear, the terms *second* and *target* language are used synonymously with the term *foreign language* throughout the text.

This book has been written in the spirit of sharing, which is such a marked characteristic of elementary school foreign language teachers when they get together. Many of the teaching ideas presented here have been shared with us in classes and workshops, and we continue to learn daily from our colleagues and from our students. We hope that *Languages and Children—Making the Match* will serve as a useful resource for teachers, supervisors, and planners, and that it will make a contribution to the number and quality of foreign language programs for children.

Introduction

This book is about the many ways in which foreign language learning with skilled teachers can enrich the world of the child. There are keys, old and new, to unlock the magic that new languages hold for children, but they have been hidden away in unlikely places, treasures collected at a time when they were not valued and left to await discovery.

With this book we offer keys that we have found as we have imagined what foreign languages for children might mean and what their potential might be for all children in our schools. These keys may be used by teachers already working with children, by those preparing to teach, and by administrators, parents, and others engaged in the planning that brings successful language programs to life and keeps them vital.

Some keys are found in the experiences of the 1960s, when elementary school foreign language programs were popular and numerous. Some serious mistakes were made during that boom-time for languages: planning was often inadequate, many teachers were poorly prepared, and goals were frequently unrealistic. By acknowledging and analyzing these mistakes, we can avoid their repetition. The 1960s left us with success stories as well, and from those experiences come examples that can guide our planning for the future.

Research in second language acquisition and in related fields, much of it done since 1970, offers other keys. Not all can be translated directly into classroom practice, but the insights provided by research can help us to evaluate programs, materials, and methodology more effectively and consistently. Perhaps the most significant key to the elementary school foreign language learning experience is a dramatic new shift in emphasis from grammar to communication in current classroom approaches. This new emphasis on communication as the governing idea in designing curricula and in classroom practice is reinforced both by research and by the experiences of successful elementary school foreign language teachers.

The emerging body of information about research and classroom practice encourages a reexamination of the assumptions and the rationale associated with foreign languages in the elementary and middle school. The FLES of the 1960s was closely associated with the audiolingual method, behaviorist psychology, and structural linguistics. Much of the current material available to teachers and school districts designing programs and curricula is still rooted in the assumptions and practices of audiolingualism. Research in language acquisition and communicative teaching and classroom practices based on that research can contribute significant new dimensions and unlock challenging new opportunities for children.

Communication is the key element, the fundamental principle of this book. It unifies the guidelines offered and the methods and materials described. Communication has long been a stated goal of the language teaching profession, but it has traditionally been cast in a secondary role to grammar as an organizing principle. The experienced teacher and the beginner alike face the challenge of adapting the methods of the past to a communicative emphasis and of developing new strategies to encourage comprehension and communication. There is no age level at which the focus on communication is more appropriate than that of the elementary school pupil, and teachers who make the adjustment can expect exciting results. This book suggests guidelines and examples to assist the teacher in creating a classroom in which communication has the highest priority.

The principles on which this book is based are summarized in the Key Concepts for Elementary and Middle School Foreign Languages printed below. They have been shaped by the collective experience of many classroom teachers, and they offer a classroom application of what many researchers have learned about languages and children. These are the keys, some new and many familiar. The door of opportunity—the magic of language acquisition—awaits their use.

KEY CONCEPTS FOR ELEMENTARY AND MIDDLE SCHOOL FOREIGN LANGUAGES

1. Children learn foreign languages best when their native language is not used for instruction.

2. Successful language learning programs emphasize comprehension rather than speaking at beginning stages and use the insights of second language research in the development of all aspects of the program.

3. Successful language learning occurs in a meaningful communicative context: social and cultural situations; subject–content instruction; games, songs and rhymes; experiences with arts, crafts, and sports.

4. Successful language learning for children is organized in terms of concrete experiences; considerable planning should go into the use of visuals, props and realia, and hands-on activities.

5. Successful language learning activities for children incorporate opportunities for movement and physical activity.

Chapter 1

Making the Case for Elementary School Foreign Language Programs

For foreign languages, as for any content area seeking a secure place in the elementary school curriculum, offering a convincing rationale holds a high priority. School boards and parent organizations need reasons and evidence before making a commitment of time and resources to a new program, and existing programs can be called into question at any time. Almost every "public" occasion—from class or program coverage by the media to party conversation—holds the potential for the common, recurring question: "Why *should* children learn foreign languages in elementary school?"

A rationale, like a program philosophy, must be developed to meet the needs and priorities of the local school and of the community that it serves. It will address both the reasons for language learning and the basis for choice of language(s) to be taught; it may also deal with the methods selected for instruction. The teacher or group developing a rationale can draw from a variety of resources to complete the task; it is the purpose of this chapter to give direction to the search for resources and to give guidance for the shaping of a rationale.

During the surge of popularity for elementary school language programs in the 1960s, it was common for schools to launch programs before setting rationale and goals. As a consequence, many programs gained public support for the wrong reasons: "catching up" with the Russians, taking advantage of government money available, providing a program like that of a neighboring school, trying to produce fluent speakers quickly because they were thought to be at the optimum age for language learning. Many administrators, parents, and teachers had unrealistic expectations of student performance. Those who had climbed on the language bandwagon out of fear or because foreign languages were a fad, or who expected fluency in weeks or months, were bound to suffer disappointment. In their eagerness to expand their offerings into the elementary schools, language teachers sometimes did not discourage such expectations. Disillusionment and lack of clear direction combined to bring an end to programs that had been too hastily begun.

It is important that any rationale for second language learning for children not be dependent on information that has been disproved or is in dispute, or on common wisdom for which there is little research support. A good example is the optimal-age issue. Claims were made in the sixties for a psychological and physiological basis for starting second language learning as early as possible. Parents and teachers often comment that children are much better language learners than adolescents or adults and that we should make the most of this special ability before it is lost. However, research evidence suggests that older learners have an advantage over children in almost every area tested—with a small advantage for children in the area of native-like pronunciation—at least in most classroom settings (Krashen et al. 1982). Some of the reasons that children are such successful language learners lie in other factors such as the amount of time spent in learning the language and the teaching methodology used.

WHERE TO LOOK FOR
A RATIONALE FOR
FOREIGN LANGUAGES

Reports and Studies

Beginning with the appearance of *Strength through Wisdom*, the report of the President's Commission on Foreign Language and International Studies (1979), a series of studies and reports on education has highlighted the need for improvement of opportunities for language study in the schools. The importance of language study has been tied to national security: ". . . A nation's welfare depends in large measure on the intellectual and psychological strengths that are derived from perceptive visions of the world beyond its own boundaries." (*Strength through Wisdom*, p. 2) Language study has been related to the success of the United States in the international marketplace and to the skills required for happy and productive living in a future of increasing global interdependence. The commission specifically recommended that language study begin in the elementary school and continue throughout the student's education. Paul Simon's book, *The Tongue-Tied American: Confronting the Foreign Language Crisis* (1980), provides a wealth of material for the construction of a rationale for language learning.

In *A Nation at Risk*, the report of the National Commission on Excellence in Education, edited by David P. Gardner (1983), the study of foreign language

6. Successful language learning activities are geared to the child's cognitive level, interest level, and motor skills.

7. Successful language learning activities are interdisciplinary.

8. Culture is learned best through experiences with cultural practices rather than through discussion and reading. Global education must be an integral part of the curriculum.

9. Successful language learning activities are organized according to a communicative syllabus rather than according to a grammatical syllabus. Grammar for its own sake should not be the object of instruction.

10. Successful language learning activities establish the language as a real means of communication.

11. Successful language programs make provision for the reading and writing of familiar material as appropriate to the age and interest of the students, even in early stages.

12. Successful language learning is evaluated frequently and regularly, in a manner that is consistent with the objectives of the program.

and culture was placed alongside the five "basics" of English, mathematics, computer science, social studies, and the natural sciences as a fundamental component of a sound education.

Other commission reports, while focusing on the general decline in the quality of the nation's schools, have also addressed the need for studying foreign languages at the elementary school level. The National Commission on Excellence in Education (1983) maintained that achieving proficiency in a foreign language takes from four to six years of study and suggested that this begin in the elementary grades. "We believe it is desirable that students achieve such proficiency because study of a foreign language introduces students to non-English-speaking cultures, heightens awareness and comprehension of one's native tongue, and serves the nation's needs in commerce, diplomacy, defense, and education." (Gardner:26)

The National Advisory Board on International Education Programs, in a report to the Secretary of Education (1983), stated that language instruction should start as early as possible. In its report, *Critical Needs in International Education: Recommendations for Action*, the board recommended that school districts should give all students the opportunity to begin learning foreign languages in the earliest years of schooling, and to continue study of the same language until they can demonstrate a functionally useful level of proficiency.

These views are reiterated in the study by the College Board (1983) which emphasizes the importance of expanding the concept of basic skills to include foreign language instruction for all students. More specifically, the report credits knowledge of a foreign language with helping students to prepare for careers in commerce, international relations, law, science, and the arts. Furthermore, the report emphasizes that the development and maintenance of foreign language skills is a valuable national resource.

General Rationale for Teaching Languages

The rationale for elementary and middle school programs is embedded in the rationale for languages generally, but it must also take into account some special characteristics of languages at that level:

1. One of the most important factors influencing the development of language proficiency is the amount of time spent in working with the language. When language learning begins earlier, it can go on longer and provide more practice and experience, leading ultimately to greater fluency and effectiveness.

2. Every skill and outcome that is important to society is introduced through the elementary school curriculum. The lists of curriculum requirements

in almost every state attest to the importance of reading, math, social studies, science, music, art, and physical education. The introduction of computers into nearly every elementary school program clearly reflects the values of our electronic, information age. Only when languages become a secure part of the elementary school curriculum will language learning begin to meet the needs so vividly described in the national reports of the 1980s.

3. The age of ten is a crucial time in the development of attitudes toward nations and groups perceived as "other," according to the research of Piaget, Lambert, and others (Lambert and Klineberg 1967). Children are in the process of moving from egocentricity to reciprocity, and information introduced before age ten is eagerly received. Carpenter and Torney (1974) suggest that exposure to a foreign language serves as a means of helping children move toward intercultural competence. The awareness of a global community can be enhanced when children have the opportunity to experience involvement with another culture through a foreign language.

Rationale from Curriculum Guides and Works on Language Teaching

Rationale statements for foreign languages can also be found in curriculum guides and works on language teaching and learning. There has been a tendency in recent statements to emphasize the holistic, global, and communicative elements of language learning. Sandra Savignon (1983) expresses it this way (p. 187):

> Learning to speak another's language means taking one's place in the human community. It means reaching out to others across cultural and linguistic boundaries. Language is far more than a system to be explained. It is our most important link to the world around us. Language is culture in motion. It is people interacting with people.

The New York State Syllabus for foreign languages, *Modern Languages for Communication* (1987) identifies the following values of foreign language study (p. 3):

> In addition to the practical application of communication skills, the benefits derived from the study of a second language are many and contribute to the attainment of the Regents' goals for elementary and secondary education. Empirical findings indicate that second language study
>
> • fosters a sense of humanity and friendship

- increases students' adaptability to different environments and modes of acting and thinking
- furnishes the key to thinking patterns, cultures, and social institutions of other peoples
- provides insights into the human mind and language itself
- prepares students for a world in which nations and peoples are increasingly interdependent
- develops the skills and habits essential to the learning process, creative inquiry, and critical thinking
- helps students to increase their sensitivity to and understanding of the language, values, customs, and traditions of others
- leads students to discover and examine their own personal values and civic responsibilities
- provides insights into America's values and an appreciation of national responsibilities in the world community
- is an additional asset to many careers and to professional advancement

In Wisconsin's *A Guide to Curriculum Planning in Foreign Language* (Grittner 1985), the following benefits of foreign language study are listed (p. 11–12):

Immediate Benefits
- Attaining greater academic achievement in other areas of study, including reading, social studies, and mathematics
- Developing clearer understanding of the English language and greater sensitivity to structure, vocabulary, and syntax
- Earning higher SAT and ACT scores, especially in verbal areas
- Sensing a greater awareness and deeper understanding of other cultures and developing a more positive interaction with persons from other nations
- Gaining advantageous qualifications for student exchange programs
- Developing a global attitude
- Improving knowledge of geography
- Exploring career opportunities involving foreign language
- Earning college credits while in high school and/or fulfilling a requirement for college entrance or graduation

Long-Range Benefits
- Facilitating the learning of additional foreign languages
- Acquiring an indispensable skill in a global world

- Preparing for travel for business, education, or pleasure
- Performing research abroad
- Qualifying for foreign scholarships and fellowships
- Qualifying for foreign-study programs

    Student exchanges

    Junior year abroad in college

    Summer courses abroad

    Business internships abroad

- Exchanging professional ideas and information in commerce, law, education, arts
- Enhancing career opportunities

    Employment abroad in business, education, or government

    Employment in the U.S. by foreign companies

    Employment in the U.S. by United States export companies

    Employment in industries dealing with foreign tourists

    Employment in social services, hospitals, law enforcement

- Appreciating the aesthetics of literature, music, art, folklore
- Exchanging professional ideas and information in commerce, science, law, education, arts
- Developing more flexibility in thinking processes through problem solving, conceptualizing, and reasoning
- Enjoying the satisfaction of achieving a personal goal—learning another language

Indiana's guide to proficiency-based instruction (Strasheim and Bartz 1984) contains the following statement of Foreign Language Philosophy (p. ix):

> The purpose . . . of foreign language education is to prepare young people to become culturally sensitive and communicatively competent travelers, students, and/or workers in other societies and cultures in the world, to interact positively and more effectively with the native speakers they meet and work with in this country, and to evolve more of those capabilities for productive citizenship in Indiana, the United States and the world.

Basic Elementary School Skills
and Goals

Some of the most powerful sources of rationale for foreign languages in the elementary and middle school are the curriculum guides of the schools themselves. Planners who truly understand both the goals of the elementary school and the potential of foreign languages can demonstrate the value of languages very convincingly by showing the relationship between the two. The local curriculum and philosophy provide the best information about the values and priorities of the school and the community in which the language program will take place.

Among the goals and philosophical positions commonly encountered in local curricula and in references to elementary school curricula, some of the following themes have particularly high potential for the developer of a rationale for languages:

1. **Basic Skills.** This is certainly not a new concern for elementary school languages. Much of the research done during the banner years of elementary school language programs, the 1960s, was concerned with the relationship of language learning to skills acquisition in English language and mathematics. The concern at that time was almost always to demonstrate that these skills areas had not suffered because of the time "lost" to foreign language instruction. The evidence was consistent: there was no sacrifice of basic skills when time was given to learning a new language. (Donoghue 1968)

   In "Tangible Benefits of the Study of Latin: A Review of Research" (1977), Rudolph Masciantonio published a survey of research which made a much bolder claim for languages. Latin instruction in the elementary grades had been shown to result in significant and dramatic gains in standardized test performance in basic-skills areas. Gains were also reported for students of French and Spanish. Research on immersion programs in Canada and the United States show that students taught *by means of* a foreign language achieve at similar *or higher* levels than their peers who are taught only in English, even when testing is done in English. Parents in Chicago, Cincinnati, and Milwaukee, for example, are known to choose metropolitan magnet schools offering languages because of the outstanding record of children in those schools on tests of English basic skills—not always primarily because of the language offerings themselves (Estelle 1985; Met 1982; Anderson 1982). A recent study in Louisiana (Rafferty 1986) showed that third-, fourth-, and fifth-graders studying French for thirty minutes per day achieved significantly higher scores on the 1985 Basic Skills Language Arts Test than did a similar group of nonparticipants. In addition, by fifth grade the math scores of language students were also higher than those of nonlanguage students.

2. **Communication.** Part of the impact of foreign language study on basic skills performance can be explained by the greater understanding students gain of their own language when they see it from the perspective of a new language. Vygotsky, a significant contributor to contemporary developmental theory, writes in *Thought and Language* (1986:160)

> . . . Goethe clearly saw it (reciprocal dependence) when he wrote that he who knows no foreign language does not truly know his own. Experimental studies fully endorse this. It has been shown that a child's understanding of his native language is enhanced by learning a foreign one. The child becomes more conscious and deliberate in using words as tools of his thought and expressive means for his ideas. . . . The child's approach to language becomes more abstract and generalized. . . . The acquisition of foreign language—in its own peculiar way—liberates him from the dependence on concrete linguistic forms and expressions.

Foreign language study has been shown to enhance listening skills and memory (Ratte 1968), and the development of second language skills can contribute a significant additional dimension to the concept of communication.

3. **Creativity.** Many of the activities common in elementary school language programs—emphasis on movement, imagination, and role play, for example—stimulate the right hemisphere of the brain, which is often underplayed in the formal school setting. Foreign language instruction can make a contribution to "whole-brain" education, and one consequence can be enhanced creativity. Elementary students attending a FLES program were reported to have greater skills in divergent thinking/figural creativity than did those who were monolingual, according to research conducted by Landry (1973).

4. **Self-concept.** Second language learning in the elementary school, especially in its beginning stages, is less dependent on previous verbal learning than are most other elements of the curriculum. This factor allows some students to succeed who have otherwise experienced repeated failure in school. Evidence from a California study shows language students to have a significantly higher self-concept than do nonlanguage students (Masciantonio 1977). Students in Cincinnati have also shown such success. In a recent study (Holobow et al. 1987) working class students did just as well in French as middle class students even though their English skills were not as good.

5. **Career Development.** The U.S. Department of Labor *Occupational Handbook* (quoted in Grittner 1985:10) suggests that future job seekers will have a better chance at any job if they also have knowledge of a foreign language. The New York State Association of Foreign Language Teachers (1982) states that ". . . the applicant with such skills in addition to others required for the position, will not only be chosen by preference over those who lack ability in a foreign language, but will probably be paid a higher salary." (Grittner 1985:10)

6. **Integration of All Areas of the Curriculum.** Every area of the curriculum can be reinforced or enriched in the foreign language classroom, and subject content can be taught through the second language. This kind of integration can foster appreciation of other cultures and can add significant dimensions to the content being taught. With close cooperation between language and classroom teachers, the second language experience can contribute directly to the mastery of first language concepts in the curriculum.

7. **Cultural Enrichment.** Most languages taught at the elementary school level can give insight into a variety of cultures, including multicultural elements in the students' own community. The positive impact of cultural information is significantly enhanced when that information is experienced through the foreign language and accompanied by experiences in culturally authentic situations.

School District Goal Statements as Sources of Rationale

The following goals—excerpted from *Outcome-Based Education Curriculum* (1987), a document from Milwaukee Public Schools—illustrate the potential of local-district goal statements as the basis for a foreign language rationale (p. 5):

> The attributes below represent those skills, attitudes, behaviors, and knowledge which the total curriculum of the Milwaukee Public Schools intends to develop in each student prior to his/her graduation from the district.
>
> Possesses skills and attitudes to enter the world of work successfully.
>
> Communicates appropriately.
>
> Gathers and analyzes information to identify and solve problems appropriately.
>
> Understands and relates constructively to the environment.

Has skills to participate fully in local, state, national, and global citizenship activities.

Possesses skills to anticipate and adapt to change.

Understands the pluralistic nature of the American society and has the skills needed to function in a multi-ethnic/multi-cultural/gender-equitable setting.

These suggestions certainly do not exhaust the possibilities for matching the values of foreign language instruction with the goals of the elementary school; rather, they are intended to suggest how elementary school goals may be used as a starting point for building a rationale. This information, paired with the understanding that a long period of exposure is required to develop fluency in a foreign language, speaks powerfully for the inclusion of foreign language instruction in elementary schools.

Other Sources of Rationale

Many of the resources listed at the end of this chapter will be useful in locating information and evidence to support a rationale. The ACTFL monograph *Second Languages and the Basics* (1984) is a particularly good summary of research and information, categorized in terms of significant outcomes of education.

In addition to examining rationale statements for languages and for elementary school programs, the developer of rationale for elementary school language programs should also seek out parent-teacher organization and community statements of philosophy. Not only do national reports on education often include information which gives strong support to teaching languages at the elementary school level; reports on international business and trade also make mention of languages and their value. Even popular magazines occasionally publish features that can be valuable sources of rationale statements and that speak clearly to local audiences.

A rationale for teaching foreign languages at the elementary school level will be the result of many resources combined to address the needs and priorities of the local school and its community. The resources are abundant and varied, and the serious program planner will find and use the most attractive and appropriate for the local situation.

SUMMARY

No single rationale for teaching of foreign languages at the elementary school level will be effective for every program in every setting. Those who develop and seek support for such programs will need to tailor their rationale to the priorities and values of the community that the program will serve. An effective rationale will be carefully developed to avoid inappropriate claims for language; rather, it will draw from a variety of recognized sources when building the case for elementary school foreign language. Many sound reasons for language study have been advanced by national reports and studies of foreign language study generally, and for elementary school foreign language in particular. The general rationale for second language study provides many reasons for beginning language study in the elementary school, and much of this rationale has been particularly well stated in recent curriculum guides and professional works on language teaching. The goals of the elementary school and the philosophy of the school district are additional resources for building a rationale, as they set the context for a holistic education to which foreign language can make a unique and valuable contribution.

FOR STUDY AND DISCUSSION

1. What reasons have you most frequently heard for teaching languages at the elementary school level? Which of these reasons do you feel would be good building blocks for a rationale statement?

2. A parent committee has asked for your assistance in convincing the school board to consider developing a foreign language program at the elementary school level. Write a memo advising the committee how they might go about building their case.

3. Choose one of the following school settings and suggest which emphases and which resources might be the most useful in the development of a rationale statement.

   - a mid-western farming community with a population of 450
   - an urban district with a large minority population
   - a suburban district with a high percentage of students who go on to college
   - a private, church-related school system with very limited funds
   - a small- to mid-sized industrial, mining, or oil town with a very high unemployment level
   - a private preparatory school with a program designed for college-bound students
   - a mid-sized community in which the local college has a great impact on the culture of the community

4. The curriculum coordinator in your district has recently discovered research indicating that children may not be better language learners

than adults, and that they are in fact less efficient learners of the grammar and structure than are older students. How do you respond to her suggestion that languages should not be taught until grade nine, based on this information?

5. Which of the reasons for teaching languages in the elementary school would be the most convincing for the faculty, administrators, and parents of the school district or school setting with which you are the most familiar?

FOR FURTHER READING

The following sources are recommended for additional information about material covered in this chapter. Chapter citations are documented in *Works Cited* at the end of the volume.

ACTFL. *Second Languages and the Basics*. Hastings-on-Hudson, NY: American Council on the Teaching of Foreign Languages, 1978, 1984.

Benevento, Jacqueline. *Issues and Innovations in Foreign Language Education*. Bloomington, IN: Phi Delta Kappa Educational Foundation, 1984.

Gardner, David P., ed. *A Nation at Risk: The Imperative for Educational Reform*. Washington, DC: U.S. Department of Education, 1983.

Harley, Birgit. *Age in Second Language Acquisition*. San Diego: College-Hill Press, 1986.

Krashen, Stephen D., Robin C. Scarcella, and Michael H. Long, eds. *Child-Adult Differences in Second Language Acquisition*. Rowley, MA: Newbury House, 1982.

National Advisory Board on International Education Programs. *Critical Needs in International Education: Recommendations for Action: A Report to the Secretary of Education*. Washington, DC: U.S. Government Printing Office, 1983.

President's Commission on Foreign Languages and International Studies. *Strength through Wisdom: A Critique of U.S. Capability*. Washington, DC: U.S. Government Printing Office, 1979.

Rafferty, Eileen A. *Second Language Study and Basic Skills in Louisiana*. Baton Rouge: Louisiana Department of Education, 1986.

Simon, Paul. *The Tongue-Tied American. Confronting the Foreign Language Crisis*. New York: Continuum Publishing Corporation, 1980.

Chapter 2

Learning from the Past to Enhance the Present and the Future

Children have been learning languages in American schools since colonial times, and the presence of these languages in the curriculum has often been the subject of controversy. Many of the concerns raised a century or more ago sound surprisingly like discussions held at contemporary staff and school board meetings at which districts consider the addition or expansion of an elementary school language program. It is important for the advocate of languages for children to understand past successes and problems, especially those of the FLES heyday of the 1960s, in order to plan and implement programs that build on the strengths and insights of the past and avoid its failures.

Foreign language instruction has been fairly common in the United States throughout its history; Latin was often taught in the early years, and German was popular after the great waves of German immigration in 1830 and 1848. French and Spanish schools developed in some areas of the country where there were concentrations of immigrants from French- and Spanish-speaking countries.

Objections to the teaching of German and other languages in the elementary schools were raised by state and territorial officials, often on the grounds that the practice was un-American, and that children in private and parochial schools were being taught by individuals who did not even speak English. However, programs persisted and grew, despite the controversies, until the United States entered World War I. At that time there was a strong reaction against everything German, especially the language, and much elementary school instruction in all foreign languages was eliminated.

In the 1940s a concern for improvement of Latin American understanding led to the development of Spanish-language programs in the elementary schools of the American Southwest. In 1957, after the stunning orbit of Sputnik, public awareness of the value of foreign language education was heightened by the jarring information that the United States could have known about the development of the Russian satellite had American scientists been regular readers of Russian journals. As a result, languages were included with mathematics and science in the generous funding of the National Defense Education Act (NDEA) of 1958. Among other provisions, the Act included matching funds for the purchase of instructional equipment and materials, and it provided for the training of teachers in "critical" languages (German, French, Spanish, Russian) at both the elementary and the secondary school level.

The national sense of urgency explains in part the haste with which many school districts launched foreign language programs at both the elementary and the secondary school level. Years of low priority for languages had failed to produce enough language teachers to meet the new demand, and most of the teachers available had little preparation for the elementary school level. These factors underscored the importance of the training provisions of the NDEA. Institutes were funded throughout the country to prepare teachers in the new aural-oral/audiolingual approach, based on the methods developed for the Army during World War II.

These NDEA institutes marked the first time in the United States that there had been a concentrated effort centered on the development of an approach to language teaching. Much of the teaching of modern languages before the 1960s, even at the elementary school level, had been modeled on the teaching of Latin and Greek, and had included an emphasis on reading, translation, and grammatical analysis using the terminology of Latin grammar. That approach may have been intended to earn academic and intellectual respect for modern languages, which had not been valued in a classical education (Grittner 1977).

In contrast, Emile de Sauzé directed a program in Cleveland for selected elementary school students from 1918 until 1949. Under the "Cleveland Plan" all instruction was conducted in the foreign language, and reading and writing were deferred until the sixth grade (Donoghue 1968).

At the end of the nineteenth century some teachers had already begun to break with the Latin-based formula for language teaching, experimenting with the "natural" and the "direct" methods. Each of these methods stressed the spoken word and de-emphasized grammar for its own sake, although the direct method approached grammar more systematically and developed more carefully constructed curricula. Both required a teacher who was fluent in the language and who was willing to use the target language almost exclusively (Zeydel 1961).

Against this background, the audiolingual method of the 1960s represented a dramatic burst of new energy for language teaching. It claimed a basis in the relatively new field of structural linguistics and in behavioral psychology, as it de-emphasized the traditional methods of grammar study and focused on language competence developed through habit formation. Elementary school children were viewed as natural candidates for this type of instruction because they were far less resistant to the repetition and drill required by the method. Oral language served as the starting point of all language study, even for those students to whom reading was a primary goal. Inductive grammar and oral drill replaced grammatical analysis in English; listening and speaking practice in the classroom and in the language laboratory replaced reading and translation exercises.

Thousands of teachers were trained or retrained in NDEA institutes, which gave teachers the opportunity to develop skills in the new method and to improve their speaking skills in the foreign language. Except for pockets of resistance or misunderstanding, a whole generation of language teachers began modeling dialogues, conducting pattern drills, and practicing the art of mimicry-memorization.

There was every reason to be optimistic that the newly attained place for languages in national priorities and the new method, supported with new opportunities for teacher preparation, would lead to a "golden age" for language programs, especially at the elementary school level. But the ambitions and good intentions of school districts often outdistanced genuine planning and the availability of well-trained personnel. The "boom" for languages in the elementary schools lasted barely five years, as programs at this level were in decline after 1964. Many of the reasons for this short period of popularity are described in "A Survey of FLES Practices," a report written for the Modern Language Association in 1961. (NOTE: This article uses "FLES" to refer to elementary foreign language programs in general, not to the specific program model referred to elsewhere in this book; see chapter 3.) After visiting sixty-two communities with reportedly good FLES programs in the spring of 1961, Alkonis and Brophy drew the following conclusions (p. 213–217):

1. A majority of the FLES programs that we observed do not fulfill the primary aim of such a program—teaching the four language skills—even when this is clearly stated as their objective . . . Sometimes the teacher is weak; just as often the weakness lies beyond the teacher's control, in the materials or the scheduling.

2. Many programs emphasized such aims as "world understanding" or "broadened horizons" to the extent that it is a clear misnomer to call them *language* programs. We saw no evidence of effective evaluation of the teaching directed toward these objectives . . .

3. There is such a diversity of linguistic content that a general evaluation of results using a single test or series of tests appears to be impracticable.

4. From the widespread emphasis upon learning lists of words, we conclude that a majority of the FLES teachers think of language as words to be learned in isolation and then strung into "conversation." They showed no awareness of the interacting systems of structure or patterns that are basic to each language.

5. Many programs, started without planning and provision for the materials, the instruction, and the eventual integration with junior- and senior-high school courses, are considered "experimental," but there is no clear statement of the conditions and terms of the experiment and no provision for an evaluation of its results.

6. The most obvious weakness is lack of teachers with sufficient skill in the language and training in methods. (This is no reflection on the sincerity, the enthusiasm, or the good will of the instructors. How many of us, with no knowledge of music and unable to play the piano, could successfully teach a roomful of little children to play that instrument?)

7. In many schools—certainly in the majority of those we visited—FLES is conceived of as merely a preview or prelude to "real" language learning (which will begin in the high school) rather than as a serious, systematic attempt to develop attitudes and skills.

8. Few programs are planned as an unbroken, cumulative sequence from the primary through the junior high school, partly because of the lack of appropriate teaching materials for the junior high school, but more because of the inadequacy of the FLES work itself.

The eight observations made by Alkonis and Brophy effectively summarized the problems that most FLES programs of the 1960s failed to resolve. As budgets tightened and priorities shifted, as promised results failed to materialize, as graduates of FLES programs failed to meet the expectations of junior and senior high teachers, language programs in the elementary school lost their credibility as well as their value as a status symbol. These programs were among the first to be cut when school systems evaluated their curricula to make room for new trends and emphases.

Although NDEA funding continued through 1968, the last institute designed specifically for elementary school teachers was held in 1965, at which time enthusiasm for the audiolingual method was also beginning to wane. While the combination of structural linguistics and behavioral psychology had focused on the external features of language, a new concern for the internal processing of language was being articulated by the rationalists and the generative grammarians. Emphasis was shifting from the manipulation of patterns that might eventually be used to convey information to the use of language as a means of communication, and from the means by which an idea was expressed to the importance of the idea being communicated.

The decline of interest and support for traditional foreign language programs in the schools, however, first evidenced by the loss of enthusiasm for FLES, had become widespread by the early 1970s. Unsettling events at home and abroad led to a period of student apathy and low motivation. The war in Vietnam and student protests at colleges and universities became the focus of public attention. School enrollments began to decline, and enrollments in language classes declined even more rapidly. Critics blamed the tedium and irrelevance of the audiolingual method for declining language enrollments, and universities aggravated the situation by dropping foreign language entrance and exit requirements.

Meanwhile, attempts to understand more about language learning and teaching were being made on behalf of language-minority students. An influx of Spanish-speaking families from Latin American countries and the arrival of refugees from Southeast Asia increased the population of non-English-speaking children in the schools in many areas in the United States and created a need for language instruction for these children.

In dealing with the challenge, teachers of English to speakers of other languages found assistance from linguists and psychologists. This alliance has resulted in a growing body of research that has shed new light on how language competence is developed. Abroad, the Council of Europe developed an approach to language teaching and learning which was based on the communication needs of the learner. *The Threshhold Level for Modern Language Learning in Schools* (Van Ek 1977), a syllabus developed for several European languages, identifies functions and vocabulary necessary to interact successfully in a variety of specific situations. Together, these developments reinforced the emerging emphasis on the messages being expressed by language and the process of language acquisition.

In Canada, the desire of English-speaking parents to increase their children's proficiency in French led to the establishment of immersion programs, an innovative educational approach in which the language of the school setting is different from the language of the home and children learn subject content through the new language. The first French kindergarten class for native speakers of English was offered in September of 1965, in St. Lambert, a suburb of Montreal. Immersion programs have spread throughout Canada and have been thoroughly researched and documented. Immersion has also spread to some parts of the United States, and according to the Center for Applied Linguistics there were immersion programs in at least thirty cities in the United States by 1987, involving 8,000 school children ("Total and Partial Immersion Programs," 1987). In Canada, immersion programs enrolled nearly 50,000 children in 1979, 150,000 in 1985, and 164,000 by 1987 (McGillivray 1985).

Another approach to teaching subject content in a new language was developing for the non-English-speaking child in American schools. Beginning with Cuban refugee children in the Dade County schools of Florida in 1963, bilingual programs helped children learn to read and write in their own language as well as introducing them to English. In most such programs subject-content material is taught in both languages, with an increasing emphasis on English at each grade level. Many early bilingual programs also include the opportunity for English-speaking children to learn the foreign language in the same setting. These programs are often referred to as two-way bilingual.

Twenty years after Sputnik, the national interest in foreign languages was again awakened by international events. The rise of multinational corporations, the increasing importance of international trade, and the oil crisis all contributed to a renewed awareness of American dependence on global relationships. The 1979 President's Commission on Foreign Language and International Studies was the first of a series of commissions on education to highlight the serious situation created by the lack of foreign language skills among Americans. Its specific recommendations included the urging of language study in the elementary school and the development of imaginative curricula dealing with other countries and cultures. Subsequent national studies and reports about education, such as *A Nation at Risk* (Gardner 1983), amplified the call for a more international vision in the schools and a higher priority for language learning.

SUMMARY

The challenge for the rest of the century is to learn from the past, to build a solid base of support for languages, and to develop programs strong enough to withstand the shifting winds of enthusiasm and fad. Many of the problems that plagued the 1960s still threaten us, especially at the elementary school level: a shortage of qualified teachers, a tendency to establish programs without sufficient planning or careful selection of teachers and materials, a lack of clarity about goals, and a willingness to promise whatever the public wanted to hear. New tools have emerged to meet the challenges: a solid base of research in psychology and linguistics, extensive experiences in immersion and bilingual education, new insights about communication, improved understanding of first and second language acquisition, and new standards for judging proficiency and progress. Taken together, the problems still in evidence and the tools available for solving them promise a stimulating period of challenge and opportunity for languages in the elementary school.

FOR STUDY AND DISCUSSION

1. What resources does the curriculum planner for elementary school language programs have available today that will help a school system avoid the pitfalls and problems encountered by earlier programs?

2. Supporting elementary school language programs might be considered "getting on another bandwagon," triggered by national reports. What lessons can be learned from the history of language teaching in the United States to help prevent the decline of support for language programs after their "fad value" has worn off?

3. What current national and international events tend to encourage support for language programs at the elementary school level?

4. Trace the history of foreign languages in the school setting you know best. What was their role in this setting during the period before and after World War I? In the 1960s? Since 1979?

5. How might information on the history of foreign language programs be of value when writing a program rationale?

FOR FURTHER READING

The following sources are recommended for additional information about material covered in this chapter. Chapter citations are documented in *Works Cited* at the end of the volume.

Andersson, Theodore. *Foreign Languages in the Elementary School: A Struggle Against Mediocrity.* Austin, TX: University of Texas Press, 1969.

Schinke-Llano, Linda. *Foreign Language in the Elementary School: State of the Art.* Washington DC: Center for Applied Linguistics, 1985. ED 264 715.

Stern, H.H. *Fundamental Concepts of Language Teaching.* Oxford: Oxford University Press, 1983.

Chapter 3

Selecting and Developing a Program Model

PROGRAM MODELS

When looking at the challenges and opportunities for languages available in the elementary school, school districts are faced with decisions as to what type of foreign language program to offer and how to staff that program. Elementary school foreign language programs can be classified into three broad categories, each with a different set of goals, a different set of expected student outcomes, and a variety of staffing options. These categories are

- Immersion programs
- FLES programs
- FLEX (Foreign Language Exploratory or Experience) programs

Outcomes from these programs range from those of exploratory programs, which are concerned with introducing students to language(s) and culture and therefore do not have language proficiency as a goal, to those of immersion programs, which have the highest goals for language proficiency. Figure 1 shows the distinctions among the various programs. Underlying every program and model description is the fact *that language proficiency outcomes are directly proportional to the amount of time spent by students in meaningful communication in the target language*. The more time students spend working communicatively with the target language, under the guidance of a skilled and fluent teacher, the greater will be the level of language proficiency which they acquire. Planners should seek to design the best possible program in terms of language proficiency that they are able to implement.

The definitions following Figure 1 further clarify the distinctions among the various programs.

Program Type	Percent of Class Time Spent in FL per Week	Goals
TOTAL IMMERSION Grades K-6 (continuous)	50–100% (Time spent learning *subject matter* taught in FL; language learning *per se* incorporated as necessary throughout curriculum)	To become functionally proficient in the foreign language (to be able to communicate on topics appropriate to age almost as well as native speakers) To master subject content taught in the foreign language To acquire an understanding of and appreciation for other cultures
PARTIAL IMMERSION Grades K-6 (continuous)	approx. 50% (Time spent learning *subject matter* taught in FL; language learning *per se* incorporated as necessary throughout curriculum)	To become functionally proficient in the foreign language (to a lesser extent than is possible in total immersion) To master subject content taught in the foreign language To acquire an understanding of and appreciation for other cultures
CONTENT-ENRICHED FLES Grades K-6 (continuous)	15–50% (Time spent learning language *per se* as well as learning subject matter in the FL)	To acquire proficiency in listening, speaking, reading, and writing the foreign language To master subject content taught in the foreign language To acquire an understanding of and appreciation for other cultures
FLES Grades K-6 (continuous)	5–15% (Time spent learning language *per se*)	To acquire proficiency in listening and speaking (degree of proficiency varies with the program) To acquire an understanding of and appreciation for other cultures To acquire some proficiency in reading and writing (emphasis varies with the program)
FLEX Grades K-6 (not continuous)	Approx. 5% (Time spent learning language and *about* language—sometimes taught mostly in English)	To develop an interest in foreign languages for future language study To learn basic words and phrases in one or more foreign languages To develop careful listening skills To develop cultural awareness

Figure 1. Elementary School Foreign Language Program Goals
Source: Center for Applied Linguistics, 1985. Adapted by permission of Nancy Rhodes.

Immersion Programs

Language immersion is an approach to second language instruction in which the usual curriculum activities are conducted in a second language. This means that the new language is the medium as well as the object of instruction. Children in immersion programs in the United States and Canada are English speakers who are learning to speak a foreign language such as French, German, Spanish, or Chinese.

Immersion Goals

The following goals are most commonly found in immersion programs.

1. Functional proficiency in the second language; children are able to communicate in the second language on topics appropriate to their age level
2. Mastery of subject–content material of the school district curriculum
3. Cross-cultural understanding
4. Achievement in English language arts comparable to or surpassing the achievement of students in English-only programs.

Immersion programs vary in the amount of time devoted to instruction in the second language (total or partial immersion), and in the level of entry (early, middle or late immersion).

The following definitions will clarify terms and concepts associated with immersion in the United States and Canada.

Total Immersion

The second language is used for the entire school day during the first two or three years. In early total immersion programs, reading is taught through the second language. Instruction by means of English is introduced gradually and the amount of English is increased until the sixth grade, where up to half the day is spent in English and half in the second language.

Partial Immersion

Instruction is in the second language for part (at least half) of the school day. The amount of instruction in the second language usually remains constant throughout the elementary school program. In early partial immersion programs, students frequently learn to read in both languages at the same time.

Early Immersion

Students begin learning through the second language in the kindergarten or first grade.

Middle Immersion

Students begin learning through the second language in the middle grades, usually fourth or fifth grade.

Late Immersion

Students begin learning through the second language at the end of elementary school, at the beginning of middle school, or in high school. Many students entering late immersion programs have had previous foreign language instruction (30–60 minutes per day) in the second language. Late immersion programs may involve 90 to 100 percent of the instruction in the second language for the first year and 50 to 80 percent for one or two years after that, or 50 to 60 percent throughout. This model is more common in Canada than in the United States.

Double Immersion

Double immersion programs are similar to other immersion programs except that instruction takes place in two new languages—for example, French in the morning and Hebrew in the afternoon. (This type of program is not common and is offered in only a few school districts in Canada.)

Two-Way Immersion

Two-way immersion, or two-way bilingual programs, are similar to regular immersion programs except that included among the students are native speakers of the target language as well as native speakers of English. The ideal goals of two-way immersion, in addition to subject–content mastery, are that the English-speaking students become functionally proficient in the second language and that the second language speakers become functionally proficient in English.

Continuing Immersion

Continuing immersion programs are found at the middle/junior high school or high school level. These programs are designed to maintain the language skills already developed in total or partial immersion programs and to further develop them to as high a degree as possible.

FLES Programs

FLES has sometimes been used as a general term to describe all foreign language programs at the elementary level. However, FLES is most appropriately used to describe a particular type of elementary school foreign language program, one that is taught one to five times per week for class periods of twenty minutes to an hour or more. Some FLES classes integrate other areas of the curriculum, but, because of time limitations, the focus of these classes is most often the second language and its culture.

FLES Goals

As with immersion programs, the goal of FLES programs is functional proficiency in the second language, although FLES students do not attain as high a proficiency level as do immersion students. The level of proficiency will vary with the amount of time available for language instruction. Listening and speaking skills tend to be emphasized more than are reading and writing. FLES programs are part of a long sequence of language study and lead to continuing courses at the secondary level.

Content-enriched FLES

Some FLES programs are "content-enriched," which means that some subject content is taught in the foreign language and that more than an hour a day (but less than half the day) is spent in the foreign language. Less time spent teaching subject content through the language distinguishes this model from the immersion models. Content-enriched FLES differs from other forms of FLES in that there is a focus on subject–content instruction rather than on language instruction alone.

   In content-enriched FLES programs, functional proficiency in the second language is possible to a greater degree than in regular FLES programs because of the greater range of topics covered and the greater amount of time spent using the language. An additional goal of content-enriched FLES programs is mastery of the subject content taught in the second language.

Exploratory Programs (FLEX)

Exploratory programs, often referred to as FLEX (Foreign Language Exploratory or Experience) programs, are self-contained, short-term programs, usually lasting from three weeks to one year. They may occur in the elementary school, but they are found most often at the middle school/junior high level. Exploratory programs have many variations, depending on the goals of the individual district. At one extreme is the course that introduces language primarily through a high-quality language learning experience. At the other extreme is the course *about* language, taught largely in English. The courses that emphasize language learning experiences hold the greatest implications for program planning. Students learn enough language in such courses to insure that they will not be total beginners the next time they take a class in the same language, and they will have been required to pay some attention to articulation of language content.

Exploratory Goals

Most exploratory or FLEX program models share many of the same goals. The differences primarily involve emphasis of individual goals within a program. Among the most common goals of exploratory programs are the following:

- Introduction to language learning
- Awareness and appreciation of foreign culture
- Appreciation of the value of communicating in another language
- Enhanced understanding of English
- Motivation to further language study

Exploratory programs generally can be categorized into three basic types, which tend to overlap somewhat in terms of goals and design. These types are the following:

The General Language Course

This is an introduction and orientation to the nature of language and language learning, which includes the goals of cultural understanding, but it provides the students with very limited speaking experiences. Such courses often include exposure to all the modern and classical languages available for later study in the school system, as well as to some related systems such as sign language for the hearing impaired, Morse code, American Indian sign language, and computer language.

The Language Potpourri

This type of course provides limited, introductory experience in the modern and classical languages that will be available later in a sequential program. It may bring several, perhaps all, languages together in a single sequence, as a part of the same learning experience, or it may provide a series of experiences with different languages over a period of a year or more. The language potpourri course is usually team taught, using specialists in each language. The effectiveness of such a course is likely to be severely limited if the same teacher is responsible for teaching all languages, especially for those languages with which the teacher has little or no experience.

The Single Language Offering

This exploratory option provides a limited, introductory experience in one language that students may later be able to choose for sequential study. In some cases there may be no opportunity for further study of the exploratory language, or any language, but the experience with the language and culture is valued for itself and for its contribution to the elementary or middle school curriculum.

Of course, some exploratory courses combine the features of the general language course, the language potpourri, or the single language course, as school districts draw from several models to meet local goals and priorities.

A comprehensive discussion of exploratory language programs and their goals is provided by Kennedy and De Lorenzo in *Complete Guide to Exploratory Foreign Language Programs* (1985).

Auxiliary Language Programs

When examining auxiliary language programs, sometimes called noncurricular programs, it is important to note that not all language programs take place within the setting of the school day. Auxiliary programs include summer camps, immersion weekends, before- and after-school programs, summer day programs, and ethnic Saturday or day schools, among others.

Auxiliary programs may be sponsored by the school district, by community groups or parent-teacher organizations, or by tuition-based private education groups. They may be structured in a variety of ways. Some auxiliary programs have been very successful and have developed sophisticated structures and curricula, while others have limited goals and are of relatively short duration. In many communities the interest generated by auxiliary language programs has led to a place for languages within the school curriculum and the school day. Some auxiliary programs, such as immersion weekends, extend the school experience into a non-academic setting.

An important strength of auxiliary programs has been their use of community resources that might otherwise remain untapped. In some situations there would be no foreign language program in the school district without them, and their role as a "foot in the door" is not to be underestimated.

Among the most serious weaknesses of auxiliary programs is that volunteers in such programs often have little or no training, and there is no agency to regulate the goals and the quality of instruction. Even under the best of circumstances, such programs place languages clearly *outside* the school curriculum and the school day, reinforcing the notion that language learning is "extra" rather than basic.

TEACHER STAFFING OPTIONS

Staffing is one of the most important components in the elementary school foreign language program. It is vital that teachers working within any of the staffing models described below have excellent language skills and that they have had training and experience in working with elementary school children. The strengths and limitations for each staffing model are described.

Staffing for Immersion Programs

The critical staff members for both total and partial immersion programs are classroom teachers and, in some programs, classroom aides. Immersion teachers are certified elementary school teachers who are native or near-native speakers of the target language. Classroom aides who are also fluent in the target language can provide an additional, authentic model for the students as well as helping with individual and small-group instruction throughout the school day. While it is considered desirable to have special subjects such as music, art, and physical education taught by specialists who are fluent in the target language, many programs find it difficult to locate staff that are appropriately trained in these areas, so these subjects are taught either by the classroom teachers or by English-speaking specialists.

In early total immersion programs all instruction takes place in the target language, so staffing consists of the classroom teacher, who is a fluent speaker of the target language, and a classroom aide. In partial immersion programs, and in total immersion beginning with the second grade, one of the following patterns is usually chosen.

Separate Teacher for Each Language

The use of the native language and the target language are kept completely separate. All instruction in the target language is given by one teacher, when possible a native speaker of the language, and all native language instruction is given by another.

Strengths:

- The native language and the target language are kept clearly separate in the minds of the students.
- The best possible language model is provided for each language.

Limitations:

- Problems of staffing, scheduling, and curriculum coordination may be aggravated by use of this model.

The Same Teacher for Both Native Language and Second Language

The instructional day is divided into native language and second language activities, and the same teacher works with both languages.

Strengths:

- The teacher has complete flexibility to adjust the amount of time used for instruction in each language according to the needs of the class on any given day.
- Only one person must be hired for each classroom.
- The classroom teacher can shape the entire classroom environment and climate according to her or his own preference.

Limitations:

- The classroom teacher may not be an equally good model in both languages.
- Greater effort is required to establish clear separation between the use of the two languages.

Staffing for FLES and Exploratory Programs

Teachers for either FLES or Exploratory programs developed to achieve communicative goals will need to have considerable fluency in the target language as well as meaningful living experiences in countries in which the language is spoken. Children will not be able to achieve fluency greater than that of their teachers. It is also important that FLES and FLEX teachers have training and experience in working with elementary school children and that they have an understanding of teaching and learning second languages.

Language Specialist Model

This is the model that has been employed most often in elementary foreign language programs. The language specialist usually teaches foreign languages only, and often has experience with children but certification at the secondary level in the foreign language. The specialist may travel from room to room, or children may come to a special language classroom for second language instruction. Many teachers see from 200 to 400 students in the course of a week.

Strengths:

- The language specialist usually has good language skills and can provide consistency of instruction.

- The potential for both vertical articulation (from one grade to the next) and horizontal articulation (within the same grade level but possibly taught by different teachers or operating in different schools) is enhanced when the entire language program is in the hands of one or more specialists.

Limitations:

- If the language specialist has secondary training only, he or she may have little experience with elementary school students and may require assistance in adapting instruction to their needs and interests.
- The specialist must deal with many students throughout the day, thus limiting the degree of personal involvement and individualization available to each child. When numbers of students mount, teacher burnout can become a risk with this model.
- In this model the language program can easily become compartmentalized: the specialist lacks both the time and the opportunity to relate the language program to the rest of the curriculum.
- Salary costs for the language specialist(s) increase the expense to the district for foreign language offerings.

Classroom Teacher Model

In this option, each classroom teacher has the responsibility for teaching the elementary foreign language program. The program is most effective when designed in cooperation with a language specialist, who also coordinates the program, provides in-service assistance for the classroom teacher, and teaches occasional class sessions in individual classrooms. In some cases, there may be media support—audio and/or video—for the classroom teacher and less actual contact with a language specialist.

Strengths:

- The classroom teacher has extensive training and experience in working with the particular age group of students in the class and is in the best position to know their needs and interests.
- The teacher is able to reenter and reinforce the language learning throughout the school day and can also teach some subject content through the foreign language, as appropriate.
- Except for the specialist-coordinator, there is no extra salary expense for language instruction.

Limitations:

- This model is highly dependent on the willingness of the classroom teacher to become proficient in the language and to devote the extra time necessary to teach it effectively.
- This model is dependent on the support of a language specialist who knows the language well, understands the school child and the school setting, and can work effectively with teachers and administrators. Individuals with these qualifications may be difficult to locate.
- It is difficult to find classroom teachers with fluency in the second language. This is especially the case during a time of low teacher mobility when the opportunities to replace present staff through natural turnover are infrequent.
- Extensive in-service training may be necessary to help the classroom teacher achieve competence in the language and in language methodology. The teacher may view this as an unwanted and unwarranted burden; the result will be unenthusiastic teaching and hostility toward the program.

Variation on the Classroom Teacher Model

A variation on the classroom teacher model includes a team approach, in which one of the team members, usually better qualified by training and/or interest, teaches the language in several classrooms; in exchange, other team members offer instruction in other areas. This arrangement often helps to alleviate the morale problem otherwise encountered in this model.

Staffing Appropriate Only for Short-term, Exploratory Programs

Certain staffing patterns that do not use certified teachers have proved to be successful over limited periods of time for programs with limited goals. The option of using nonspecialist and volunteer teachers and cross-age tutors can meet the needs of specific programs when the programs are carefully planned by language specialists who train and monitor the teachers carefully. *The staffing options described below are not suitable for long-term, articulated FLES programs.*

Nonspecialist Teacher/Volunteer

Nonspecialist teachers could be college students studying languages, pre-service teachers enrolled in teacher education programs, parents, or other interested and qualified adults. They lead short-term language programs, singly or in pairs, under the supervision of a language specialist who assists in planning the program with the capabilities of these teachers clearly in mind.

Strengths:

- The use of the nonspecialist tutor in a short-term language experience has possibilities for bringing languages that would otherwise never be considered into the curriculum. For example, an exchange student from Africa might offer a nine-week course in Swahili; a former Peace Corps volunteer might offer a six-week class in Hindi.
- The use of nonspecialists identifies and takes advantage of community language resources that might otherwise remain untapped.

Limitations:

- Speakers of other languages may not have teaching background or training, and if they are from abroad, they may have difficulty adjusting to the American elementary school setting. They will require carefully planned assistance from language specialists and a well-developed format.
- In some cases, the district language specialist may not speak the language being taught by the volunteer, but the specialist can serve as a resource for the volunteer teacher and develop a course framework.
- Finding a dependable supply of qualified and suitable volunteers and auxiliary personnel who are willing to maintain a long-term commitment to a program is an inherent problem.

Cross-age Tutors

Cross-age tutors are usually intermediate or advanced students in successful foreign language programs who work on a short-term basis with students in the elementary school. The programs are developed by a language specialist, usually the secondary teacher, often in collaboration with the secondary students themselves.

Strengths:

- Children wish to identify with the high school tutors, who thus provide powerful models for future language learning.
- The tutors learn as much as, or more than, the elementary school children, as they go through the process of planning and presenting the lessons.

- This type of *very limited*, low-cost program can demonstrate interest in, and the success of, a second language program; thus, it can serve as a starting point for consideration of a professionally staffed curricular program.

Limitations:

- Success depends on the quality of direction provided by the language teacher and on adequate preparation of secondary students for their role as tutors. Not every secondary school language teacher has the background, time, or interest to provide the necessary training and direction.
- In many school settings the problems of distance and schedule make a cross-age tutoring arrangement impractical or impossible.

Other Instructional Models

The following are alternatives to the staffing models described above. In most cases they are implemented as stop-gap alternatives because of budgetary limitations or because of difficulty in locating teachers.

Media-based Model

In this model, the primary vehicle for teaching the language is some form of media, usually videotape (or television), audiotape, or microcomputers and videodiscs. Follow-up and reinforcement are handled either by the classroom teacher or by a traveling specialist.

The key to success of media-based programs is the quality and intensity of the follow-up. In a successful program, the media will supplement and not replace time spent with a foreign language teacher. Media-based programs in the past that haven't adequately provided for classroom interaction with a qualified teacher have been extremely disappointing in their results and have disappeared, leaving behind an extremely negative attitude toward foreign language instruction.

Strengths:

- Videotapes can present some aspects of culture with great imagination, and media programs can use special effects to lighten and enliven drill and practice sessions.

Limitations:

- The success of a media-based program is almost totally dependent on the goodwill of the classroom teacher. Students do not have the opportunity to interact with their primary source of instruction except in the case of the computer.

- Students often feel a detachment from the medium and are adept at shutting it out.
- The cost of buying, maintaining, and upgrading media equipment and software tend to offset the fact that fewer teachers are required for this model.
- High-quality media programs for teaching second languages at the elementary school level are difficult to find.

Interactive Video

In a foreign language program using interactive video, the teacher is located at one site (the base site), usually with a group of students, and one or more groups of students are located at a remote site or sites. Remote sites usually are located in another school building some distance away. Video cameras, monitors, and microphones are located at the base and remote sites so that the teachers and groups of students can see and communicate with each other. While this model is most frequently used at the high school level, it can be adapted for use with elementary school students when adequate supervision is provided at the remote sites.

Strengths:

- Small school districts can combine resources to offer a second language at the elementary school level, or even to offer more than one language.
- A single, talented teacher can reach many more students with this model than would otherwise be physically possible.

Limitations:

- It is impossible to engage in many valuable context-embedded, activity-oriented activities when all of the students and the teacher are not physically in the same place.
- Opportunities for students to produce oral language and teacher evaluation of individual progress are severaly limited in this model.
- Teaching on camera requires extensive preparation, skillful planning, and a high level of technical quality. Careful management is required to bring all these factors together. It is critical that the teacher receive adequate preparation time to insure a quality program.
- Supervision of students at the remote site(s) is an additional cost factor.

SUMMARY

In this chapter, various program models and staffing options have been presented. School districts and program planners must choose among them according to the language proficiency outcomes they desire and the budgetary and staffing circumstances in which they find themselves.

Underlying every program and model description is the fact that *language proficiency outcomes are directly proportional to the amount of time spent by students in meaningful communication in the target language.* The more time students spend working communicatively with the target language, under the guidance of a skilled and fluent teacher, the greater will be the level of language proficiency which they acquire. Planners should seek to design the best possible program in terms of language proficiency that they are able to implement.

FOR STUDY AND DISCUSSION

1. Discuss which models described in this chapter you would recommend to a school committee that has set the following priorities for its planned elementary school language program.
   a. Maximum, functional fluency in the second language
   b. Development of interest in languages so students will elect to study them at the secondary school level
   c. Fluency in a language and improved basic skills and subject–content skills
   d. Global awareness and some degree of language fluency
   e. Language introduction for highly verbal, gifted students
   f. General exposure to all aspects of language learning

2. Describe an elementary school level foreign language program that you know in the greatest detail. Explain how it fits into the categories of this chapter, and identify its strengths and its limitations. What particular aspects of the model account for the program's strengths? What changes in the model might bring about improvements in the program?

3. An influential elementary school principal has taken the position that an exploratory program is too limited in its objectives to justify its inclusion in the elementary school day. Yet, this appears to be the only feasible option for the immediate future for any form of language study at the elementary school level in this district. How would you respond to this principal's objections?

4. Your school district has had a very successful "traditional" FLES program for several years; it is staffed by several traveling specialist teachers, and follow-up programs at the middle school and at the high school are well designed and effective. Many parents and teachers would like to make an even stronger commitment to languages in the elementary school. What options and suggestions would you offer to the parent planning committee?

5. Because there are a number of international companies located in your community, as well as a college with a large population of international students, there is a strong interest in foreign languages and cultures throughout the district. How might you tap the international resources of the community to provide language learning experiences for elementary school children?

FOR FURTHER READING

The following sources are recommended for additional information about material covered in this chapter. Chapter citations are documented in *Works Cited* at the end of the volume.

California State Department of Education, Bilingual Education Office. *Studies on Immersion Education: A Collection for United States Educators*. Los Angeles: California State University; Evaluation, Dissemination, and Assessment Center, 1984.

Gray, Tracy C., Russell N. Campbell, Nancy C. Rhodes, and Marguerite Ann Snow. *Comparative Evaluation of Elementary School Foreign Language Programs*. Final Report to the U.S. Department of Education. Washington, DC: Center for Applied Linguistics, 1984.

Kennedy, Dora F., and William De Lorenzo. *Complete Guide to Exploratory Foreign Language Programs*. Lincolnwood, IL: National Textbook Company, 1985.

Lipton, Gladys C. *Practical Handbook for Elementary Language Programs*. Lincolnwood, IL: National Textbook Company, 1987.

Lipton, Gladys C., Nancy C. Rhodes, and Helena Anderson Curtain, eds. *The Many Faces of Foreign Language in the Elementary School: FLES, FLEX and Immersion*. Champaign, IL: American Association of Teachers of French, 1986. ED 264 727.

Met, Myriam. "Decisions, Decisions, Decisions!" *Foreign Language Annals* 18 no. 6 (December 1985): 469–473.

Rhodes, Nancy, and Audrey Schreibstein. *Foreign Language in the Elementary School: A Practical Guide*. Washington, DC: Center for Applied Linguistics, 1983. ED 225 403.

Schinke-Llano, Linda. *Foreign Language in the Elementary School: State of the Art*. Washington, DC: Center for Applied Linguistics, 1985. ED 264 715.

Snow, Marguerite Ann. *Common Terms in Second Language Education*. Los Angeles: UCLA, Center for Language Education and Research (CLEAR), 1986.

Snow, Marguerite Ann. *Innovative Second Language Education: Bilingual Immersion Programs*. Los Angeles: UCLA, Center for Language Education and Research (CLEAR), 1986.

Strasheim, Lorraine A. "FLEX: The Acronym and the Entity." *Die Unterrichtspraxis*. 15:60–62.

Williford, Mary L. "The Answer: High School Foreign Languages Tutoring Program," *Foreign Language Annals* 12 no. 3 (May 1979): 213–214.

Chapter 4

Planning the Program: Budgets, Staffing, and Other Practical Matters

PLANNING PROCESS

Planning, the most crucial element in the success of any language program at the elementary or middle school level, is often given the least disciplined attention. Programs at this level are frequently initiated because of the enthusiasm of an individual or a group, and in many cases the eagerness to implement the program competes with the need to plan carefully. A thoughtful, thorough planning process that involves all the affected members of the community can build a support system for the program which will help it to weather shifting fads and priorities in the curriculum, the school, and the community.

Pressure to implement programs prematurely was a common problem with the short-lived experiments of the 1960s. As Theodore Andersson pointed out in his thorough account of the history of elementary school foreign language programs (1969:138),

> Many communities, enchanted by the promise that a FLES program offers, set out with a minimum of preparation, only to find later that, to endure, a FLES program requires hard work, time, money, and expertise. A minimum commitment—a late start, doubtful continuity, too little class time, overloading the teacher, leaving the teacher to work in isolation— leads to almost certain disenchantment.

At a minimum, a planning group should include parents; elementary, middle/junior high school and high school administrators; language teachers; and classroom teachers at the affected levels. The planning group should make recommendations to the administration, which in the end will carry the responsibility for effectively implementing the elementary foreign language program.

The elementary or middle school language program that begins with planning for the entire language sequence, not just for the initial year, is most likely to succeed. Language teachers from all levels can contribute to planning and program development, and they can work together in staff development activities designed to facilitate a smooth transition from one grade to the next. All members of the group should be involved in planning from the beginning so that together they can address these concerns:

Philosophy

Goals

Budget

Resources

Staffing

Support of existing staff

Choice of language(s)

Who should study languages?

Scheduling

Curriculum

Integrating second language learning into the basic curriculum

Articulation with later language programs

Building public relations

Evaluation

Sharing experiences and ideas

Philosophy

The statement of philosophy for the elementary school foreign language program must be congruent with the statement of philosophy or mission statement of the school or the district. This statement of philosophy is the starting point for program planning and will shape many of the responses to the planning considerations outlined in this chapter. The following statement of philosophy from New York State can serve as a model for formulating a local statement:

> . . . language is our connection to our community and to the world. Through language, we identify the world around us, express our concerns and dreams, and share our experiences and ideas.

The ability to communicate in a second language increases the opportunities to interact with other peoples and to understand other cultures. As the world becomes increasingly interdependent, it is important for every person to acquire the skills for communication with others and for cross-cultural understanding.

. . . In light of these benefits, the study of a second language should be an integral part of every student's educational experience. All students deserve the opportunity to study a second language in order to prepare themselves for an informed and productive role in tomorrow's world community. (*Modern Languages for Communication*, 1987:3)

Goals

In order to decide which type of program to offer, planners must determine the expected educational outcomes of the program. As outlined in chapter 3, the broad spectrum of potential outcomes could include, at one end, simply exposing students to foreign language study in an effort to motivate them to study further, and at the other end, a program in which functional proficiency in listening, speaking, reading, and writing is the goal. *The level of fluency a student will gain in an elementary foreign language class is directly related to the amount of time students spend using the language.* For example, students in a program that meets two or three times a week will not acquire the same level of proficiency as will students enrolled in a total immersion program in which they are in contact with the language for the entire school day. Reading and writing the foreign language are realistic goals only for FLES programs that provide more than brief exposure to the language, and for those programs that involve full or partial immersion. If new programs at the elementary or middle/junior high school level are to succeed, their positive features and their distinctive goals must be clearly identified and articulated.

Functional language proficiency is a goal that can only be accomplished in programs where there is sufficient time available. Students have achieved functional language proficiency when they are able to communicate in the foreign language on any topics appropriate to their age and grade level. This level of proficiency could not be attained in a FLEX or an Exploratory program and would be difficult to attain in most FLES programs. It *can* be accomplished in total and partial immersion programs in which half the school day or more is devoted to second language learning.

The community in which the language program is being planned will have a strong influence on the goals that are chosen. For example, it may provide a more favorable climate for one language over another, or community values could very well determine what level of language proficiency is seen as desirable or worthy of support. In some communities a heavy cultural emphasis might seem very important, while in other communities a heavy career orientation might be seen as important, giving other directions to the program.

As program goals emerge, specific program models will suggest themselves. At this point, planners can identify existing programs built on models similar to those they are considering. Planners should correspond with people involved in these programs and try to visit them in order to determine whether the goals they are reaching are comparable to the results they hope to achieve themselves. Study and visits of this type will make it clear that *programs must offer languages for a significant amount of time in order to achieve significant goals.* School districts should be encouraged to begin programs that will result in as much language learning as possible for the students.

It is vitally important to set realistic program goals and to communicate them to parents, teachers, administrators, the school board, and the community. *The language proficiency students attain in any elementary school foreign language program is a direct result of the goals of the program and of the amount of time they spend in language study.* The program models chart in chapter 3 graphically illustrates the variety of goals in elementary school programs; the chart shows that achieving each level of fluency depends on the amount of time available for study.

Budget

The level of funding that a school system is willing to commit to a language program will be the final determiner of the shape and scope of a program. It is imperative to plan with budget factors in mind, developing a program that will make the best use of the funds available. The most carefully planned "dream" program will suffer if shortcuts and compromises must be made in order to stretch an inadequate budget. A realistic proposed budget will take the following factors into account:

1. Start-Up Costs

FLES or FLEX Programs

Start-up costs for a FLES or Exploratory program will include realia, materials, a collection of resource books and sample programs for teacher use, some audiovisual equipment, and other nonconsumable classroom materials. These costs may also include additions to the instructional resource center such as filmstrips, slides, library books, and displays.

Immersion Programs

In an immersion program the start-up costs are significant, because target language materials must be purchased for all elements of classroom instruction and library supplementation, and some may have to be developed locally.

Media-based Programs

Media-based formats, such as interactive cable programs, will also have relatively high start-up costs for materials and equipment.

2. Salaries

Language Specialists

Schools choosing a language specialist model will immediately add the expense of salaries for the language teacher(s). As the program develops, more teachers will be hired to staff new levels and new sections.

Nonspecialist Tutors

Programs which use nonspecialist tutors will require a professional coordinator to supervise the program at some percentage of a full-time salary.

Immersion Teachers

Immersion programs have no additional salary costs since the immersion teacher replaces a regular classroom teacher, rather than supplementing that teacher. It should be noted, however, that the most successful immersion models include a native-speaking classroom aide in each classroom, for at least part of each day.

3. Curriculum and Staff Development Time

There are few investments that can yield a greater return than planning time for teachers. If at least some of the initial planning is done by an entire language department, the commitment to the total program and the chances for smooth articulation are both improved. Schools should budget to fund at least several weeks of planning time before beginning a new program, and regular summer planning time each year thereafter.

Curriculum Development

Although commercial materials are available for some FLES programs, most schools will find that they need to develop at least some part of the curriculum to meet the particular needs of the local community. There is very little available commercially for FLEX programs or for the less-commonly taught languages, so local planning will consume considerable time and energy. Immersion programs generally require extensive locally developed materials.

Staff Development

Teachers in elementary school foreign language programs will need regular staff development opportunities, separately and with secondary school language faculty. Especially with the classroom-teacher model, staff development opportunities should not intrude on regular planning time or on what would otherwise be free time.

Attendance at Conferences

Because elementary school language teachers often feel very isolated, some of the best staff development support for teachers comes from attendance at foreign language conferences such as the annual meeting of the American Council on the Teaching of Foreign Languages and the annual conference of Advocates for Language Learning, which feature workshops and sessions on languages at the elementary school level. Travel and registration costs for these conferences are valuable additions to the language budget.

4. Materials

After the start-up costs for materials, there will be ongoing expenditures for the following:

Consumable Materials

- Worksheets, workbooks, crafts materials and food items fall into this category.
- Language teaching in the elementary and middle/junior high school relies heavily on visuals and realia, so costs for realia and visuals needed for each language and each level may well be greater than in other curricular areas.

Import Costs

- Costs of imported materials may be 10 to 20 percent higher than costs of domestic materials.

Textbook Costs

- When texts are available, these costs will increase with each grade level added to the program.

Duplication Costs

- The costs for ditto, mimeograph, or photocopying will be proportionally higher in programs for which there is no textbook.

Software, Hardware and Repair

- Media-based programs will have recurring expenditures in this area.

5. Miscellaneous Costs

There may be various miscellaneous costs to be considered:

- Travel between schools for language specialist teachers, when they are assigned to more than one school
- Travel from base site to receiving sites, in programs that use interactive cable

- Travel for the language coordinator for supervision purposes
- Delivery costs, when languages are taught by means of interactive cable, for transporting materials and student work from school to school
- Mailing costs for programs that incorporate systematic contacts with schools or children in foreign countries
- Admission fees, speaker's fees, and field trips
- Costs of making connections with language speakers or other representative elements of the target culture (gift shops, restaurants, museums, festivals, art galleries, etc.)
- Food and craft activities

It is sometimes possible for a school system to receive government assistance or a foundation grant for beginning a language program at the elementary school level. While this eases the impact of the start-up costs and initial planning, it is critical that there be a school commitment to a realistic level of long-term funding for the program.

Resources

Interesting and appropriate instructional materials are an important part of any language program, but up-to-date commercial materials for most program models described here may be difficult to find. Many school systems have developed their own curriculum and materials for FLES and FLEX programs, especially in French, German, and Spanish, and these can serve as a starting point for local materials development. Immersion programs in French often draw on resources created for Canadian programs, although these must usually be adapted somewhat for use in the United States. Spanish immersion programs can often make use of some materials developed for bilingual programs, but these materials, too, must be adapted to suit the different language sophistication of the learner. Immersion programs in other languages must rely on locally developed materials and on those developed in already-existing immersion programs. Materials suitable for elementary school children in less commonly taught languages such as Arabic, Chinese, Japanese, and Russian are the most difficult to obtain.

The choice of a program model for which few existing curriculum materials are available requires a commitment to the time and expertise necessary for materials development. Since the goals are so limited, creation of materials for a short-term FLES or FLEX program may well be a realistic task for a few teachers working with locally available native speakers during several weeks in the summer. Developing an articulated FLES program, however, will require skilled and experienced teachers and the cooperation of native speakers over a significant period of time, probably including regular released time during the school year. The planning time and start-up curriculum costs for an immersion program that has to be developed locally will represent a major investment for the district.

As more school systems make a commitment to languages at the elementary school level, and as more teachers are able to articulate clearly what kinds of materials they need for these programs, publishers are more likely to produce materials that are usable. That development will make planning a program at the elementary or middle school level an easier and more efficient process.

Staffing

There is no single decision that will affect the success of the language program more than the choice of teachers. School districts will want to insure that the teachers they select have had training and experience in working with elementary school children, that they have excellent language skills, and that they have had training in the teaching of a foreign language. In states that have a certification category for elementary school language teachers, only licensed/certified teachers should be hired. The best insurance for the success of a language program is the hiring of skilled and talented teachers.

Teacher Skills

Skills and classroom practices commonly found at the secondary school and college level do not transfer directly into the elementary school classroom. Even teachers who are very successful at the higher levels will require additional background and training before they attempt to work with elementary school children. Successful elementary teachers who are fluent in a foreign language will require some background in foreign language methodology before they can reach the same high level of effectiveness in foreign language teaching as they have attained in other subjects. Because so much of the instruction in the elementary school is oral, and because the teacher is the only model for the children most of the time, it is especially important that the teacher have excellent oral language skills.

Teacher Availability

The short-term and long-term availability of teachers will influence the selection of both the program model and of the language(s) to be taught. An articulated FLES program in Japanese would be a questionable choice in an isolated rural community that finds it difficult to attract new teachers, while a FLEX or FLES option in French, German, or Spanish could be realistic in the same community. Searching for a teacher of Japanese might be very manageable in a large, cosmopolitan urban system where the supply of teachers would be more reliable.

Immersion Teachers

Immersion programs require teachers who are fluent in the target language and are also certified elementary school teachers. They must be capable of teaching the entire curriculum in the foreign language, and they must understand the process of second language acquisition. Some school districts with immersion programs have found it necessary to recruit teachers abroad in order to find staff with adequate background and language skills—and then they have faced the challenge of orienting foreign staff to the realities of the American school and the psyche of the American child. Many teachers in Spanish immersion programs have been drawn from a background in bilingual education, but some readjustment of attitudes and assumptions is necessary before these teachers adapt smoothly to an immersion approach.

Support of Existing District Staff

Support of Elementary Principals and Teachers

The success of a language program is closely tied to the environment of the school in which it is placed. It is vital that the principal and the teachers in the school be in favor of the program, that they share commitment to its goals, and that they participate in program planning.

In programs using a language specialist model, classroom teachers who feel themselves to be a part of the language teaching team can extend the language learning into the regular school day. They may suggest curricular areas for reinforcement or vocabulary development in the language classroom, encourage the use of the foreign language during other school activities, and participate in language classes with the children, thus serving as powerful models of interest and enthusiasm.

In programs using a classroom teacher model, tremendous responsibility for success of the program rests with individual teachers for whom language instruction is only one component in a busy, demanding schedule. Teachers with a commitment to the language program will find ways to use the language communicatively throughout the day and will be in a position to give individual students the special attention they may need in order to succeed to the level of their own potential. Without real commitment to the program, participation may be grudging, and results from the students will be disappointing.

Immersion programs, in particular, require the coordinated efforts of the principal and all of the staff to create a second language environment and to work toward unified goals.

Support of Existing
Foreign Language Staff

The success of an elementary school language program also depends to a great extent on the support and expertise of the existing foreign language staff in the school system, who will work with the students from the elementary and middle school/junior high program once they reach the secondary school levels. If teachers at later levels are unsupportive or ineffective, the program at the elementary school will eventually suffer.

A case in point is a medium-sized Midwestern district that taught three languages at the senior high school; one of the languages, French, had very low enrollments and dissatisfied students. In the 1960s an elementary school program in French was introduced by a talented and innovative teacher, and junior high enrollments soared when students reached that level. As soon as these students entered the senior high school, however, they dropped French, sometimes after a week or two, or did not ever register, on the basis of the "grapevine" alone.

After a year or two of this type of enrollment pattern, the school board discontinued the entire French program on the grounds that they could not justify continuing a feeder program without the senior high school culmination. The elementary school program was blamed by some for giving children "false" expectations that language learning would be fun, that the work would be meaningful and enjoyable, and that everyone could learn a language. By the mid-1980s, French had been reintroduced in the district, but no languages had returned to the elementary school.

Choice of Language(s)

Which language to offer is often a difficult and emotional issue at the beginning of the planning process. Community interest, availability of materials and staff, and potential for articulation must all be taken into consideration. When none of these factors plays a determining role, many school districts have chosen to advertise a "foreign language" position rather than to indicate a specific language. The best available candidate is hired, regardless of the language, and the quality of the resulting program lays a foundation for long-term success. Compelling rationale can be developed for *any* of the commonly taught languages, and any language, when well taught, can provide children with the benefits of global awareness, enhanced basic skills, identification with other cultures, self-esteem, and communicative language skills.

If the elementary school program is implemented in only one language, a possible adverse effect on enrollments in other languages at the middle school/junior high and high school levels must be considered. On the other hand, implementing an elementary language program in more than one language may fragment the district's program and compound articulation problems. This is one of the most difficult issues to wrestle with. There is some justification for the fear that students will choose the elementary school language for continuation at the high school level, thus crowding out the other languages. In many districts, however, all languages have benefited from an increased interest in learning languages, and students entering high school choose to add a third language, or to explore a different language. It is important to provide more than one entry point into the district's language program in order to accommodate students who would like to study an additional language or who were not able to enroll in the elementary language program.

It is especially desirable to introduce the less-commonly-taught languages, such as Arabic, Chinese, Japanese, and Russian, into the elementary school because of their critical importance to the national interest. These languages are more difficult for the English speaker and thus require a much longer exposure before competence can be attained than is the case with the more common school offerings. Their introduction early in the curriculum would make it much more likely that students could develop usable communication skills in them.

Who Should Study Languages?

"Inclusive education" is a concept that has grown increasingly significant during the 1980s. This may be an excellent time to shed the "elitist" image that foreign languages have borne for most of this century in the United States. Evidence from the inner-city schools of Philadelphia, Milwaukee, and Cincinnati, among others, supports the idea of including learners of all levels of ability and background in foreign language study. Students with poor skills may even have the most to gain from the opportunity to study languages (Masciantonio 1977). The practice in some schools of reserving foreign language study for children who are reading at or above grade level stands in direct contradiction to the information obtained from the Masciantonio study. Such practices may be taking away opportunities for foreign language study from those children who could benefit from it the most.

Teachers in Chicago (Estelle 1985), New York State (Schnitzler 1986), and in other areas, have reported success in teaching foreign languages to learning-disabled and to mentally handicapped students, especially when they employ an oral, communicative methodology. A special education teacher in Glyndon, Minnesota verified an observation made by many elementary school language teachers when she noted that some of her students were achieving school success and satisfaction for the first time in their French classes, and that as a result their overall attitude and performance had improved in other school subjects as well.

At the other end of the scale, the gifted child is often selected first to be given the opportunity to study a language. Language teachers are caught in a conflict regarding programs for the gifted child. While there is evidence that languages can be of value to every child, and programs offered exclusively to the gifted tend to reinforce an elitist image for languages, it is also true that many language programs that were begun only for the gifted have led to programs for all children because of their success and popularity.

Gifted children are often especially good language learners as a result of certain frequently observed learning characteristics: retentiveness, a high degree of verbal ability, persistent goal-directed behavior, ability to work independently. For the gifted child, languages can be a key to unlock new dimensions of learning and new perspectives. With the foreign language as a tool, the gifted have the opportunity to explore a new system of thinking, a new cultural context, and, at advanced levels, even new literary and political perspectives.

The academically talented are among the nation's most precious resources, the pool from which our strongest leaders are likely to come. In an increasingly interdependent global community, these leaders of tomorrow cannot afford to be monolingual. Programs designed specifically for the gifted must be designed to meet their specific needs and must capitalize on their particular abilities, and they should be supported by an appropriate rationale and curriculum. Coordinators of programs for the gifted, working together with knowledgeable language teachers, can design the best possible program for this group.

Scheduling

The way in which the elementary language program is scheduled is also an important consideration. Will the program be offered once a week, every other day, or daily? How much time will be allotted per class? For optimal learning to take place, elementary foreign language programs should meet for a minimum of twenty to thirty minutes per day, five days per week, with as much additional reinforcement of the language throughout the school day as possible. For Core French programs in Canada (equivalent to FLES programs in the United States), forty minutes per day is the recommended standard. Programs that do not meet daily will be required to devote a large proportion of class time to review activity to compensate for the long periods of time between language classes.

Another important point to consider is how the foreign language program fits into the total elementary school curriculum. One frequent obstacle to beginning foreign language programs at the elementary level is the complaint from classroom teachers and administrators that there is not enough room in the school day for the present curriculum, let alone enough time to add another subject to it. Many school districts have addressed this problem by allotting some of the language arts or social studies time for the foreign language program. Some districts take a little time from each subject area in order to make a place for languages. When going through the difficult process of finding time for an elementary school foreign language program, it is important to stress the interdisciplinary aspects of foreign language learning and the well-documented benefits to first language skills.

Another way to deal with the scheduling problem is to plan a content-based curriculum that interfaces with the basic curriculum at various points and that is planned in such a way that many objectives from the basic curriculum are clearly defined in the second language curriculum. Too often, elementary foreign language programs state that the program is interdisciplinary or that subject–content instruction is included, but in reality these turn out to be only token activities. (For information on effective use of content-based instruction see the discussion in chapter 7.)

Curriculum

Once the goals of the program have been set, it is necessary to formulate a curriculum to meet these goals. There are three avenues to approaching curriculum development:

1. *Choosing Curriculum*
   The first and easiest approach is to locate already-prepared curriculum that is basically compatible with the program goals and that is suitable for the age level of the students.
2. *Adapting Curriculum*
   The second approach is to locate curriculum that is close to what is desired but that needs to be adapted in some way.
3. *Writing Curriculum*
   The third avenue, and the most difficult, is to begin from scratch to write curriculum.

Each of these three options is discussed more fully below.

Curriculum Sources

Sources of curriculum for elementary language programs from outside the district include commercial materials and those developed by other school districts. You may find commercial materials by writing to publishers or by contacting them at foreign language conferences, and through contacts with existing programs. (See appendix C) Many materials developed by existing programs to meet local needs are available through ERIC (Educational Resources Information Center), which can be accessed at most public and university libraries (microfiche and paper copy), through the Kraus Curriculum Library, and through contacts with individuals in existing programs.

Other sources of curriculum may include commercial or locally-developed materials for ESL and bilingual classes. Many of these materials demonstrate the application of linguistic and psychological research to the language learning process and they can be successfully adapted to a foreign language format.

Screening Curriculum Sources

Key factors in determining the appropriateness of materials for adoption in the local program include the following:

Publication date

Many materials with publication dates in the 1960s and early 1970s do not reflect the insights gained through research and experience during the late 1970s and the 1980s. It is important to note, however, that a recent publication date does not guarantee that materials have been developed in harmony with current research and practice.

Compatibility with philosophy and goals of the local program

Because goals and circumstances in each local situation differ so markedly, especially at the elementary school level, the transfer of a curriculum from one setting to another is especially problematical. Also, publishers find it difficult, especially at this level, to produce materials that will meet all the needs of the wide variety of programs being developed.

Age-appropriateness

In some programs teachers have attempted to solve the problem of materials by adapting high school or college texts, or using texts developed at a much earlier date. We do not recommend the adaptation of high school and college texts because topics and activities covered are inappropriate to the interests of children, and there is often a strong grammatical bias in upper level textbooks of this type.

Adapting Curriculum

Whatever curriculum is chosen, be it commercially prepared or developed by another school district, it must be adapted and modified to fit the local situation. For example, a curriculum planned for a daily program would have to be modified to fit the needs of an alternate-day program. A curriculum written for a regular classroom group might have to be modified for use with students in a gifted and talented program, or for a class with a high proportion of special-education students.

Specific interests and priorities of the local school or community must also be taken into account. Children in a rural community will probably not relate well to a program designed to capitalize on the city environment of the school system for which it was created. A school in which many children have realistic expectations of traveling abroad will want to incorporate much more information about life and travel in other countries than might be appropriate in another setting. The background and interests of the teaching staff should influence which countries and which aspects of culture will be emphasized in a specific program.

Writing Curriculum

Successful local curriculum writing requires the talents of a skilled teacher, or, preferably, a team of teachers who are very familiar with the principles of second language acquisition, communicative language teaching, curriculum development, and child development. In addition, all materials must be screened for linguistic and cultural accuracy by at least one native speaker of the language.

Curriculum writers need to examine a wide variety of available materials, both from commercial sources and from other districts, in order to emulate the strengths and avoid the pitfalls represented there. No curriculum will be in its final form until it has been field tested and revised as a result of student and teacher reaction.

The development of local curriculum is a time-consuming, costly, and rigorous process. It requires strong support from the district and from the administration, through released time and/or summer writing time, and there must be financial recognition of the high degree of skill and dedication involved in the task. The reward can be an exemplary program that meets the needs of the district in a very precise way—which also makes a contribution to the development of elementary school foreign languages in other communities.

Integrating Second Language Learning into the Basic Curriculum

Mathematics, science, and social studies curricula at the elementary school level contain many topics and units of study that can be incorporated into the foreign language curriculum. A language program in which the subject matter taught in regular academic subjects is reviewed and reinforced is more likely to be welcomed as a positive contribution to the school day. Mathematics concepts can be taught with limited vocabulary and with considerable use of manipulative experiences. Science at the elementary school level is primarily based on experience and discovery, and many of these experiences and discoveries can occur through the foreign language with no risk to the pupils' ability to understand the concept. The goals of social studies and foreign language instruction intersect at many points, especially in the early grades when both subjects deal with the individual student and the immediate environment of school, home, family, and community. At later grade levels the geography, culture, and customs of foreign peoples are natural areas in which language instruction can make a contribution. Art, music, and physical education classes also lend themselves to reinforcement in the language classroom, and they may offer opportunities for extending language learning beyond the limits of the language class itself. To identify areas in which basic curricula and second language learning can be integrated, see the mathematics, social studies, and science learner expectations in appendix D. (See also chapter 7, *Drawing on the Whole Curriculum: Content-Based Instruction.*)

Articulation with Later Language Programs

Students leaving the elementary school foreign language program must have an appropriate course available to them in order to continue their language study. One of the reasons that earlier FLES programs failed is that the language ability the children had acquired was not taken into account when the students were programmed into middle school or junior high language courses. Often, elementary school foreign language students were forced to begin the language again when they entered junior high school or high school, because the oral proficiency they had attained was not valued in the grammatically–based secondary school program. These experiences discouraged enrollments at the elementary school, discouraged continuation of study at higher levels, and ultimately raised the question of the effectiveness of the FLES programs themselves.

The middle school/junior high program for continuing FLES students must be visibly and substantively different from the program for students who are beginning language study at that level. School districts must either establish a separate track for the continuing elementary school foreign language students, or they must insure that the content of the middle school/ junior high school courses in which they are enrolled builds on and is complementary to the knowledge they have already obtained. When full or partial immersion has been implemented at the elementary school level, middle/junior high school programs must provide some content instruction in the target language as well as advanced language instruction. As students reach the senior high school with extensive foreign language background, curriculum at that level must also change in significant, substantive ways.

Outcomes that are expected among language programs at the elementary school, middle school/junior high school, and high school levels differ because the focus at each level is different. Attempts to describe progress at one level in terms of another level must take into account the differences among programs at each level. Some of these differences are listed here:

1. Elementary school foreign language programs emphasize listening and speaking skills, while an increasing proportion of class time at the middle/ junior high school and high school level is devoted to reading and writing.

2. Elementary school students have very limited experience with grammatical analysis, an area that is addressed more formally at later levels.

3. Language skills at each level are developed to deal with different settings and different interests, in response to the interests and experiences of students at different age levels. The range of vocabulary and situations with which students at various levels can function comfortably will differ accordingly.

Successful articulation, and especially the building of a successful middle school/junior high link for a program, can be accomplished only with the full participation of the elementary school teachers together with the middle school/junior high teachers in planning the program. Adjustments in both programs may have to be made in order to insure a continuous development of language skills.

Building Public Relations

When planning the foreign language program, you must involve parents, the community, the staff, and the school board in every step of the process. Their support will be the decisive factor in the later success of the program. Once the program is in progress, spending the time and effort necessary to develop a broad support base in the school and the community will prove to be very rewarding. Some of the activities that can contribute to this support include the following:

- Making use of the media to provide publicity
- Taking field trips
- Inviting parents and others to visit classes
- Videotaping classes
- Reporting class activities to parents, to the principal, and to other teachers

- Sending out a monthly newsletter
- Taking part in school programs
- Putting on a special program for parents and/or for the community
- Sending second language invitations and greeting cards

These activities give the program visibility and communicate the activities and accomplishments of the elementary school foreign language program. They also serve as an effective recruitment tool for languages at all levels.

Evaluation

Program Evaluation

Evaluation must be an integral part of curriculum design. If impact on basic skills, on attitudes, or on performance in other content areas is to be measured, pretests will have to be designed and administered before the beginning of the program. The goals of program evaluation should be determined at the outset, so that specific instruments can be developed and a time line for evaluation can be built into the school schedule. Types of program evaluation include the following:

- Pupil language skills performance
- Pupil attitudes toward other languages and cultures
- Pupil attitudes toward the course
- Pupil performance in other content areas
- Teacher performance checklists
- Teacher evaluation of program
- Parent attitudes
- Outside consultant observation
- Teacher-peer observation and review
- Administrator observation and review

Pupil Evaluation and Testing

Although some school districts have chosen to give pupils in elementary school foreign language classes a pass/fail grade, or no grade at all, a program that seeks parity with other courses in the curriculum should be treated like other content areas in terms of grading. Both children and parents tend to perceive classes for which grades are not given as less important, as peripheral to the basic curriculum. The basis for evaluating student progress and for awarding grades must be compatible with the goals and the philosophy of the program. That is, if oral skills are emphasized, evaluation will be based on listening and speaking performance, even though reading and writing skills might be easier to measure objectively.

Sharing Experiences and Ideas

Sharing the experiences and good ideas that you have gained from developing an elementary school foreign language program will enable others interested in starting a program to build on what has already been done and will prevent their being forced to make the same discoveries and the same mistakes in isolation. Materials that have been painstakingly developed should be put into the ERIC system so that others may take advantage of what has been done. (See the explanation of the ERIC system in "Works Cited," page 339.) They might also be shared with the state foreign language consultant and with the state foreign language organization. Presentations at local, regional, and national conferences, newsletter articles, and contacts with professional associations are also effective ways of giving program experiences and ideas an impact beyond the local setting.

SUMMARY

This chapter has outlined the concerns you must address in the planning process for any elementary school language program. There is no factor in the program that will be more crucial to its success than a careful and thorough plan that addresses the key areas of program philosophy and goals, program model, time allocation, budget, staffing, materials, articulation, evaluation, and staff and community involvement and support. A successful plan requires a significant investment of planning time and the unqualified support of the administration and school board. When it is the product of the cooperation, research, and insight of staff, community and administration, the design of the elementary school program can be carefully tailored to local needs and priorities. Only then is the program likely to become an integrated and lasting component of the basic elementary school curriculum. The following checklist provides useful guidelines for applying the principles of this chapter.

Elementary Foreign Language Program Planning Checklist

1. _____ Hold district-wide planning meetings

   _____ Involve community

   _____ Involve classroom and language teachers, administrators

2. _____ Complete mission statement, program philosophy
3. _____ Select program model and goals

   _____ Identify pupils

   _____ Schedule plan for amount of instructional time: days per week, hours per day, years

   _____ Develop patterns of organization for staffing

   _____ Allocate budget for staff, materials, in-service and miscellaneous costs

4. _____ Identify staff
5. _____ Select language(s)
6. _____ Develop curriculum

   _____ Locate and adapt materials

   _____ Plan scope and sequence, classroom activities

7. _____ Plan articulation with secondary school programs
8. _____ Develop evaluation plan
9. _____ Design public relations activities
10. _____ Disseminate program information

FOR STUDY AND DISCUSSION

1. Which program-planning considerations might weigh most heavily in each of the following settings?

   - an isolated rural community
   - a community with a rapidly expanding suburban population
   - a small town near a medium-sized city in the American Southwest
   - an urban district with many elementary and secondary schools
   - a medium-sized city near the Canadian border
   - a private school
   - a K–12 school housed in a single building

2. You are a middle school foreign language teacher in a system with a strong secondary school program in your language and reasonably successful programs in three other foreign languages including Latin. You have just been asked to chair a committee to plan an elementary

school foreign language program. You have the freedom to choose your own committee and set your own agenda. How will you proceed?

3. An elementary school curriculum coordinator has agreed to support a new elementary school foreign language program but she believes strongly that the elementary school day is already too fragmented. She asks you to design a program that will require the minimum time out of the school day. How will you respond to her request?

4. Use the ERIC data base or the Kraus Curriculum Library to locate at least one curriculum resource in your language for the elementary school level. What adaptations would you have to make in it if you wanted to use it to teach your language in a first-grade exploratory program?

5. If you could design the ideal program for the school setting that you know best, what would it be like?

FOR FURTHER READING

The following sources are recommended for additional information about material covered in this chapter. Chapter citations are documented in *Works Cited* at the end of the volume.

Gray, Tracy C., Russell N. Campbell, Nancy C. Rhodes, and Marguerite Ann Snow. *Comparative Evaluation of Elementary School Foreign Language Programs*. Final Report to the U.S. Department of Education. Washington, DC: Center for Applied Linguistics, 1984.

Lipton, Gladys, Nancy C. Rhodes, and Helena Anderson Curtain, eds. *The Many Faces of Foreign Language in the Elementary School: FLES, FLEX and Immersion*. Champaign, IL: American Association of Teachers of French, 1986.

Masciantonio, Rudolph. "Innovative Classical Programs in the School District of Philadelphia," *Foreign Language Annals* 3 no. 4 (May 1970): 592–595.

Rhodes, Nancy, and Audrey Schreibstein. *Foreign Language in the Elementary School: A Practical Guide*. Washington, DC: Center for Applied Linguistics, 1983.

Schinke-Llano, Linda. *Foreign Language in the Elementary School: State of the Art*. Washington, DC: Center for Applied Linguistics, 1985. ED 264 715.

Chapter 5

Building Programs on a Sound Foundation: From Theory to Practice

Children have a reputation for being natural language learners, for very good reason. Almost without exception they have learned their native language with apparent ease, and by the time they are six years old they have brought it to a level of fluency that is the envy of non-native speakers. Parents who bring their children into a second language setting and immerse them in a new situation, for example, an elementary school class taught in the foreign language, often experience a kind of miracle. After around six months their child begins to function successfully in the new setting and at a linguistic level to which the parents cannot hope to aspire, even when they have been studying the language seriously for a similar period of time.

These examples of children's natural language learning ability might seem to suggest that the best thing to do to help a child learn a language is simply to place the child in the target language setting and then stay out of the way to let the miracle happen. Unfortunately, this is not an approach that will make it possible to bring languages to every child. There is, however, both linguistic and psychological theory to help explain children's seemingly effortless second language acquisition and to provide insights that can make the classroom a better place for such language acquisition to take place. An understanding of this theory, together with an understanding of the principles of child development and of the characteristics of children at different stages of development, will help prepare the teacher to create a curriculum and activities that bring languages and children together effectively.

SECOND LANGUAGE ACQUISITION

Second language acquisition theory may help to explain the puzzling situation of children who acquire languages more quickly, and apparently with much less effort, than do their parents, when placed in a local school in the second language environment. The children are in a setting in which they are surrounded by language that is made meaningful because of the context and because of the way teachers speak to them. They are given time to sort out the language that they hear and understand, until they are ready to begin to use it for their own expressive purposes. Their parents, on the other hand, are usually busy learning rules, and they attempt to apply them later to a setting in which they have something to say. For Stephen Krashen, a linguist who has synthesized much of recent second language acquisition research in his writing, the children would be *acquiring* language, the parents would be *learning* it. A review of several of Krashen's theories follows.

Acquisition vs. Learning

The distinction between *acquisition* and *learning* illustrated above is the first hypothesis of second language acquisition, as explained by Krashen (1981b). A second hypothesis, *The Natural Order Hypothesis*, suggests that the structures of a language will be acquired in approximately the same order, regardless of what is being taught in a formal setting.

Monitor Hypothesis

Krashen's third hypothesis describes the functions of the *monitor*. The monitor is the trigger in the brain which applies rules that have been learned in order to accurately produce or interpret a message in the target language. The monitor at work makes the speaker aware of a mistake after it has been made, or it triggers awareness of the error in time to prevent its being spoken aloud. For the monitor to work effectively, the speaker must know the rule, have time to think of the rule and apply it, and be in a setting in which it is appropriate to focus on form. These conditions do not usually apply in the normal conversational situations in which a child is most commonly exposed to the target language.

Input Hypothesis

Krashen's fourth hypothesis of second language acquisition probably has the most direct application to the elementary school foreign language classroom. The *Input Hypothesis* suggests that the most important factor in the amount of language acquired by a learner is the amount of *comprehensible input* to which that learner is exposed. *Comprehensible input* is understood to be the amount of language which the learner can fully understand, plus just a little more: $i + 1$. The "i" represents the level at which the student is now; " + 1" is just a little beyond. As with Piaget's cognitive theories, for Krashen,

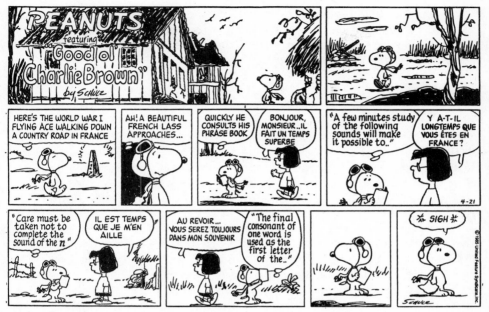

Worrying about rules and accuracy can impede communication!

the learner must always be challenged, but never to a point at which frustration sets in.

The Input Hypothesis provides a powerful reason for the exclusive use of the target language for all classroom purposes. However, simply deciding to use the target language is not enough. It must be used in such a way that the message is understood by the student at all times, even though every word of the message may not be familiar. This is accomplished through the use of gestures, examples, illustrations, experiences, and caretaker speech, as described below. When teachers complain that children do not understand them when they use the target language, it may well be because they are using the target language at a level that is too far beyond the child's current ability to understand—$i + 10$ or perhaps $i + 50$. Learners who are presented with language too far beyond their current level may well conclude that they are not good language learners and/or that this language is simply too hard to be learned. An important part of the teacher's planning time for a classroom based on the principles of second language acquisition will be devoted to strategies for making the target language comprehensible to the students.

The Input Hypothesis, while currently the subject of lively professional discussion, has brought new attention to the importance of listening skills and to the potential benefits that can come from increased listening opportunities for all students, especially those at the beginning level. An extended listening period gives learners the opportunity to gather meanings and associate them with language. They can give their full attention to understanding the messages that are being communicated, without the pressure to imitate or respond immediately.

Affective Filter Hypothesis

A fifth hypothesis Krashen presents describes the *affective filter*, a highly visual term for a phenomenon that has been observed in all forms of education. Children and adults alike are known to resist learning when learning is unpleasant, painful, or being attempted in a punitive environment. Students' ability to learn more readily those things they *want* to learn is well recognized. Krashen relates these experiences to language acquisition by describing a filter that the brain erects to block out second language input, no matter how carefully designed that input may be. The filter goes up in the presence of anxiety or low self-confidence or in the absence of motivation. The filter goes down and the input can come through when motivation is high, when a student is self-confident, and when the learning takes place in a relatively anxiety-free environment. The filter plays an important role in planning lessons for adult learners, to whom a major source of anxiety is the pressure to speak a second language early in the learning experience. Although most children seem not to have the same anxiety about speaking in a foreign language, an environment in which children feel self-confident, free, and highly motivated is certainly desirable.

Conditions for Second
Language Acquisition

According to Krashen and other researchers, language acquisition takes place most effectively when the input is meaningful and interesting to the learner, when it is comprehensible ($i + 1$), and when it is not grammatically sequenced. These ideas contrast sharply with some practices that have been common in language teaching. Language acquisition theory suggests that the language to which learners are exposed should be as natural as possible—that the past tense, for example, should not be postponed until students are able to analyze the past tense themselves. The key factor in the usefulness of input is whether or not it is comprehended. In general, the grammatical details of a message do not have as much impact on comprehensibility as do the context surrounding the message and the vocabulary with which the message is communicated, especially in the early stages of language acquisition.

Michael Long (1983) and others suggest that acquisition takes place best in a setting in which meaning is negotiated through interaction, so that the student has influence on the message being communicated. Of course, the greater the language skills of the listener, the more effectively the interaction can influence the message. This suggests to the teacher that there must be early attention to providing students with the ability to communicate messages such as these: "I don't understand"; "Could you please repeat that?"; "Did you mean that . . .?"; "Could you please speak more slowly?"; and so forth.

Comprehensible Output

Merrill Swain (1985) has taken Krashen's idea one step further with her suggestion that students acquire language most meaningfully when they also have the opportunity for comprehensible "output." That is, they need to have a setting in which their attempts at communication are valued and shaped to make them acceptable and understandable, through communicative rather than grammatical means of correction. There is mounting evidence to suggest that direct error correction has little or no influence on the accuracy of messages (Dulay, Burt, Krashen 1982). Correction that responds to the *meaning* of a message, however, has a much greater likelihood of making a difference for the speaker. Frequently correcting grammatical errors and

THE FAMILY CIRCUS **By Bil Keane**

"You corrected my English so much I forgot what I was goin' to say!"

interrupting to prod for accuracy tends to shift students' attention away from
the message being communicated and to inhibit their willingness to speak.

Use of Language

In a classroom designed to encourage second language acquisition, there will
be an emphasis on communication. The teacher will provide students with
an environment in which they are surrounded by messages in the target
language which communicate interesting, relevant information—in language
they are able to understand, language that is comprehensible to them. The
teacher will use natural language, not contrived language intended to
incorporate all the most recently-learned grammar points. It will differ,
however, from the language which the teacher might use with a native-
speaking peer, in the same way that the language a mother might use with
a young child who is just beginning to speak differs from the language she
uses with her peers. Part of creating comprehensible input for language
acquirers consists of using strategies for making the message understood,
variously known as "motherese," "caretaker speech," "teacherese," or
"foreigner talk." Some of the characteristics of this speech, as it occurs
naturally, are the following:

1. A somewhat slower rate of speech (still with the normal rate of speech
   for that speaker, but at the lower end of the range).
2. More distinct pronunciation (not distorted pronunciation, which actually
   changes the sounds of the language). For example, most American
   speakers of English pronounce the *tt* in the word *letter* as if it were
   spelled *dd*. When asked to pronounce clearly, they often change their
   pronunciation of the sound to "tt," thus distorting the language through
   an attempt to pronounce it "accurately." Such distortions are not in the
   long-range best interests of the learner.
3. Shorter, less complex sentences.
4. More rephrasing and repetition.
5. More frequent meaning checks with the hearer to make sure that he or
   she is understanding.
6. Use of gesture and visual reinforcement.
7. Greater use of concrete referents.

PAYING ATTENTION TO
THE BRAIN

The study of the brain and intensive work in cognitive psychology have
resulted in a significant shift in orientation away from the behaviorist

principles that once dominated educational thought and practice. Rote learning, habit formation, and observable outcomes are being replaced by an emphasis on meaningfulness, metacognition, and process. For the behavioral psychologist, the student is considered to be a relatively passive subject, to be manipulated through reinforcement techniques and drill. The cognitive psychologist, in contrast, sees students as active participants in the learning situation, controlling and shaping their own learning processes. In the behaviorist classroom the student responds to stimuli and reinforcement, while in the classroom based on cognitive psychology the students' own internal motivation drives the learning process. One of the most important principles of cognitive psychology for the foreign language teacher is that information is best learned and retained if it is made meaningful to students.

Glover and Bruning (1987) have summarized six major principles of cognitive psychology as they relate to instruction:

1. Students are active processors of information.
2. Learning is most likely to occur when information is made meaningful to students.
3. How students learn may be more important than what they learn.
4. Cognitive processes become automatic with repeated use.
5. Metacognitive skills can be developed through instruction.
6. The most enduring motivation for learning is internal motivation.
7. There are vast differences in students' information-processing abilities.

Elementary school foreign language teachers can apply these principles in the classroom as they engage their students in meaningful situations and make them full participants in the communication of the classroom. They can work together with teachers across the curriculum to help children understand what it is they need to learn and how their own learning best takes place—to help children become aware of the process of language acquisition and to enjoy their own progress. At the very beginning of a language sequence, for example, children can learn the importance of paying careful attention to both the language and the context in which it occurs, a first step in the process of understanding their own learning.

Attention to cognitive processes has also resulted in a new appreciation of the variety of learning styles and learning rates present in every classroom. James Asher (1986) developed his Total Physical Response approach (TPR) to language teaching as a response to the different tasks performed by the left and right hemispheres of the brain. Students respond with physical activity to increasingly complex teacher commands, and they are not expected to speak until they feel ready. TPR was intended to encourage use of right-hemisphere processes, which some have theorized to be more open to the new habits that foreign language study requires. Others have advocated the use of music, rhythm, drama, and games as methods to stimulate the right hemisphere and thus facilitate language acquisition.

COGNITIVE DEVELOPMENT

The teaching of children has been profoundly affected by the work of Jean Piaget, who identified four stages of cognitive and affective development in childhood and adolescence. The child develops cognitively through active involvement with the environment, and each new step in development builds on and becomes integrated with previous steps. Because two of the four developmental stages normally occur during the elementary school years, it is important for language teachers working with children to keep the characteristics of each cognitive stage in mind (Wadsworth 1984: 26-7). They are as follows:

1. *The stage of sensory-motor intelligence (0 to 2 years).* During this stage, behavior is primarily motor. The child does not yet internally represent events and "think" conceptually, though "cognitive" development is seen as schemata are constructed.

2. *The stage of preoperational thought (2 to 7 years).* This stage is characterized by the development of language and other forms of representation and rapid conceptual development. Reasoning during this stage is prelogical or semilogical, and children tend to be very egocentric.

3. *The stage of concrete operations (7 to 11 years).* During these years, the child develops the ability to apply logical thought to concrete problems.

4. *The stage of formal operations (11 to 15 years or older).* During this stage, the child's cognitive *structures* reach their greatest level of development, and the child becomes able to apply logical reasoning to all classes of problems.

The thinking skills of most children in elementary school foreign language programs are at the concrete stage, and experience plays a major role in all learning. Piaget points out that children are not simply miniature adults who have less experience and thus less knowledge to work with as they approach problems and new situations. They do not think like adults because their minds are not like adult minds. It is the privilege of the elementary school teacher to share their world and learn to work with it. Characteristics of children as learners at different ages and implications for foreign language teaching are described below.

CHARACTERISTICS OF ELEMENTARY AND MIDDLE SCHOOL LEARNERS

Preschool Students (ages 2 to 4)

These students are in a sensitive period for language development. They absorb languages effortlessly and are adept imitators of speech sounds. Because they are very self-centered, they do not work well in groups, and they respond best to activities and learning situations relating to their own interests and experiences. Although they have a short attention span, they have great patience for repetition of the same activity or game. Preschoolers respond well to concrete experiences and to large-motor involvement in language learning.

Primary Students (ages 5 to 7): Kindergarten and Grades 1 and 2

Most of these children are still preoperational, and they learn best with concrete experiences and immediate goals. They like to name objects, define words, and learn about things in their own world. Primary-age children learn through oral language; they are capable of developing good oral skills, pronunciation, and intonation when they have a good model. They learn well, especially beginning in first grade, through dramatic play and role play. Because of their short attention spans, they need to have a great variety of activities, but the teacher must keep in mind that children of this age tire easily. They require large-muscle activity, and they are still rather unskilled with small-muscle tasks. Teachers of primary students must give very structured and specific directions and build regular routines and patterns into the daily lesson plan.

Intermediate Students (ages 8 to 10): Grades 3, 4, and 5

Children at this age are at a maximum of openness to people and situations different from their own experience. For these students, a global emphasis is extremely important, because it gives them an opportunity to work with information from all parts of the world. As intermediates develop the cognitive characteristics of the concrete operations stage, they begin to understand cause and effect. Students in intermediate grades can work well in groups. They can begin a more systematic approach to language learning, but they continue to need first-hand, concrete experiences as a starting point and continue to benefit from learning that is embedded in context. The phenomenon of "boy germs" and "girl germs" begins to develop during these years, and children may resist partner situations with children of the opposite sex.

Transescent Students (ages 11 to 14): Grades 6, 7, and 8

During the middle school and junior high school years, students are undergoing more dramatic developmental changes than experienced at any other time in life, and on widely differing timetables. The transescent must learn to deal with a variety of experiences: emerging sexuality in a changing and often unpredictable body; reaching a cognitive plateau for a time, and then finding new, adult intellectual tools; multiplying and rapidly shifting interests; a fluid and flexible self-concept; a need to rework interpersonal relationships with adults; turbulent emotions; extreme idealism; a need to assert independence; and a powerful peer group. A major goal of all schooling for children of this age is the encouragement of positive relationships and positive self-image. Transescent children need the opportunity for broad exploration, as well as an introduction to the demands of academic disciplines.

SUMMARY

Teachers of languages for elementary school children can draw on a variety of resources as they seek to gain greater insight into their task. Second language acquisition theory, brain research, cognitive psychology, and information about child development all contribute to a greater understanding of languages and children. Information in these areas is always evolving and is subject to new questions and interpretations as understanding of human development and the mind continues to change and grow. Each teacher will find individualized ways to use theoretical insights to enhance language learning for the children of each classroom.

FOR STUDY AND DISCUSSION

1. What can the elementary school foreign language teacher do to create a classroom climate that promotes language acquisition? Identify specific actions and techniques that will be helpful.

2. How can the teacher plan a lesson to make sure the language presented will be comprehensible to the students? How can the classroom environment contribute to comprehension?

3. How might an awareness of current theories of brain functioning influence how you plan a language class?

4. Choose a topic or a lesson (such as animals, foods, geography) that could

be of interest to children at several age levels and explain how you would approach it differently at each of three different levels:

a. Kindergarten

b. Grade 3

c. Grade 6 or 7

FOR FURTHER READING

The following sources are recommended for additional information about material covered in this chapter. Chapter citations are documented in *Works Cited* at the end of the volume.

Asher, James J. *Learning Another Language Through Actions: The Complete Teacher's Guidebook*. 3rd ed. Los Gatos, CA: Sky Oaks Publications, 1986.

Burling, Robbins. *Sounding Right*. Rowley, MA: Newbury House, 1982.

California State Department of Education, Bilingual Education Office. *Schooling and Language Minority Students: A Theoretical Framework*. Los Angeles: California State University; Evaluation, Dissemination and Assessment Center, 1981.

Cummins, James. "The Influence of Bilingualism on Cognitive Growth: A Synthesis of Research Findings and Explanatory Hypotheses." *Working Papers on Bilingualism* 9 (1976): 1–43.

Dulay, Heidi, Marina Burt and Stephen Krashen. *Language Two*. New York: Oxford University Press, 1982.

Gaarder, Bruce. "The Golden Rules of Child Second Language Acquisition." *NABE Journal*, March 1978.

Gass, Susan M., and Carolyn G. Madden, eds. *Input In Second Language Acquisition*. Rowley, MA: Newbury House, 1985.

Glover, John A., and Roger H. Bruning. *Educational Psychology: Principles and Applications*. 2d ed. Boston: Little, Brown, and Company, 1987.

Krashen, Stephen D., and Tracy Terrell. *The Natural Approach: Language Acquisition in the Classroom*. Hayward, CA: Alemany Press, 1983.

McLaughlin, Barry. *Children's Second Language Learning*. Language in Education: Theory and Practice, No. 47. Washington, DC: ERIC Clearinghouse on Language and Linguistics, 1982. FL 012 964.

Rivers, Wilga M. "Comprehension and Production in Interactive Language Teaching." *The Modern Language Journal* 70, i (1986): 1–7.

Savignon, Sandra J. *Communicative Competence: Theory and Classroom Practice: Texts and Contexts in Second Language Learning*. Reading, MA: Addison-Wesley, 1983.

Stevick, Earl W. *Teaching Languages: A Way and Ways*. Rowley, MA: Newbury House, 1980.

Ventriglia, Linda. *Conversations of Miguel and Maria—How Children Learn a Second Language: Implications for Classroom Teaching*. Reading, MA: Addison-Wesley, 1982.

Vitale, Barbara Meister. *Unicorns are Real: A Right-Brained Approach to Learning*. Rolling Hills Estates, CA: 1982.

Winitz, Harris, Paul A. García, and Renate Frick. "Teaching Language through Comprehension." In Patricia B. Westpfahl, ed. *Meeting the Call for Excellence in the Foreign Language Classroom*. Lincolnwood, IL: National Textbook Company, 1985: 14–29.

Chapter 6

Learning from the Experiences of Immersion Programs

IMMERSION: WHAT IS IT?
WHAT MAKES IT WORK?
WHAT ARE THE RESULTS?

In Chapter 3, immersion was presented as the program model that has the greatest success in terms of language outcomes. Students in immersion programs become functionally proficient in the second language at a level appropriate to their age and grade in school. Immersion students not only become bilingual but also master the subject content of the regular elementary school curriculum that is taught through the second language. As an approach to elementary school foreign language education, immersion is easily able to provide a holistic language learning experience for second language students since the teachers and students are able to communicate throughout the entire school day on topics spanning the entire range of the curriculum.

The purpose of this chapter is to expand on the overview of immersion given in chapter 3, to provide answers to the most frequently asked questions about immersion, and most important, to relate what is known about immersion to other types of elementary school foreign language programs. Key instructional concepts of immersion are presented in the latter half of the chapter. This group of principles and strategies identifies some of the features of immersion programs that make them so successful. These concepts can provide insight and direction for the redesigning of other types of elementary school foreign language programs to make them even more effective.

In immersion, the focus of instruction is on the curriculum (social studies, science, mathematics, language arts, health, art, music), and the second language is used as a tool to teach the curriculum. It has been said that immersion teachers are elementary teachers 100 percent of the time and are also language teachers 100 percent of the time. Language arts is approached in an immersion classroom very much as it would be approached in a regular monolingual classroom, except that it is taught in the target language. Since the syllabus is oriented toward the regular curriculum of the school district, and since the students need the language to communicate on a daily basis, immersion programs are usually able to avoid the pitfalls of many second language programs that are solely grammar-based. They are truly able to base language learning on real communication needs.

Immersion students are generally monolingual English speakers who are learning another language for enrichment purposes, and immersion teachers are elementary-certified teachers who are native or near-native speakers of the second language.

As outlined in chapter 3, there are several variables in immersion program design. Programs can vary as to the entry point (early, middle, or late immersion), as to the amount of time each day that is spent using the second language, and as to the point at which English reading is introduced (total or partial immersion).

Immersion Goals

Immersion program goals may be summarized as follows:

1. Functional proficiency in the second language
2. Maintenance and development of English language arts skills comparable to or surpassing the achievement of students in English-only programs
3. Mastery of subject–content material of the school district curriculum
4. Cross-cultural understanding

HOW DID IMMERSION START?

The idea of immersing second language learners in an environment in which they must use the language is certainly not a new one. This is something which has happened throughout history and is evidenced in many international private schools throughout the world. The first public school immersion program in recent times began in 1965 with a kindergarten in St. Lambert in Quebec. It was prompted by a group of English-speaking parents who were concerned that traditional French programs were not sufficient to meet their children's needs for greater comprehension of and fluency in French, at a time when bilingualism in French and English had become a necessity in Canada.

As research information from Canadian immersion programs began to be disseminated, and as immersion programs were spreading rapidly in

Canada, similar programs began to be established in the United States, where a different set of realities regarding second language learning existed. Whereas Canadian immersion programs were developed because of a demonstrated need for bilingualism, immersion programs in the United States were established for a variety of reasons, most of which centered on a search for alternative approaches to successful second language teaching for young children.

The first immersion program in the United States was started in 1971 in Culver City, California, with the help of professors at the University of California at Los Angeles (Campbell 1984; Cohen 1974). They had observed the St. Lambert Elementary School immersion program, were familiar with the Lambert and Tucker research project (1972), and were excited by the possibilities of establishing such a program in the United States. The Culver City Spanish Program, like many immersion programs in the United States, is modeled after the St. Lambert program.

The number of immersion programs in the United States grew slowly: in 1974, a total immersion program in French was started in Montgomery County, Maryland, near Washington, D.C.; in 1974 a partial immersion program in French, German, and Spanish began in Cincinnati, Ohio; in 1975 a total immersion program in French was started in Plattsburgh, New York; and in 1977 the Milwaukee Public Schools opened the German component of its immersion program, and San Diego Schools began a program in Spanish. Immersion programs have continued to spread until, in 1987, there were a total of thirty such programs in the United States, with approximately ten thousand students, in locations ranging from small rural areas to large urban school districts. The new programs are spread across the country in California, Louisiana, Maryland, Massachusetts, Michigan, New York, Oklahoma, Oregon, Texas, Utah, and Washington, D.C. Canadian programs also continue to grow, so that currently there are over 170,000 students involved in immersion programs in Canada.

The programs have been initiated in a variety of ways: in some cases the school principal, in other cases parents, teachers, or the district foreign language coordinator have been the most influential at early stages. An interesting historical note is that at least three of the city-wide immersion programs were developed as part of voluntary desegregation efforts. District administrators in large urban school districts such as San Diego and Milwaukee planned the immersion programs as magnet schools to attract students from all over the district.

HOW DOES IMMERSION WORK?

In early total immersion programs students begin their study of the second language in kindergarten or first grade. When the children arrive at school in the morning, they hear the teacher speak only the second language. All classroom conversation and instructions are in the second language. In this way the children acquire the second language in play and work situations that are related to meaningful communication. The emphasis is on the learning activity (reading, mathematics, social studies, art, etc.) and not on the language. Even though the teacher is constantly using the second language, the students may use English among themselves and also in speaking to the teacher. This reduces anxiety and frustration and allows the children a period of time in which they can build up comprehension skills in the second language. Within one to two years in the program, the children move rather automatically into speech production.

Since most of the students in an immersion class are monolingual, they begin on an equal footing with each other with regard to second language skills. The children tend to show little anxiety or frustration about learning in another language because the things they learn are within their experience and because every effort is made to put messages into a meaningful context. For example, they learn to speak and write about things they understand: in kindergarten a lesson on objects that sink and float, in first grade a trip to the fire station, in second grade a lesson on magnets, in fifth grade a lesson on geography, and so forth. In the beginning stages of the program they learn to say things like "I have hot lunch today"; "Can we go out for recess?"; "I want to be first"; "Give me the ball."

Children in total immersion programs learn to read through the second language rather than through the first. They read about things they have been exposed to through various experiences and can already speak about. This approach is markedly different from that used in most bilingual education programs, in which reading is always introduced in the first language. Parents of kindergarten and first grade students in immersion programs are advised that they should feel free to encourage any natural interest in reading expressed by their child, but that they should not try to formally teach English reading at home.

After two or three years in a total immersion program, formal English language arts is introduced for about thirty minutes to an hour each day—in the second or third grade, depending on the school district. A few districts wait until fourth or fifth grade to introduce instruction in English. Children continue to study the remainder of their subjects through the second language. Once children begin to read in English, the many skills that transfer from the second language enable most of them to "catch up" in English reading within one or two years. In some immersion programs, as the students progress through the middle grades, the amount of English is gradually increased until by fifth or sixth grade, there is a balance of instruction in the second language and in English. In other immersion programs, such as the one in Milwaukee (see discussion below), once students have been exposed to English for one hour per day, the amount of English continues at one hour per day for the duration of the program. The result is that 80 percent of the student's day is spent in the second language and 20 percent of the day is spent in English through the sixth grade. Variations in program design reflect the needs, desires, and resources of the individual school district.

WHAT ARE IMMERSION RESULTS?

Parents and school administrators have frequently expressed fear that students will not achieve well in the basics and will fall behind their peers in monolingual English classes. Abundant research reports on immersion programs in Canada have thoroughly described and documented the positive effects of the immersion approach since the original St. Lambert study (Lambert and Tucker 1972).

Second Language Skills

Immersion students acquire remarkable proficiency in the second language compared with students in other second language programs. But it must be noted that this proficiency is not nativelike in every aspect. Immersion students are able to communicate on any topic appropriate to their level of intellectual development, but they do make grammatical errors, and they have to use circumlocutions and other strategies to express themselves when they are lacking the appropriate vocabulary.

One reason that immersion students do not have nativelike speech in every respect is that they do not usually have the opportunity to interact with native speaking peers. Often the only native speaker model that the immersion students have available to them is their classroom teacher. The other models that they hear constantly are their non-native speaking classmates. Immersion students who have moved into a native speaking environment, however, have been able to adjust their speech successfully.

English Skills

Research results (Swain 1984) show that students in early immersion programs perform as well as, or often out-perform, their English-educated peers on tests of achievement in English. Immersion students are initially behind in their English skills but catch up within a year after the English component is introduced into the curriculum.

Subject-Content Mastery

Immersion students perform as well as or better than their monolingual English-speaking peers on tests of subject–content mastery in mathematics, science, and social studies. It is interesting to note that these achievement tests are administered in English even though the students have been taught through the second language.

Cross-Cultural Understanding

Results from research show that Canadian immersion students "develop more friendly and open attitudes toward French-Canadians" (Lambert 1984). Genesee (1987:105) suggests two reasons for this outcome. First, the acquisition of a second language results in perceptions of oneself as bilingual, as similar to those who speak the target language. Familiarization with French-Canadian culture through class materials and contact with French teachers may also help English speakers realize the fundamental similarities between the two groups.

Differences between Partial and Total Immersion Programs

As would be expected, the language skills of students in partial and total immersion programs are found to differ: the more contact hours students have with the second language, the better their second language proficiency (Campbell, Gray, Rhodes and Snow 1985).

Results from Late Immersion Programs

The outcomes from late immersion programs with respect to subject content mastery, maintenance of first language skills, and development of second language skills are difficult to summarize because of the large variation in formats which are available. Swain (1979) for example, states that if there is sufficient core French instruction prior to the program, and if sufficient additional courses are taken in French following the program, high levels of French proficiency can be attained, with no loss to the mastery of content material or native language proficiency.

Benefits of Early Immersion

One of the most obvious benefits of early immersion education is the long time it allows the student to achieve proficiency in the second language. It prepares the students to survive communicatively in a native-speaking environment, with the expectation that the student's speech will become more and more nativelike. Early immersion makes bilingualism possible for the largest number of students because functional proficiency in the second language at that level is not necessarily tied to literacy skills.

Since early immersion develops proficiency in the second language very quickly, it is possible for children to acquire the fluency they need to deal with subject content areas without any difficulty. This is not the case in partial or late immersion programs in which the level of vocabulary required in a subject–content course may be beyond the language ability of the students. In early immersion much less time is required than is required in partial immersion programs to develop the equivalent results on tests of achievement in English.

A final point in favor of early immersion programs, that should not be discounted, is the apparent enthusiasm and aptitude which young children demonstrate for language learning. Swain (1979:26) characterizes this as "feelings of ease, comfort and naturalness in using the second language." In contrast, older students may have had experiences or may have formed negative attitudes that could jeopardize second language learning (Genesee 1984). Also, since early immersion programs are an integral part of the elementary school day, they do not compete with other activities for prominence.

The Immersion Program in Milwaukee

The Milwaukee experience with immersion is representative of many of the programs that have developed in the United States since the first program in Culver City in 1971. The Milwaukee Public Schools began a total immersion program in German in 1977 as part of the integration plan for the city. German was chosen because of the strong German ethnic background present in the city. French was added in 1978, Spanish in 1980. Like its earlier counterparts in Culver City and in Montgomery County, Maryland, the program modeled its goals and structure on the St. Lambert experiment.

Students who complete the kindergarten through fifth grade sequence of the Milwaukee immersion program in French, German, or Spanish will be able to do the following:

1. Communicate (understand, speak, read, and write) in the second language about topics appropriate to their age level with ability approximating that of a pupil who is native to that language

2. Perform in English language arts and in subject–content areas as well as or better than their monolingual peers on standardized achievement tests administered in English

3. Acquire greater understanding, knowledge, and appreciation of other cultures

4. Achieve such proficiency in the second language and in English that
they are able to continue their studies in both languages (Curtain 1987:4)

According to data collected by the author (Curtain), the student population in the immersion schools represents diverse geographical and socioeconomic backgrounds and a wide range of intellectual ability. Approximately
40 percent of the students are black, and about 10 percent are Spanish-
surnamed, Native American, and Asian students. The remaining 50 percent
of the students are white. There are no criteria for entrance into the immersion
program except for parent interest and maintenance of racial balance. Students
are randomly selected from lengthy waiting lists.

Data from Milwaukee's standardized testing program, which has been
collected both from the Metropolitan Achievement Test and the Iowa Test of
Basic Skills, have been excellent since the beginning of the program. These
test results over the years have been consistent with student performance in
the Canadian immersion programs, even though the Milwaukee program
may reflect an even greater socioeconomic and intellectual diversity than do
some of the Canadian programs.

Milwaukee's immersion students consistently score well above city-wide
and national averages in standardized tests in English language arts and
mathematics. For example, in the 1981 grade three results from the German
program, 100 percent of the pupils scored in the average to above-average
range on the Metropolitan Achievement Test for Reading (in English),
compared to 70 percent for Milwaukee Schools as a whole and 77 percent
for norm groups throughout the United States. Similar results were found
in mathematics test scores and in each subsequent yearly testing program
(author).

The following generalizations apply to the test results of immersion
students in Milwaukee:

1. Students in the immersion program are achieving at or above ability
level.

2. Immersion students at every grade level are performing much better on
achievement tests administered in English than are students in English-
only programs whose performance was measured in city-wide or national
samples.

3. Student test scores are increasing grade by grade.

To further exemplify immersion test results, the table below, taken from
the Spanish immersion program, shows a sample of the patterns that
consistently appear in immersion-program testing. It can be seen that students
in grade one who have had no English instruction show a slight lag at first
but that their scores tend to increase grade by grade so that more and more

GRADE BY GRADE TEST RESULTS: IOWA TEST OF BASIC SKILLS
VOCABULARY AND READING COMBINED
Milwaukee Spanish Immersion Program 1985

Performance Categories	National Sample	Vocabulary and Reading Combined			
		Grade 1	Grade 2	Grade 3	Grade 4
HIGH	23	18	26	41	48
AVERAGE	54	60	61	54	52
LOW	23	22	13	5	0

Figure 2.   Grade by Grade Test Results: Iowa Test of Basic Skills
Source: Milwaukee Public Schools, 1985. Used by permission.

students are scoring in the high category. Since the immersion program attracts students from every ability level, it is even more significant that the numbers of students scoring in the low category decrease year by year. By fourth or fifth grade, immersion students of every ability tend to perform at average or above average levels.

In conclusion, it is important to note that while there is a great variety in the types of immersion programs now functioning, and while there are still areas that need to be investigated further, it is apparent that the immersion concept in second language education is a sound one. Extensive studies have shown that children benefit from this approach to second language acquisition, and do not suffer a loss in native language skill development. They not only become functionally proficient in a second language, but they also develop average or above-average skills in their native language.

THE IMPLICATIONS OF
IMMERSION FOR FLES CLASSES

The immersion program model offers optimum results due to the amount of time available, the ease of integration with the remainder of the elementary school curriculum, and the limitless opportunities for meaningful communication. It comes as no surprise that the study of children in immersion, partial immersion and FLES programs by the Center for Applied Linguistics (Campbell, Gray, Rhodes and Snow 1985) found immersion and partial immersion students to be far ahead of FLES students in listening, speaking, reading and writing. Furthermore, their speaking skills were much more flexible and wide ranging than were those of the FLES students, to a degree not measurable with the test instrument used for the study. The impact of this report in some circles has been for teachers, parents, and administrators to question the value of FLES programs, since the results appear to fall so short of those experienced in immersion. They have sometimes chosen to offer no language at all, when immersion was not feasible or desired.

This is a very unfortunate decision, for several reasons. First, while immersion is a powerful and very successful way for children to learn languages, it will never be able to reach every child. Immersion will continue to be an elective program, often very popular and competitive, but it will not be implemented in every school or in every community. The shortage of qualified teachers alone precludes this possibility. If every child is to have the opportunity of acquiring a second language in the elementary school, there must be a variety of high-quality options available.

Second, a well-designed, successful FLES program can prepare a school or a community for a stronger commitment to second language learning. Once children have demonstrated their interest and ability in a FLES program, parents and administrators may be willing to consider adding an immersion option to the program, or they may choose to support language learning in other significant ways, such as planning trips and developing exchange programs or building short-term immersion opportunities into the extracurricular schedule.

Third, and most important, a well-planned and skillfully taught FLES program can produce significant language outcomes. Children can acquire an impressive amount of a new language that will be of high quality in well-taught FLES programs, even under the severe time limitations which often characterize them. Graduates of such programs can have a stable foundation on which to build further skills in their second language, as well as an enriched cultural understanding and a broader perspective of the world.

The amount of time available is both the most obvious and one of the most important differences between immersion and other elementary school foreign language programs. An example of the importance of time can be seen in the fact that in most immersion programs known to the authors, the children are not given foreign language names, although this practice is common in FLES programs. One explanation may be that a FLES teacher has to use every moment and every possible opportunity to model and reinforce the target language in the short teaching time available, whereas time for immersion teachers is an ally rather than a constraint and they do not have to contrive uses of the target language. As teachers in FLES and FLEX programs seek to make the best possible use of their limited class time with students, examining other features of immersion that contribute to its remarkable success may be helpful. They may find it practical to organize their teaching around the key concepts of immersion which follow.

KEY CONCEPTS OF IMMERSION—PRINCIPLES

As FLES programs are redesigned to bring them to optimal effectiveness, these key concepts can provide insight and direction. They may be regarded as building blocks of an immersion approach.

Principle 1: Communication motivates all language use.

- There are myriad opportunities to communicate throughout the school day.
- The need to communicate is strong and ongoing.
- Pupils are encouraged to communicate in the target language, using vocabulary and structures they know.
- Communication results from a need to bridge an "information gap" or an "opinion gap."

This may be the single most important and distinctive feature of an immersion approach. In contrast to the recitation orientation of traditional FLES classrooms, the language activities in immersion are based on exchange of information. Prominent in the thrust toward communicative language teaching is the idea that for communication to take place there must be either an "information gap" or an "opinion gap" (Morrow 1981). In the immersion classroom these conditions are continually present, a natural and normal part of the entire school day.

Applications to FLES

In the FLES classroom, in contrast, the need to communicate must usually be created, and the teacher must take full advantage of every naturally occurring communicative situation. Giving directions, disciplining, and performing standard classroom routines are all recurring opportunities for communication. When access to the drinking fountain, the bathroom, and the pencil sharpener is dependent on conversations in the target language, the need to communicate is strong and genuine. Many teachers have found that Total Physical Response strategies, in which children respond to teacher commands, are a useful first step in creating a climate of communication.

Principle 2: There is natural use of oral language.

- Language use is not grammatically sequenced.
- Program design takes into account natural stages of second language acquisition:

- There is an initial listening period when students are not expected to respond in the target language.
- The ability to speak emerges and develops in a predictable manner.
- The target language is used for all classroom management.
- Classroom routines provide students with clear clues to meaning.

Applications to FLES

The elementary school foreign language teacher has often felt obligated to restrict the language used in the classroom to that which the students can understand fully and attempt to produce themselves. When teachers follow the immersion model, they enrich the language environment and surround the activity of the classroom with speech. Instead of calling for immediate imitation of words and patterns, they allow for an initial period when students are not expected to respond in the target language, thus encouraging the children to listen for *meaning* rather than listening for *speaking*. As children accumulate a stockpile of language meanings, they will also begin to speak, using vocabulary and structures drawn from the treasury of their own experience to express personal meanings. The teacher has already demonstrated that the target language has real value for expressing important ideas, as the teacher uses the language for discipline and for praise, for routine and for change of pace, for venting frustrations and for teasing and joking.

This exchange of personal meanings in natural situations is very difficult to achieve in the limited setting of the FLES classroom. If it is to occur at all, it must be a planned part of classroom activity, and it will no doubt displace some traditional "learning" activities.

Principle 3: Language is a tool of instruction, and not just the object of instruction.

In the immersion classroom this principle is clear from the first day, when the language used with the children is based entirely on practical needs—how can we communicate about the ideas and the routines of the classroom? Language becomes the object of instruction only when students have acquired enough language for the teacher to be able to approach it in the same way language arts is approached in the English track.

Applications to FLES

While this principle may seem difficult to translate fully into the FLES setting, it does suggest the possibility of choosing initial language content based on utility for the school and community setting rather than on grammatical sequencing or other factors.

Principle 4: Subject content is taught in the target language.

One of the clearest implications of immersion for all other forms of language programs is that of the value of subject–content instruction. Dulay, Burt, and Krashen (1982) suggest that the addition of even one area of subject content taught *in* the target language can have a dramatic impact on the rate and quality of second language acquisition. Simply adding a class in mathematics, music, art, social studies, science, health or physical education taught in the target language could multiply the effects of a FLES program several times over.

Applications to FLES

Within the FLES class itself, the implementation of this principle is somewhat harder, but very rewarding. One of the best features of teaching subject content in the target language is that it provides something meaningful and real to talk about. Cultural concepts are in themselves subject content and can be taught effectively in the target language. Close cooperation with teachers in other content areas will suggest concepts that can be reinforced or enriched in the language classroom. In FLES programs, the willingness of the language teacher to take responsibility for specific concepts from another subject area may ease the problem of finding time in the school day for the second language.

Principle 5: The sequence of grammar instruction follows the developmental sequence of the elementary school language arts curriculum, or may be dictated by communication needs.

Teaching of the target language structure in an immersion program is integrated into the rest of the curriculum and is not presented in isolation. Structures are modeled and introduced as they are *needed* to express meanings important to the children and to the content being addressed. This is a very different approach to grammar from what has been the practice in most language classrooms at any level—in fact, grammar has been the primary basis for curriculum and daily activities in many cases.

Applications to FLES

There is very little place for formal grammar instruction in FLES instruction. When it occurs, it should be presented as a means for communicating messages which have importance to both the speaker and the listener.

Principle 6: Error correction is minimal and focuses on errors of meaning rather than on errors of form.

- Correction should not interrupt the student flow of talk.
- Classroom activities should be developed to address recurring errors.

In the immersion classroom children are exposed to a great deal of meaningful, natural, accurate language modeling before they are expected to speak, in a setting that focuses on meaning rather than on form. When children begin to speak they naturally make errors, but early correction efforts also focus on meaning rather than on form. Teachers work with individual children to help them clarify their messages, but they do not interrupt with corrections when the child does not request assistance. Frequently, in the process of reflective listening, the teacher uses indirect error correction:

Student: I eated at McDonald's last night.

Teacher: Oh, you ate at McDonald's? What did you have?

The day-to-day need to clarify grammatical errors children make will be addressed in the interest of communication, by working with children individually or in a group to correct recurring problems that prevent them from getting their ideas across to others.

Applications to FLES

Formal error correction has little place in the FLES classroom, especially in the first several years. That does not mean that teachers cannot occasionally plan activities in which the focus is on the form of the language rather than on the meaning of the language. Such activities will be most successful when their goals are made clear to the students and when they take place in a communicative context.

Principle 7: Use of the native language is kept clearly separated from use of the target language.

In many Canadian immersion programs, the separation of languages is made very clear: classes in French are taught by a French teacher, classes in English are taught by an English teacher. In most adaptations in the United States the classroom teacher is responsible for both the target language and the English parts of the curriculum. Evidence from bilingual classrooms in the United States reinforces the idea that a clear division between the use of the native language and the use of the target language results in significantly improved second language acquisition (Wong–Fillmore 1983, 1985). Many teachers in the United States have found the simple device of using a sign to indicate the present language of communication to be very successful in maintaining a clear separation of languages. The sign, for example, reads *"English being spoken now"* on one side, *"On parle français maintenant,"* on the other. Whenever the language of classroom communication changes, the sign is flipped over.

Applications to FLES

Elementary school foreign language teachers will find that creating a tangible, visible reminder, like a sign, or raising a flag, or putting on a "French" apron, will encourage cooperation from the children—and even reminders from them when the teacher or a fellow student slips. Teachers who have tried this technique have found it to be very effective.

Principle 8: Reading instruction begins with previously mastered oral language.

As is the case in first language instruction, children in immersion programs learn to read about things they can already understand and respond to in the target language.

Applications to FLES

In elementary school foreign language classrooms in which language use has been determined by the communication needs of the immediate environment, reading will begin with the same emphasis: reading will be a natural reinforcement of the spoken word, presented and practiced as a form of communication. The kind of delay in reading in the target language that has sometimes been suggested for the FLES program—up to several years, according to some sources—does not seem to be compatible with an immersion model.

Principle 9: Literacy skills are transferred from the language in which they first are learned to the next language. In early total immersion programs students learn to read first in the target language.

Applications to FLES

The tasks of the immersion teacher and of the FLES teacher are clearly very different in the area of reading. The FLES teacher is not responsible for teaching the child to read, since reading has already been taught in the first language. It is the role of the FLES teacher to assist the child in the transfer of the reading skill from the native language to the target language, and then to develop reading as an additional tool of communication. Reading and writing will be used to extend and reinforce the oral material from the classroom experience and will be integrated into the total FLES curriculum.

Principle 10: Culture is an integral component of language learning.

The presence of cultural content in every aspect of curriculum may be more common in Canadian immersion programs than is sometimes found in the United States, at least partly because of the intimate relationship between French-Canadian culture and the Canadian identity. In programs in the

United States, in which considerable energy must be directed toward developing a curriculum that reproduces the English-language concepts taught in other schools in the district, it sometimes happens that culture is an overlay rather than an integral program component.

Applications to FLES

The message of immersion for FLES is that culture must be embedded in the curriculum, infusing instruction at every point along the way—from the choice of the content that will be discussed to the use of gestures and exclamations in dealing with everyday events. As children acquire language through meaningful experiences surrounded by language, so also do they acquire cultural awareness and the ability to function in a new cultural setting—also through meaningful experiences surrounded by language.

Principle 11: The second language atmosphere permeates the classroom and the school.

The immersion classroom provides a rich visual environment for the language learner, much as the primary classroom uses wall, hall and ceiling space to reinforce the concepts and the relationships being developed there. This atmosphere also reinforces the importance of the group and enhances the attractiveness of being a part of the group: "We belong to Mrs. Nelson's second grade, and that's a good place to be! We are all learning Spanish, and that's a good thing to do!"

Applications to FLES

This atmosphere can also be developed through a FLES program—and as this atmosphere develops, so does the perception of the program's importance. Labeling classroom objects in the target language, developing displays for the classroom and the hallways, celebrating target culture holidays, publishing the school lunch menu in the target language, labeling items all over the school building in the target language—all these techniques and many more may be used to reinforce the idea that the target language is something valuable, and that studying that language is an important thing.

KEY CONCEPTS OF IMMERSION—STRATEGIES

The above principles of immersion offer a rich resource for the elementary school foreign language teacher, but willingness to apply them may be overcome by questions and uncertainties: "How can I make them understand? Shouldn't I have them talking right away? Will I really know they have the right concepts if I don't check in English? Is everything I've been doing wrong? Why should I change when the children like things just the way they are—and so do I?!" The immersion strategies listed below are intended to answer some of those questions.

Strategy 1: Teachers make regular use of contextual clues such as gestures, facial expressions and body language; and of concrete referents such as props, realia, manipulatives, and visuals (especially with entry-level students).

Kindergarten and first-grade teachers are natural users of body language and manipulatives, even in native language instruction. These techniques link language very clearly to its meaning, and the use of the native language to clarify meaning becomes an unnecessary intrusion in the concrete situations most commonly encountered in early second language instruction. Use of extensive body language and a variety of props and realia also appeal to the right hemisphere of the brain, thus adding to the impact of the information for the learner at any stage of language instruction.

Applications to FLES

This strategy can be adopted fully by teachers in FLES programs, with the confidence that it is an extension of the natural mode of learning for elementary school children.

Strategy 2: Teachers provide hands-on experiences for students, accompanied by oral and written language use.

Language acquisition in the immersion classroom is based on experiences the children share in the course of a school day rich in activity. Teachers surround these experiences with language, and language and content skills grow at the same time.

Applications to FLES

The choice and range of available experiences is much more limited in the FLES program. This suggests that teachers need to be deliberate about planning experiences which have the maximum potential for language use.

Strategy 3: Teachers use linguistic modifications when necessary to make the target language more comprehensible for the students in the beginning stages of the program, such as:

- controlled, standardized vocabulary
- controlled sentence length and complexity
- slower speech rate
- restatements, expansions, and repetitions

The special modifications of language used by immersion teachers in order to make the target language comprehensible represent the natural use of language by a fluent speaker who takes into account the limitations of a conversation partner in order to help the partner understand. A slower speech rate in this context, for example, does not mean exaggerated slow speech, which distorts the natural features of the language. The speaker simply operates at the slower end of the normal range for that speaker.

Applications to FLES

The FLES teacher can make conscious application of these modifications in order to avoid translation, on the one hand, or to avoid overwhelming the children with a stream of language, on the other.

Strategy 4: Teachers accelerate student communication by teaching functional chunks of language.

Immersion teachers in Milwaukee have developed an extensive list of "passwords", phrases that are necessary for students to use in the normal course of day-to-day school life. (See page 132 for a partial list). One such phrase is taught each day, with a clear indication of the need it will resolve for the children, and then the phrase is posted on the bulletin board. In order to leave the room at any time during the day—whether to go to lunch, the playground, or the bus—each child must be able to say the passwords. Motivation to learn these chunks of language is high, because they obviously will meet a specific need in the child's daily school life. While much other language is acquired through experience surrounded by language, these high-frequency items are directly taught and practiced.

Applications to FLES

This procedure is clearly applicable to the FLES classroom, where it will hasten the active involvement of the children in classroom communication.

Strategy 5: Teachers constantly monitor student comprehension through interactive means, such as:

- checking comprehension with nonverbal responses
- personalizing questions
- using a variety of questioning types

Many of these strategies are drawn not only from immersion teaching, but also from effective teaching strategies in general. The immersion teacher must do far more monitoring of student comprehension than is usual in the content teaching of the first language classroom because the immersion teacher must determine whether the student understands the concept *and* the language in which the concept is communicated. This careful monitoring may be one reason for the impressive record of immersion students in tests of content–area mastery.

Applications to FLES

The principle of checking comprehension by means of application, when adopted for the FLES classroom, will eliminate the temptation to check if the student *really* understands by asking for translation.

Strategy 6: Teachers use the language–experience approach to reading instruction.

The language–experience approach, or whole–language approach, to reading is an extension of the principle that language acquisition grows out of experiences surrounded by language. Its application is just as appropriate in FLES programs, in which the task is to assist students in transferring reading skills from their native language, as it is in immersion programs, in which students are learning to read for the first time. The teacher guides children in their description or narration of an experience they have shared and then writes the children's sentences as a record of the event. Children read and later copy these sentences and associate the content with their own words and their own experiences. A more extensive discussion of the language–experience approach is found in chapter 8.

Applications to FLES

Students in FLES programs may require more oral discussion of an experience, with indirect correction and guidance from the teacher, before they are able to provide the language for an adequate written record.

Strategy 7: Teachers draw classroom techniques primarily from elementary school methodology.

The overwhelming impression from visits to immersion schools is at the same time the most obvious and the most unexpected: *Good immersion teachers ARE good elementary school classroom teachers.* The same qualities observed in teachers and student teachers in native-language elementary schools are evident in immersion classrooms. Successful immersion teachers use the finest elementary school methodologies; less successful immersion teachers would probably have just as much difficulty teaching students in their native language. Immersion teachers need to read as much as possible about current first language methodology for elementary school subject content and language arts. Immersion teachers are full-time language teachers—and also full-time elementary school teachers.

Applications to FLES

The FLES teacher who wishes to develop the strongest possible program will draw heavily on the ideas and the methodology of the elementary school such as literature-based reading, the process approach to writing, and cooperative learning.

The above list does not exhaust, by any means, the strategies used by immersion teachers which might enhance the teaching of FLES, but it establishes a direction in which to search for ideas and resources for developing ever more effective programs. Met (1987), Schinke-Llano (1984), and Snow (1987) provide more extensive descriptions of immersion strategies and techniques.

Where do we start in applying immersion principles to FLES programs? It seems clear that the first requirement is the conviction that the insights of immersion teaching can be applied even in a more limited setting. For some teachers and administrators this may require a first-hand experience, such as a visit to an immersion school. For others it may be enough just to read as much as possible, as background. The language teacher with a limited elementary school background will also find it helpful to read extensively about first language methodology in the language arts and other content areas. Visits to kindergarten and first grade classrooms will yield valuable insights about strategies for using contextual clues and for tying language to experience. Classroom visits at other grade levels will suggest subject content appropriate for the second language classroom. Immersion materials obtained from programs in the United States and Canada may serve as a resource for developing classroom activities and approaches in the FLES classroom.

SUMMARY

Immersion programs place children in a school environment in which all subject content is taught in a foreign language, beginning as early as kindergarten or grade one. Carefully designed immersion programs in Canada and the United States have produced remarkable results, both in terms of the amount and quality of the second language acquired and in terms of the level of achievement in subject content and native language skills. Children who are given the opportunity to learn in an early total immersion program can achieve a degree of fluency in the target language that would otherwise by attainable only through an extended period of study in the target culture. In addition, their performance in first language basic skills and their mastery of subject content is as good as or better than that of their peers who are studying in an English-only curriculum. Research results in Canada have been replicated in immersion programs in the United States. The Milwaukee example presented in this chapter is representative of many successful programs in the United States.

While intensive, long-term exposure to a second language is available only in an immersion program, other distinctive components of immersion instruction can be applied in every FLES classroom. Eleven principles and seven strategies are listed in this chapter as key instructional concepts of immersion, with suggestions for applying the concepts to other program models. Even though immersion instruction will always be a limited program option, available only to some students in some school systems, insights from immersion can contribute to improved foreign language instruction for all children.

FOR STUDY AND DISCUSSION

1. As the new curriculum coordinator for your district, it is your job to present an information session for parents who are considering enrolling their children in a *new* immersion program in your language in the district.

   a. Outline the information you will include in your presentation.

   b. What questions do you expect the parents to raise? How will you answer them?

2. Despite the compelling research evidence of success, immersion programs are found in relatively few locations in the United States. Why do you think this is the case?

3. Adaptation and change in teaching practice never happen all at once. Teaching a FLES class according to the insights of immersion may have to proceed as a step-by-step process, especially for the experienced teacher who has been relatively successful using more traditional, grammar-oriented methodology. As a consultant to the FLES teachers in your district, choose one or two of the key concepts of immersion that you think would be important first steps toward teaching within the immersion philosophy, and explain how you would present them to the teachers. Use concrete examples in your explanations.

4. What implications would the implementation of an early immersion program in one elementary school in a mid-sized American city have for the language offerings in other schools and at other levels in the same school system?

FOR FURTHER READING

The following sources are recommended for additional information about material covered in this chapter. Chapter citations are documented in *Works Cited* at the end of the volume.

General Resources

California State Department of Education, Bilingual Education Office. *Studies on Immersion Education: A Collection for United States Educators.* Los Angeles: California State University; Evaluation, Dissemination, and Assessment Center, 1984.

Center for Language Education and Research. "Total and Partial Immersion Language Programs in U.S. Elementary Schools." Unpublished list. 1987.

Genesee, Fred. *Learning Through Two Languages: Studies of Immersion and Bilingual Education.* Cambridge, MA: Newbury House, 1987.

Lambert, Wallace E., and G. Richard Tucker. *Bilingual Education of Children: The St. Lambert Experiment.* Rowley, MA: Newbury House, 1972.

Lapkin, Sharon, Merrill Swain, and Valerie Argue. *French Immersion: The Trial Balloon That Flew.* Ottawa: The Ontario Institute for Studies in Education, 1983.

McGillivray, W. R. *More French, S'il Vous Plaît!* Ottawa: Canadian Parents for French, 1985.

Met, Myriam, and Eileen Lorenz. "What It Means to Be an Immersion Teacher." In preparation.

Mlacak, Beth, and Elaine Isabelle, eds. *So You Want Your Child to Learn French? A Handbook for Parents.* Ottawa: Canadian Parents for French, 1979. ED 213 248.

Snow, Marguerite Ann. "Immersion Methodology: How Do Immersion Teachers Make Instructions in a Foreign Language Comprehensible?" *FLES News* 1 no. 1 (Fall 1987).

Snow, Marguerite Ann. *Immersion Teacher Handbook.* Los Angeles: UCLA, Center for Language Education and Research (CLEAR), 1987.

Stern, H. H., ed. "The French Immersion Phenomenon." *Language and Society* (Special Issue). Ottawa: Minister of Supply and Services, 1984. Available from Office of Commissioner of Official Languages, Ottawa, Canada, K1A0T8.

Swain, Merrill, and Sharon Lapkin. *Bilingual Education in Ontario: A Decade of Research.* Toronto: Ontario Institute for Studies in Education, 1981.

Readings Regarding Immersion and Language Minority Students

Dolson, David P. *The Application of Immersion Education in the United States.* Rosslyn, VA: National Clearinghouse for Bilingual Education, 1985.

Met, Myriam. *Immersion and the Language Minority Student.* Midwest National Origin Desegregation Assistance Center, Milwaukee: University of Wisconsin-Milwaukee, 1984.

Schinke-Llano, Linda. *Programmatic and Instructional Aspects of Language Immersion Programs.* Unpublished manuscript, 1984. Available from SRA Technologies, 2570 W. El Camino Real, Suite 402, Mountain View, CA 94040.

Chapter 7

Drawing on the Whole Curriculum: Content-Based Instruction

Regarding language as a medium of learning naturally leads to a cross-curriculum perspective. We have seen that reading specialists contrast learning to read with reading to learn. Writing specialists contrast learning to write with writing to learn. Similarly, language education specialists should distinguish between language learning and using language to learn. Helping students use language to learn requires us to look beyond the language domain to all subject areas and to look beyond language learning to education in general. Outside the isolated language classroom students learn language and content at the same time. Therefore we need a broad perspective which integrates language and content learning (Mohan 1986:18).

CONTENT-BASED PROGRAMS

The goals of second language teachers and content–area teachers have not always been congruent. Too often, the second language curriculum has been conceived and taught independently from and to the exclusion of the content–area curriculum. This situation accounts in part for the resistance classroom teachers in many districts raise to the addition of second languages to an already crowded school day.

The integration of language and content instruction is a positive step toward meeting the goals of both language and content teaching and toward identifying a place for languages in every child's program. In fact, integration of language and subject content has already been successfully accomplished in several types of programs, including the following:

- Immersion programs
- Two-way immersion/bilingual programs

- Content-enriched FLES and partial immersion programs
- Sheltered English programs for Limited English Proficient (LEP) students
- English for Specific Purposes (ESP) programs

In all of the above programs students succeed not only in acquiring a second language, but also in acquiring subject–content knowledge at the same time.

Immersion Programs

Immersion programs have demonstrated for a period of over twenty years that students can learn subject content and language simultaneously and successfully. As discussed in chapter 6, immersion students achieve at the same level or often at higher levels than students in English-only classes on standardized tests administered in English (Swain 1984).

Two-Way Immersion/Bilingual Programs

Two-way immersion or bilingual programs (sometimes also referred to as interlocking programs) are content-based programs that are very similar to the immersion model, except that the students are both native and non-native speakers of the second language.

Content-Enriched
FLES/Partial Immersion

A third example of successful content-based instruction can be found in content-enriched FLES programs or in partial immersion programs, in which students receive some subject-content instruction in a second language in addition to formal instruction in the language.

Examples of such programs can be found in Cincinnati, where elementary school students are learning Arabic, Chinese, Japanese, or Russian through art, music, and physical education classes, and in Milwaukee, Wisconsin, where a group of middle school students are learning Spanish and mathematics taught through Spanish. Elementary school students in the Maple Dale-Indian Hill School District in Wisconsin participate in an interdisciplinary Spanish program; Spanish, along with selected science, art, and social studies lessons are taught through the second language. Students in St. Lambert, near Montreal, receive all instruction in physical education in French, in addition to regular French instruction each day.

Sheltered English Programs or Sheltered Language Instruction

Immersion programs are not alone in providing successful content-based instruction for second language learners. Sheltered English programs, as a component of bilingual education, have also proved to be very effective in this regard. Sheltered English programs are designed to teach English and subject content to limited English proficient (LEP) students using specially adapted (but not watered down) curriculum and materials. Students in these classes learn the subject content in the target language, but they are not required to compete with native speakers nor work with the same linguistic tools that are used by native speakers. In the sheltered English class, as in the immersion class, language is a tool through which subject content is learned and not primarily the object of instruction.

English for Specific Purposes Programs

English for Specific Purposes programs teach the language needed for communication in certain fields and academic disciplines such as engineering or science.

COMBINING LANGUAGE AND CONTENT

Bernard Mohan (1986) has outlined three types of relationships between language teaching and content teaching. They are as follows:

1. Language teaching *by* content teaching in which the focus is on content, and the language skills develop almost incidentally. The intention is that the student will learn the second language by participating in the content instruction. Students will learn language through exposure to modified content alone.

2. Language teaching *with* content teaching in which the focus is on teaching both language and content. In such an approach the language and content objectives need to be in close alignment. Language learning in the language classroom can further the goals of content teaching by giving learners help with the processes of content learning.

3. Language teaching *for* content teaching, in which students learn the specific language needed for success in various subject areas as quickly as possible.

Immersion and two-way immersion/bilingual programs focus on the first area of language and content teaching—language teaching *by* content teaching. Content-enriched FLES, partial immersion programs, and sheltered English programs focus on the second area—language teaching *with* content teaching. English as a Second Language and English for Specific Purposes classes focus on the third area—language teaching for *content* teaching.

Early immersion programs that are extremely successful in teaching language by content are able to do so because in early immersion the language curriculum and the content curriculum are so closely intertwined. English for Specific Purposes programs (language teaching *for* content teaching) are mostly in effect at the high school and especially at the university level and do not have applicability at the K through 8 level.

The focus of this chapter is on exploring ways to accomplish the second of the relationships between language and culture outlined by Mohan (language teaching *with* content teaching) in the belief that it best demonstrates the principle of holistic integrated language teaching. The principles at work in content-enriched FLES, sheltered English and partial immersion programs have the broadest applicability since they can be put into effect at almost any level.

SUPPORT FOR CONTENT-BASED INSTRUCTION

Communicative Competence Movement

One reason for the success of content-based instruction can be found in what we know about communicative competence. In order for communication to take place, there must be some knowledge or information to be shared. Communicative competence can be developed as students feel the need to exchange information with one another or with the teacher in a setting that has significance for all of the participants in the communication. Incorporating subject–content instruction into the elementary school second-language class-room puts language into a meaningful context and provides a situation that requires language *use* rather than just talking about language.

Second Language Acquisition Theory

Subject–content instruction fills the need for "comprehensible input" as described by Stephen Krashen (1981). When providing subject–content instruction, the teacher surrounds the students with language to which they can relate by means of a concrete experience, or on the basis of their previous experiences with the information. Lessons on mapping and graphing, estimating, measuring, or on properties of matter such as hard, soft, big, little, provide rich opportunities for making language input comprehensible through visual and tactile experiences. Teachers also need to make modifications in the target language used to explain ideas and concepts, to make sure that the concepts and the language itself are being communicated clearly.

Studies reported by Dulay, Burt, and Krashen (1982) lead clearly to the conclusion that time spent in experiencing the target language as the medium of instruction is much more effective in producing language proficiency than is time spent in direct language instruction alone. The addition of a class taught in the target language to the experiences of the child already enrolled in a conventional FLES class, or the addition of subject content to the goals of the FLES class itself, can more than double the effectiveness of second language instruction for each student.

Holistic Education

Support for integrating subject–content instruction into the elementary foreign language curriculum also comes from the move toward more holistic education. Since, in content-based instruction, the teacher is not dealing with language that is isolated and reduced to small pieces, students see the language and concepts to be learned as part of an integrated whole. This movement toward holistic, integrated education is seen in the recent interest shown in reading, writing and thinking across the curriculum, and the inclusion of critical thinking skills such as analysis, synthesis and evaluation in all areas of the curriculum (Holdzkom, Reed, Porter, Rubin 1982).

Time in the Curriculum

The perennial question asked by administrators and classroom teachers is: "What will we have to take out of the curriculum in order to include foreign language instruction? There is currently not enough time in the curriculum for us to accomplish our existing goals." A foreign language curriculum that introduces or reinforces some mathematics, social studies, and science concepts, and that incorporates study skills and thinking skills, provides a powerful rationale for justifying a stable place in the curriculum for elementary foreign language instruction.

CONSIDERATIONS IN CONTENT-BASED INSTRUCTION

The work of James Cummins (1981) is very helpful in explaining some of the strategies found in subject–content instruction. Cummins states that first or second language proficiency can be looked at in terms of the degree of contextual support available for expressing or comprehending through a language. He describes "context-embedded" language, which is supported by a wide range of clues, and "context-reduced" language, which has very little extra support, so that everything depends on the words themselves. Cummins also says that language proficiency can be viewed in terms of cognitive involvement, or the amount of information a person must process simultaneously or in close succession in order to do an activity.

According to Cummins's model, tasks involving language use can be classified into four categories, as seen in the four quadrants in the chart below (Figure 3). These categories are as follows:

(A) Cognitively undemanding and context-embedded (embedded in context that helps to make the meaning clear)

(B) Cognitively demanding and context-embedded

(C) Cognitively undemanding and context-reduced (little context provided)

(D) Cognitively demanding and context-reduced

The chart helps to illustrate the level of contextual support and academic complexity found in various areas of the curriculum. They range from quadrant A, in which the activities are context-embedded and relatively simple, to quadrant D, where the activities are more language-dependent, context-reduced, and relatively difficult. As concepts characteristic of quadrant B and quadrant D emerge in the course of instruction, the teacher can make them more accessible to students through the incorporation of extensive visual and concrete referents and through the careful establishment of a context. The math story problem from quadrant D can be made intelligible through visual or graphic representation by the teacher. Conceptual explanations can be made more vivid with the addition of appropriate graphs, charts, and illustrations. With the addition of context, materials which would otherwise be unintelligible in the target language can contribute to student learning. (See Chamot and O'Malley, 1986:13 for further discussion of this concept.)

Sample activities for each of the quadrants are the following:

Quadrant A (Context-embedded and cognitively undemanding)

Physical response activities (TPR)

Demonstrations and descriptions

Following simple directions

Art, music, physical education

Face-to-face conversation

Simple games

Map skills

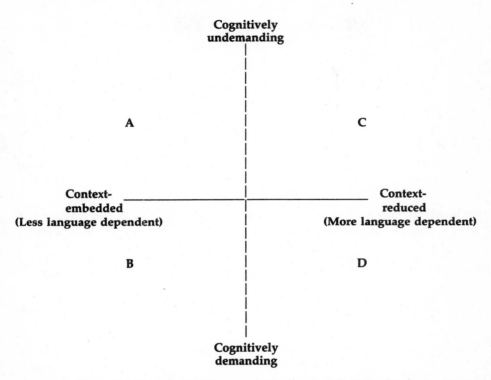

Figure 3. Range of Contextual Support and Degree of Cognitive Involvement in Communicative Activities

Source: From J. Cummins "The Role of Primary Language Development in Promoting Educational Success for Language Minority Students," in *Schooling and Language Minority Students: A Theoretical Framework.* Los Angeles: California State University; Evaluation, Dissemination, and Assessment Center, 1981. Used by permission.

Quadrant B (Context-embedded and cognitively demanding)

Mathematics computations

Hands-on activities such as science experiences

Social studies projects of a concrete nature such as models, charts, and graphs

Quadrant C (Context-reduced and cognitively undemanding)

Routing telephone conversations

Written directions (without diagrams or examples)

Notes, lists, and recipes

Completing forms

Quadrant D (Context-reduced and cognitively demanding)

Subject–content presentations without visuals and demonstrations

Mathematics word problems without illustrations

Explanations of new abstract concepts

Standardized testing

The characteristics of content-based foreign language instruction—language teaching combined with content teaching—and the strategies used by teachers are those described in the discussion of immersion programs in chapter 6.

CURRICULAR AREAS WITH POTENTIAL FOR CONTENT-BASED INSTRUCTION

Many curricular areas are well suited for content-based instruction in a second language. Each area has a variety of possibilities to offer.

Social Studies

The social studies curriculum for the elementary school deals with many of the same concepts often taught in elementary school foreign language programs, but in a less systematic way. Some of these topics are home, family, community, social patterns, and comparative cultures. Map skills are also easily incorporated into content-based elementary school foreign language instruction. Many of the techniques and resources frequently used for the teaching of social studies are also very appropriate for presenting the same concepts in a second language—for example, the use of media; the inquiry method; the use of photos, pictures and study prints; the use of historical artifacts; and the availability of colorful periodicals such as *National Geographic* can provide a rich stimulus for meaning-based language instruction. Although social studies offers a wealth of language and materials for content-based instruction, there are advantages and disadvantages of using social studies as a basis for partial immersion and content-enriched FLES courses. On the one hand, there is the potential for a great deal of meaningful language and vocabulary use; on the other hand, there may be a concern that more vocabulary is required for the content than beginning foreign language students can adequately develop.

Mathematics

Abstract concepts at higher levels of mathematics instruction may pose difficulties, but computations and concrete problem-solving situations can be very useful in content-enriched instruction. Concepts of size and shape are easily communicated in the target language, and elementary school foreign language teachers have long used simple computation as a means of practicing number concepts.

To show how mathematics can be compatible with elementary school foreign languages, we have chosen here some learner expectations from the Milwaukee Public Schools' mathematics curriculum which seem to have particularly good potential for introduction or reinforcement in the foreign language classroom. When planning to incorporate mathematics activities (or activities from other areas of the general curriculum), the teacher should look at the objectives for at least one grade level *above* and one *below* the grade in question. In grade five, for example, the teacher might plan to review time-telling (grade four expectation), introduce duration of events by means of an activity in which the children plan a program (grade five expectation), and should be aware of working toward estimation of time and other measures (grade six expectation). All of the learner expectations below would be helpful to the teacher planning mathematics activities for a fifth grade foreign language class. (See appendix D for more samples of subject-content objectives, grades 1 and 4.)

Possible Mathematics Activities for Content-Based Foreign Language Instruction in Grade 5

GRADE SIX LEARNER EXPECTATIONS

Measurement

- Estimate measure with resonable accuracy, using appropriate unit (length, mass, area, volume, time, temperature)
- Identify standard measures and intra-system equivalencies

Statistics

- Read, interpret, and construct graphs
- Given a set of data, determine the mean or average of that data

Arithmetic

- Classify numbers as prime or composite

GRADE FIVE LEARNER EXPECTATIONS

Measurement

- Determine duration of an event

Statistics
- Interpret various graphs
- Construct picture graphs

Arithmetic
- Read, write, and say whole numbers 0–100 billion
- Round numbers to nearest 10, 100, 1,000, 10,000 or 100,000
- List multiples of a given number
- Find products and quotients of whole numbers

GRADE FOUR LEARNER EXPECTATIONS

Measurement
- Tell, read, and write time to the nearest minute

Statistics
- Construct a bar graph

Arithmetic
- Multiply mentally by 10, 100 or 1,000

Geometry
- Identify congruent figures including segments and angles

Graphing Activities

Graphing is an excellent mathematics-related activity that can be used with many different themes in a language classroom, even when children have relatively limited expressive language ability.

A first experience with graphing might be entirely teacher directed and involve only physical responses on the part of the children. (Children have already learned to understand colors and various items of clothing when the teacher describes them.)

Teacher: Everyone who has brown shoes on, stand up.
Hold up your left foot so we can see your brown shoe.
(Walks around class to check for shoes and to comment)
Yes, Mary has brown shoes—they look new, Mary!
Look, Tom has brown shoes.
Let's see how many people have brown shoes (counts)
1-2-3-4-. . . (or children may count along)
(Goes to prepared chart on overhead projector, chart paper or chalkboard)

Seven children have brown shoes.
(Colors in graph—seven squares, perhaps with brown marker
 or places colored shoes on the graph)
Everyone who has brown shoes, sit down.
Everyone with black shoes, raise your hand.
Wave your hand back and forth!
Lift up your feet so we can see your black shoes.
(Continues in this way, changing things slightly with each
 color)

At the end of this activity there will be a completed graph that the children can talk about. If the activity is used with more than one class during the day, the graphs for the different classes can be compared, and such concepts as *more* and *less* can be practiced.

Another type of graphing activity involves food (or other item) preferences. Pictures of different foods might be placed on each of the walls of the room, and children "vote" for their favorite first by pointing to it and then by walking to that section of the room. (In a class in which children are already doing a lot of speaking, they might express their preferences orally.) The children might themselves place a square representing their choice on the chart, perhaps with their name printed on it, to help build a graph.

Once the graphing activity has been completed, it can be the basis of discussion, used for comparisons, for recalling favorite foods of individual classmates, for games, and for a variety of other communicative activities.

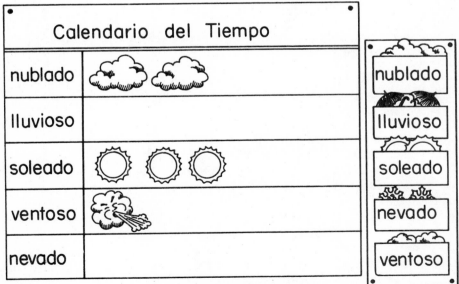

Sample Graphing Activity

At more advanced speaking stages, children might take surveys among their classmates about topics that interest them and graph the results, using their graphs to help explain their discoveries to their classmates.

Science

Science is especially well suited to content-enriched foreign language instruction. Hands-on science activities involve many opportunities for interaction and meaningful exchange of language. Activities such as formulating and reformulating hypotheses when the outcomes vary are important opportunities for the exchange of real information. Science instruction incorporates the use of many graphics and charts, which also contribute to understanding.

Other Curricular Areas

Other curricular areas such as physical education, vocational subjects, health, art, and music have potential for content-based instruction. Because they deal with highly experiential, often very visual learning, the use of a second language in communicating the concepts could be a natural and successful alternative for instruction. (See appendix D for sample objectives in mathematics, science, and social studies for grades 1 and 4.)

SOURCES FOR INFORMATION AND PLANNING FOR CONTENT-BASED INSTRUCTION

In planning a content-based lesson, teachers need to develop the curriculum with these three areas in mind:

1. The language skills needed
2. The content-area skills that will interrelate with the language skills
3. The cognitive skills that are necessary to perform the tasks in the lesson

Once teachers have planned one or two content-based lessons, this new task will become easier and the ideas will come quickly. It is useful to initially plan short units and then to plan larger units as teachers become comfortable with the concepts and become experienced in putting them into action. The best resources for the teacher who is interested in content-based instruction are the curriculum documents for the elementary school level of the school district in which the second language program takes place. If such materials are not current or are not available, the state department of education may be able to provide recent guidelines for each content area and each grade level. The teacher's edition for each subject at each grade level may also yield useful information.

Language teachers should first examine curriculum documents to discover which concepts are already being addressed or reinforced in the language classroom in an unsystematic way. The context in which these concepts are developed may suggest methods for expanding these concepts to enrich their presence in the language classroom. For example, the teacher who regularly teaches the location of French-speaking countries in a fifth-grade class may choose to expand these lessons to include locating capital cities on simple maps using elementary grids, thus reinforcing additional map-reading skills taught at this grade level.

The language teacher may also look for concepts that lend themselves especially well to teaching through experience, or which are readily clarified by the use of visuals and artifacts. In the fourth-grade science curriculum of Minneapolis, for example, the unit on rocks and charts was chosen as a likely candidate for Spanish instruction in the first year of a content-enriched, partial immersion program, because so many of the activities involved handling and observing characteristics of rocks and then classifying the rocks according to visual criteria. A unit on magnetism, however, was determined to require an inappropriately sophisticated command of the target language because of the expectation that conclusions would be evaluated and discussed in great detail. In any program with children who had been using Spanish for several years, both units might have been appropriate choices for Spanish instruction.

USEFUL TECHNIQUES FOR CONTENT-BASED INSTRUCTION

The following list of strategies is intended to be just a sampling of possible content-based activities for the elementary school foreign language classroom that deal with specific areas of the curriculum.

Thematic Webbing

The unit, or theme, approach to teaching is an excellent way to provide for integrated holistic instruction and at the same time incorporate subject content in its interdisciplinary dimensions so that students can see the relationship of the theme or unit to many areas of the curriculum. In this approach, the teacher chooses a word or theme, or a book or story, as a central focus from which to develop a "web" of oral and written language activities. Within the web, language arts, visual arts, fine arts, and subject content can be coordinated in an integrated language process and not pursued as separate skills. The web is a graphic representation of how the pieces of the unit or theme fit together. There is no limit to teacher and student creativity in interrelating activities around a theme to develop a web or cluster that fosters language development.

Some Web Examples

An example of a rather uncomplicated web might be one built around the color green. Parts of the web might include these activities:

Music

Sing songs that include the color.

Science

Add blue and yellow food coloring one at a time to a beaker of water on the overhead projector to see how they combine to make green.

Language Arts

Read or tell a story in which the color green has a prominent role.

Mathematics

Declare a "green" day, on which children wear as many green clothing items and accessories as they can. Then discuss the items and graph the number of different green items.

Social Studies

Look at flags that contain the color green and locate them on a map or a globe.

Art

Locate the color green on the color wheel, identify its complementary color (or other related colors) and draw a picture using only those colors; perhaps students can relate their picture to the story or the song that is part of the unit.

Health

Place pictures or models of foods that are green in color into their appropriate food groups.

A more complicated and larger web built around the popular topic of bears, might include these activities:

1. Read or tell the story of the three bears.
   a. Cook and eat porridge.
      1) Classify porridge by food group.
      2) Build a breakfast around porridge that includes all four food groups.

b. Play games using opposites: hot, cold; hard, soft.

c. Categorize objects as small, medium or large.

d. Distinguish between real bears and bears in the story, between stories that are true and stories that are make-believe.

2. Learn the vocabulary for discussing the color and size of bears.

a. Identify a variety of types of bears (polar, panda, grizzly, koala, brown, black).

1) Locate on the globe the homes of different types of bears.

2) Develop a mural of different bear habitats around the world.

b. Have children bring their own bears to school and describe them.

1) Classify bears by small, medium, and large.

2) Classify by properties such as soft, hard, by color, by type of bear.

3. Describe a bear habitat in the nearest location where bears are found.

a. Name and describe other woodland animals.

1) Distinguish between wild animals and pets and classify them.

2) Classify woodland animals by size.

3) Describe body parts of bears, and other animals.

b. Build a diorama of a bear habitat.

4. Use teddy bear counters (readily available manipulatives) for mathematics activities.

5. Use a large model of a bear, and dress the bear for the weather.

6. Discuss the hibernation of bears.

a. Relate hibernation to seasons, temperature, duration.

1) Create a year time line tracing the bear cycle.

2) Compare the sleep of humans and other animals to the hibernation of bears.

b. Build a model of a bear's den.

7. Learn songs and rhymes about bears.

8. Read or tell stories about bears.

a. Illustrate a story about a bear.

b. Make puppets and act out a story about bears.

Semantic Mapping

Semantic mapping provides a way for students to structure information in graphic form that is very much like the thematic teacher-produced webs that

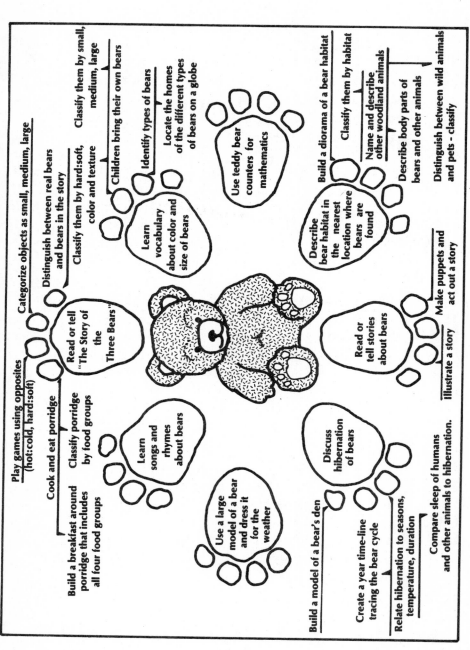

Bear Web

Categorize objects as small, medium, large

Distinguish between real bears and bears in the story

Classify them by hard:soft, color and texture

Classify them by small, medium, large

Children bring their own bears

Identify types of bears

Locate the homes of the different types of bears on a globe

Learn vocabulary about color and size of bears

Use teddy bear counters for mathematics

Build a diorama of a bear habitat

Classify them by habitat

Name and describe other woodland animals

Describe body parts of bears and other animals

Distinguish between wild animals and pets – classify

Describe bear habitat in the nearest location where bears are found

Make puppets and act out a story

Read or tell stories about bears

Illustrate a story

Read or tell "The Story of the Three Bears"

Play games using opposites (hot:cold, hard:soft)

Cook and eat porridge

Classify porridge by food groups

Build a breakfast around porridge that includes all four food groups

Learn songs and rhymes about bears

Use a large model of a bear and dress it for the weather

Discuss hibernation of bears

Build a model of a bear's den

Create a year time-line tracing the bear cycle

Relate hibernation to seasons, temperature, duration

Compare sleep of humans and other animals to hibernation.

have just been discussed. Semantic maps display words, ideas, or concepts in categories and show how words relate to one another or how they go together. A semantic map helps students in content-based elementary school foreign language classes because it encourages them to make the bridge from the abstract to the concrete.

At the center of the map is the key word or question that establishes the topic for exploration. Both students and teacher put the map together by brainstorming and then relating their ideas visually to the topic.

Procedures for Webbing/Mapping/Clustering

Procedures for semantic mapping are presented here (from Los Angeles County Office of Education 1983, and Cook 1986).

1. Choose a simple topic or vocabulary concept such as *river* and write it on the board, or in the center of a piece of paper and circle it.

2. Have students brainstorm (within the limits of their target language vocabulary; or, in very early stages of language instruction, have them provide the English equivalent that you then write down in the target language) and have them tell what they think of when the word *river* is mentioned).

3. Accept student responses; such a brainstorming session might yield words such as the following:

fish	raccoons	frogs	beavers
boat	ducks	clams	running
swimming	water	logs	rocks
muddy	town	sailboat	leeches
wide	dirty	bicycling	snails
deer	wet	trees	houseboat
algae	plants	grass	

4. Determine secondary categories or related words, and write them around the central idea or word, connecting them to the central idea and to each other with lines. The categories might look like this:

Things you can do along the river
    running
    boating
    bicycling

Things that cross the river
    bridge
    cars
    trains
    people

Things that live along the river
    plants
    beavers
    ducks
    deer
    raccoons
    trees
    grass

Things that travel on the river
    ferry boats
    barges
    sailboats
    houseboats

Things in the river
    plants
    logs
    rocks
    fish
    turtles
    frogs
    ducks
    snails
    beavers
    algae
    clams
    leeches

Depicted graphically in a simple map format, the ideas could be represented as on the following page.

Mapping activities can be extended into writing activities, with the various categories serving as organizers for simple paragraphs. A second language student can write a meaningful composition based on one or more elements of the map.

An extension of the mapping activity, and another organizer for writing, is the use of a Venn diagram for making comparisons and contrasts (Winocur, 1985). A Venn diagram consists of two or more intersecting circles which graphically depict logical relationships among concepts (see Figure 4). In the case of the river map, using a Venn diagram, for example, in circle A students could list things that live in the river and in Circle B the things that live along the river. Students then identify the things that can live in either habitat and list these overlapping items in the intersection of the two circles, AB. This activity serves as an exercise in logical thinking, and can also be

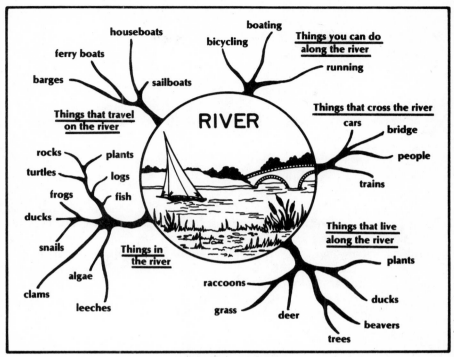

River Mapping Activity

the basis of a meaningful writing exercise with each area of the diagram serving as the starting point for a separate paragraph.

THE APPLICATION OF GENERAL ACADEMIC SKILLS

As second language teachers begin to incorporate content teaching into the class period, their planning will take on a three-dimensional character. Lessons will be designed to develop the student's skills in the content area, their intellectual or general academic skills across the curriculum, and the language skills necessary for them to achieve both of the preceding goals.

Especially important in the area of academic skills are thinking skills. Many schools are including a thinking component in their curriculum, and this component can become a vital part of the second language curriculum. Teaching children thinking skills enables them to manipulate information in order to plan, make judgments, decide, and solve problems. Children need thinking skills so that they can raise questions as well as support possible answers. They also need to become aware of their own mental processes

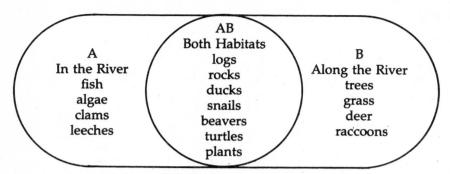

Figure 4. Venn Diagram Activity

and need to assess what they know so that they can determine what they still need to learn. Bloom's Taxonomy of Thinking Processes outlines six levels of skills, including *knowledge, comprehension, application, analysis, synthesis*, and *evaluation*. Figure 5 outlines the levels and the diverse teacher and student activities associated with various levels of thinking. This chart should be helpful to teachers looking to incorporate thinking skills into their teaching. There is currently much information available on thinking skills since this has been a major thrust in the general curriculum.

SUMMARY

The successes of content-based instruction as evidenced in immersion programs, sheltered English programs and other second language programs need to be carried further into foreign language programs, at the elementary, middle school/junior high, and high school levels. Especially in the area of elementary school foreign language programs, the incorporation of content-based instruction can give increased impetus to language study at that level, not only because of the more effective language learning it will bring, but also because it offers a solution to the perennial problem of how to find time for elementary school foreign language instruction. When content-based instruction is incorporated into elementary school foreign language programs, the classroom teacher who must struggle to schedule a multitude of curricular areas into a limited amount of time will see the elementary school foreign language teacher as an ally in this effort, rather than as someone who is taking away another valuable block of time. Incorporating content-based instruction into elementary school foreign language programs is a powerful way to provide a stable place in the curriculum for such instruction.

FOR STUDY AND DISCUSSION

1. Examine an elementary or middle school/junior high foreign language curriculum to identify concepts from other subject–content areas that are

BLOOM'S TAXONOMY OF THINKING PROCESSES

LEVEL OF TAXONOMY	DEFINITION	WHAT THE STUDENT DOES	VERBS TO HELP YOU DESIGN ACTIVITIES
Knowledge	Recall or location of specific bits of information	responds absorbs remembers recognizes	tell - list - define - name - recall identify - state - know - remember repeat - recognize
Comprehension (understanding)	Understanding of communicated material or information	explains translates demonstrates interprets	transform - change - restate - describe explain - review - paraphrase - relate generalize - summarize - interpret infer - give main idea
Application (using)	Use of rules, concepts, principles, and theories in new situations	solves novel problems demonstrates uses knowledge constructs	apply - practice - employ - use demonstrate - illustrate - show report
Analysis (taking apart)	Breaking down information into its parts	discusses uncovers lists dissects	analyze - dissect - distinguish examine - compare - contrast survey - investigate - separate categorize - classify - organize
Synthesis (creating new)	Putting together of ideas into a new or unique product or plan	discusses generalizes relates contrasts	create - invent - compose - construct design - modify - imagine produce - propose - what if . . . .
Evaluation (judging)	Judging the value of materials or ideas on the basis of set standards or criteria	judges disputes forms opinions debates	judge - decide/select/justify evaluate - critique - debate - verify recommend - assess

Figure 5.   Bloom's Taxonomy of Thinking Processes

Source: From Building Competency in Reading Through the Improvement of Thinking Skills, Milwaukee Public Schools, 1985. Reprinted by permission.

already present there. What role do they play? How could the teacher increase their importance within the existing curriculum?

2. Locate a curriculum guide for social studies, science, language arts, mathematics, health, or physical education at the elementary level with which you are most familiar. What concepts do you find that are already touched on in foreign language classes? What concepts lend themselves to instruction in a second language? What criteria did you apply for choosing these concepts? List five of the concepts that you feel have the best potential, and give reasons for your choice.

3. Using the curriculum guide in number 2, choose two concepts that are located in quadrant D (context-reduced, cognitively demanding) of Cummins's chart (Figure 3), and explain how you would develop lessons and materials to move them to quadrant B (context-embedded, cognitively demanding) in order to include them in a foreign-language curriculum.

4. Which of the advantages of content-based FLES instruction do you feel would be most important in the elementary school language situation you know best? What obstacles will need to be confronted in order to implement it?

5. Choose a common topic or theme that you would expect to teach in an elementary school foreign language classroom at the grade level with which you have the most experience. Develop an interdisciplinary web of activities centered on this topic.

FOR FURTHER READING

The following sources are recommended for additional information about material covered in this chapter. Chapter citations are documented in *Works Cited* at the end of the volume.

Baron, Joan Boykoff, and Robert J. Sternberg, eds. *Teaching Thinking Skills: Theory and Practice.* New York: W.H. Freeman and Company, 1987.

Cantoni-Harvey, Gina. *Content-Area Language Instruction: Approaches and Strategies.* Reading, MA: Addison-Wesley, 1987.

Chamot, Anna Uhl, and J. Michael O'Malley. *A Cognitive Academic Language Learning Approach: An ESL Content-Based Curriculum.* Rosslyn, VA: National Clearinghouse for Bilingual Education, 1986.

Chamot, Anna Uhl, and J. Michael O'Malley. "The Cognitive Academic Language Learning Approach: A Bridge to the Mainstream." *TESOL Quarterly.* 21 no. 2 (June 1987).

Costa, Arthur L., ed. *Developing Minds: A Resource Book for Teaching Thinking.* Alexandria, VA: Association for Supervision and Curriculum Development, 1985.

Crandall, JoAnn, ed. *ESL Through Content-Area Instruction: Math, Science, Social Studies.* Englewood Cliffs, NJ: Prentice Hall, 1987.

Cummins, James. "The Role of Primary Language Development in Promoting Educational Success for Language Minority Students." in *Schooling and Language Minority Students: A Theoretical Framework.* Los Angeles: California State University; Evaluation, Dissemination, and Assessment Center, 1981.

Curtain, Helena Anderson. "Integrating Language and Content Instruction." *ERIC/CLL News Bulletin* 9 no. 2 (March 1986).

Global Perspectives in Education. Intercom: Moving Toward a Global Perspective: Social Studies and Second Languages. New York: Global Perspectives in Education, 1983.

Met, Myriam, Helena Anderson, Evelyn Brega, and Nancy Rhodes. "Elementary School Language: Key Links in the Chain of Learning." *Foreign Languages: Key Links in the Chain of Learning.* Middlebury, VT: Northeast Conference on the Teaching of Foreign Languages, 1983.

Mian, Claire. "Integrating Language and Content Through Skill Development." *Contact* 5 no. 3 (October 1986).

Northcutt, Linda, and Daniel Watson. *S.E.T. Sheltered English Teaching Handbook.* Carlsbad, CA: Northcutt, Watson, Gonzales; 1986 (Available from PO Box 1429, Carlsbad, CA 92008).

Rigg, Pat, and D. Scott Enright, eds. *Children and ESL: Integrating Perspectives.* Washington, DC: TESOL, 1986.

Willets, Karen F., ed. *Integrating Language and Content Instruction.* Los Angeles: UCLA, Center for Language Education and Research (CLEAR), 1986.

Winocur, S. Lee. "Developing Lesson Plans with Cognitive Objectives." In Arthur S. Costa, ed. *Developing Minds: A Resource Book for Teaching Thinking.* Alexandria, VA: Association for Supervision and Curriculum Development, 1985.

Chapter 8

Creating an Environment for Communication

There is a compelling thrust from the insights of second language acquisition research, from the communicative competence movement, from experience with immersion programs, from cognitive psychology, and from content-based instruction toward a new organizing principle for language instruction: meaningful communication in the context of a holistic approach to learning. This principle replaces the grammatical focus so common in secondary and post-secondary language programs, and the emphasis on memorization and recitation that has frequently characterized language instruction in the elementary school. The orientation toward communication places language learning in a living laboratory, in which *process* is the primary focus of planning and instruction.

As communication takes on a central position, it is important to agree on what it is and how it can be encouraged. Rivers (1986:2) explains that "students . . . achieve facility in using a language when their attention is focused on conveying and receiving authentic messages—messages that contain information of interest to speaker and listener in a situation of importance to both—that is, through interaction . . . *interaction between people who have something to share.*" Krashen and Terrell (1983:55) refer to the "Great Paradox of Language Teaching: Language is best taught when it is being used to transmit messages, not when it is explicitly taught for conscious learning." Savignon (1983:vi) reports that "the development of the learners' communicative abilities is seen to depend not so much on the time they spend rehearsing grammatical patterns as on the opportunities they are given to interpret, to express, and to negotiate meaning in real-life situations." The sociolinguist Fernando Peñalosa (1981), describes communicative competence as "the speaker's knowledge of what is appropriate to say, how it should be said, and when, in the different social situations in which he finds himself." (p. 50). Canale and Swain (1979) contribute the idea that communicative competence is actually the combination of competence in four areas: (1) grammatical competence, the ability to apply the rules of grammar to produce or interpret a message correctly; (2) discourse competence, the ability to connect several ideas together appropriately and to maintain an extended exchange of messages; (3) sociolinguistic competence, the ability to choose language usage according to the social situation; and (4) strategic competence, the ability to understand a basic meaning or to be understood, even when adequate vocabulary and structures are lacking.

A common danger for every innovation is that it will be trivialized into a slogan and robbed of its power for genuine change. Not every text, drill, or activity now bearing the label "communicative" is an example of communication. Many attempts to "personalize" activities in a language classroom are actually thinly disguised drills, which provide no opportunities for actual sharing of information. For example, the question "What is your name?" has no communicative value when the name of every student in the class is already known to every other student. The notorious question "Are you a boy or a girl?" would be considered both ridiculous and insulting to a student of any age if it were asked in the native language instead of the target language. If, on the other hand, one student is blindfolded and trying to guess the identity of another student in a game setting, both the questions "Are you a boy or a girl?" and "What is your name?" could be genuine requests for information; the questions and the answers would have a communicative purpose.

The gap, described by the Center for Applied Linguistics (Campbell et al. 1985) between the results of immersion and those of FLES (or "core" programs, as they are called in Canada) may have been aggravated by the noncommunicative ways in which instruction has frequently been organized in these more limited programs. FLES programs have typically had the following characteristics:

1. An emphasis on recitation

    - Lists
    - Labels
    - Memorized patterns and dialogues, usually cued by a teacher question
    - Songs, many of which are not integrated into the rest of the language curriculum
    - Games, used as change of pace or for grammar practice
    - Rhymes and poems
    - Reading for recitation; reading aloud

2. Pervasive use of English during the class

    - For discipline

- For giving directions
- For clarifying the target language
- For checking comprehension
- For teaching culture

In content–based classroom settings, like immersion, the context within which communication takes place is well established. The context is the regular day and the regular curriculum of the school with all of its givens. The language becomes a tool of instruction and information exchange is assured. In most FLES and FLEX classrooms, however, in order to avoid the emphasis on recitation, a context for communication must be created, and the FLES teacher must be the one to create it.

A parallel can be drawn between elementary school foreign language programs and elementary school music programs with regard to creating a communicative setting. In a music program, the goal of every music teacher is to provide students with the skills necessary to perform music written for aesthetic purposes, both for the sake of their own enjoyment and to communicate a musical experience to others. This process takes a long time and many years of practice, even for very talented students. However, students in a successful music program are not limited to practicing skills, drills, and scales for all those years without any actual musical experiences. In the absence of music originally written at a level that enables children to perform it, sensitive teachers have prepared music at the ability level of the students—music that students can perform with enjoyment and with an authentic musical message for the listeners. These selections are planned and chosen carefully, taking into account the skills of the musician and the limitations of the school setting. Young people in programs like these gain both pleasure and confidence from their experiences with performance and with the communication of musical ideas.

There is a marked analogy between the music setting described above and the foreign language classroom. While the elementary school child in the foreign language program has neither the skills nor the opportunity to use the target language in a natural communicative setting, the teacher can create settings within the classroom that will satisfy the learner because there is a genuine exchange of information taking place. These experiences also prepare the learner for the day when the opportunity for natural communication will be available. The elementary school foreign language teacher who thinks only in terms of lists and drills, of mastering a body of grammatical forms, of a series of pronunciation tasks, and of memorizing lists of basic vocabulary, is not giving the students any opportunity for authentic messages and is not providing inherently motivating tasks.

DEVELOPING COMMUNICATIVE MATERIALS

Revision of Traditional Activities

Since the shift to communication as an organizing principle is just now taking place, materials available from commercial sources or through exchanges among school districts frequently provide little help in developing communicative tasks. The teacher who has made a commitment to communication as an organizing principle must do extensive adaptation of materials in order to provide opportunities for communication. The teacher might go about revising materials, as in the following example.

> A suggested game from the teacher handbook for a textbook series calls for identification and guessing. As one child leaves the room, the other children choose a classmate to lie down on a piece of butcher paper and then outline the child with a felt pen. The child who is IT returns to the room, looks at the picture, and asks "Is it the teacher?" "Is it Mary? John? Is it Miss Jones?" until the child has guessed the identity of the outlined figure. The child then goes on to ask questions like "Is it a teacher or student? Is it a boy or a girl? Does the person have red hair or green hair?" and so on.

Revision

In its present form, about half of the game is noncommunicative because once the name of the person is known all the other information is clearly known to all participants as well. If the questioning had started by identifying first the role, then the sex, and then other information such as hair color, color of clothing, and so forth, the entire task might have been communicative.

Of course there is a place in a communication-based classroom for practice and drill; the difference is in the motivation for the practice and drill. In a communication-based classroom, the practice and drill take place not for their own sake but in order for a student to participate in a specific communicative setting: to talk about classroom material, to discuss information related to specific interests, or to contribute in some other way to an information exchange that is meaningful to all the participants.

As another example, the teacher may wish to have the children practice the phrase "My name is" (for example, in German *"Ich heisse"*). This phrase will enable them to introduce themselves, perhaps to a visitor in the class, to members of a partner school on a videotape, or in some other natural communication setting. The children in most cases already know each other's names, so to go around the class and have each child say "Ich heisse Fritz,"

"Ich heisse Maria," carries no communication value. The teacher may choose to create a context within which "Ich heisse Maria" is a genuine exchange of information. One possibility would be for the teacher to put on the name tag of one of the children in the class and claim to be that child. The teacher persists until the child responds with her or his own name. This can be done until every child in the class has had a chance to practice. Another possibility, after the phrase is well established but still needs practice, would be to blindfold the children one at a time and create a game in which they must identify speakers by voice who claim to be the teacher, a favorite fairy tale character, or a famous person.

Games

Games are a familiar method by which elementary school teachers create a setting for second language acquisition. In addition to context, games also provide motivation and a sense of play that brain research and teacher experience indicate can enhance both learning and memory. Teachers interested in communication will choose or invent games for introducing and practicing the language students will need in natural contexts for communicative purposes. They will also try to develop and use games that are in themselves communicative rather than heavily drill oriented. Often, a form of practice with just a simple twist, as exemplified above, can change a drill or exercise enough to provide a context that makes it consistent with communicative goals for the classroom.

Games can also provide a structured setting for the practice of common social and conversation-starting formulas for which there is not sufficient opportunity in the everyday classroom. A good example of this is one of the New Games (Fluegelman 1976), which is easily adaptable to any target language:

> Children stand in a circle, facing the center with hands joined. A child who is IT walks around the outside of the circle, touches another child on the shoulder, and begins to run in the same direction around the circle. The child who has been tapped runs in the opposite direction around the circle. At whatever point the children meet, the two must shake hands, greet one another in the target language, perhaps even adding "How are you? I'm fine" and then race to see who can be the first back at the empty place left in the circle.

There are a number of New Games that build on everyday social language and can easily be adapted to the foreign language setting. These can be very useful as a way of providing context for practice of language that will later be used in a genuine communicative situation.

Language–Experience Activities

Another strategy for creating context is the use of language–experience activities that involve children in concrete experiences surrounded by language. Many content-based activities fall into this category. The teacher in any elementary school foreign language program, from immersion to FLES or FLEX, can choose a group activity as an organizing principle that gives context to all of the language that is practiced. For example, in a French classroom the lesson might be centered around the French food *crêpes*. The children work through the steps in making crepes, if possible by actually preparing the crepes themselves, in small groups, or through pantomine as the teacher gives a demonstration in front of the class. The teacher surrounds the activity of the crepes preparation with descriptions and explanations in the target language. Some part of this language use might involve invitations for students to imitate phrases, to respond to questions, or even to initiate comments in the language as they participate in the activity.

Later, in recall of the entire experience, the language is reentered and reactivated. Language used to recall the experience provides the basis for discussions, for demonstrations, for a videotape or a slide series, for scrapbook activities, for class group-story books, and for a variety of other possibilities. Within the context of this experience, the teacher can embed functions or purposes that are transferable to future settings. The link between language and action enhances the impact of the language itself and encourages its retention in long-term memory.

Songs, Rhymes, and Finger Plays

Other powerful vehicles for linking language with action include songs, rhymes, and finger plays that involve large- and small-motor physical actions. Many songs and rhymes for young children are designed to incorporate actions, and the finger play is a rhyme built entirely around the use of the hand and the fingers to enter into the performance of a rhyme. The power of these vehicles is clear when one considers how many adults, at least with the authors' Midwestern backgrounds, can respond without thinking to the following:

> Here's the church,
> Here's the steeple,
> Open the doors and
> See all the people.
>
> * * * *
>
> Where is thumbkin?
> Where is thumbkin?

Here I am.
Here I am. . . .

*　*　*　*

Teddy bear teddy bear
Turn around.
Teddy bear teddy bear
Touch the ground.
Teddy bear teddy bear
Show your shoes.
Teddy bear teddy bear
Read the news.

These rhymes are just a few examples of the shared language experiences which unite many adult speakers in the United States. Songs, rhymes, and finger plays can be located in the target language to bring concepts and common expressions to life for children and to add a cultural dimension to the lesson. In some cases, songs and rhymes may also be adapted from their English counterparts. In an elementary school foreign language classroom action-oriented songs and rhymes, especially those with humorous actions, become favorites of the children, who want to recite or sing them again and again.

Props and Concrete Materials

Another important factor in creating context for communication is the use of props and concrete materials. Children throughout the elementary school years continue to learn best from concrete situations; the more frequently the manipulation of actual objects can accompany language use, especially objects representing the cultures being taught, the greater the impact of the language itself. Examples of concrete objects and suggestions for their use will be found in chapter 11.

Dialogs

Another cluster of strategies for creating context to motivate communication is the development of simulations, dialogs, role plays, and the use of small–group and pair work. Dialogs, the hallmark of the audiolingual method, have value in the elementary school because they provide a structure for a series of utterances that combine to develop a situation, an idea, or an experience. When they are carefully constructed and chosen, dialogs can provide an outlet for children's natural love of dramatization and role play. A dialog can prepare students for conversations and situations that will later be part of a story or a fairy tale in the curriculum. The dialog can also develop as a means of re-creating a story that the children loved when the teacher read it or when they saw it in a filmstrip or a movie.

The following guidelines will assist teachers in the choice or creation of a dialog:

1. It should be short, including short utterances for the children to say.
2. It should feature natural use of language that is not restricted by artificially imposed grammatical limitations.
3. It should be open to many variations so that it can be recast to serve as the basis for future dialogs in other settings.
4. It should be flexible so that children can shape it according to their own creativity and senses of humor.
5. It should incorporate a large proportion of previously learned vocabulary and functions so that children are not overwhelmed by the quantity of new language to be learned.

Role Play

Role play moves a step beyond the dialog and places students in a situation in which they are called on to cope with the unexpected or with a new setting, using the material they have memorized through dialogs and other classroom activities. For example, after working with a dialog drawn from a shopping situation, students of Spanish might be called on to develop a role play in which they go into a Peruvian market to buy an item that represents new vocabulary or a new challenge. Perhaps they look for their favorite American brand of breakfast cereal at the food store, or the clerk has only sizes that are too large or too small in the clothing store. They then work together in a group to develop an unscripted conversation around the new situation.

Small-Group or Pair Work

Another very powerful context for communication in the classroom involves the use of small-group or pair activities. Students can work together to solve a problem or develop a response to a situation the teacher designs. There are many patterns for pair work; for example, each student might be given part of the information necessary to find a location on a map, to choose an appropriate gift for a parent, to identify another member of their class, and so on. As they share the information orally, the children solve the problem and also practice the language involved. In a pair or small-group setting of three to four children, they might work with a "jigsaw": each child has a certain amount of information that, when combined with the rest of the groups', will lead to the completion of an assignment.

Students in a classroom might be divided into long term groups by "family." This allows children who are going to be given target language names to have a last name as well as a first name. Within the small group each member might be assigned a role: mother, father, sister, brother, grandparent. The teacher can use the family groupings to assign tasks within the group: today the mother will be the leader, the father will be the recorder, and so forth. The small group could form the basis for a simulation in which one family encounters another family on an outing and introductions are made all around. This type of simulation allows for meaningful use of language in an imaginary setting.

A pair or small group might design a series of commands to give to another small group or to the teacher, orally at first and perhaps later in writing. The members of the small group might rehearse one another to make sure that everyone in the group is able to ask to go to the bathroom or to sharpen a pencil, to ask to have something repeated, to agree or disagree. The shared teaching task creates a kind of validity for the communication in and of itself, and practice takes on a different texture because it is being directed toward a goal and being managed and monitored by the children themselves.

THE ROLE OF LISTENING, SPEAKING, READING, AND WRITING

Even though the skills groups of listening, speaking, reading, and writing are treated separately in the pages that follow, this in no way implies that the authors intend them to be treated in isolation in the classroom. *These skills must be regarded as an integrated whole in the elementary school foreign language classroom.* At various times one or another of the skills groups may receive more attention than others, as is the case with listening for general understanding in early stages, but *the total instructional program should include activities involving all four groups of skills.*

LISTENING

Within the framework of communication, listening skills take on a very important role. They are both the basis for the development of all other skills and the main channel through which the student makes initial contact with the target language and its culture. Because of a tendency since the early 1960s to equate foreign language skills development only with the development of speaking, the teaching of listening has often been neglected. There has been a common assumption that real language learning is learning to speak, leading naturally to a great deal of classroom time used to teach speaking. It now seems clear that time spent in listening comprehension activities has a direct and important relationship to the amount and quality of speaking skill that is later acquired. Even at more advanced levels students will benefit from an initial emphasis on comprehension in two ways. First, they will be listening for meaning, rather than listening for speaking, when new information is presented. They will not be preoccupied with pressure to parrot back the language they have just heard. Second, leaving a period of time for comprehension to take place allows students to respond to the new information in a natural, communicative way rather than by imitation. Students will begin to make active use of the language because they have something to communicate rather than because they are forced to imitate the sounds and the structures they have heard.

Sometimes listening has been treated as if it were an unfortunate necessity that must be moved through as quickly as possible in order to get to oral expression. For that reason, most teachers will need to give focused attention to granting more opportunities for the development of listening skills. Since information regarding comprehension-based instruction is relatively new, the background of many teachers includes little experience with listening comprehension, and there is even less modeling to help them in this area. Consequently, these teachers need to significantly expand their repertoire of activities and ideas for developing listening skills. There are a number of tools that can be used for listening practice, several of which have been frequent components of elementary school foreign language instruction over the years.

One important step toward emphasizing listening skills is the establishment of a target language environment in the classroom. Even in an exploratory program the target language can be the primary or even the exclusive means of communication in the language class. The predictable activities and verbal routines of the classroom provide useful meaning clues to accelerate the comprehension of classroom-related vocabulary and structures, and these then become the basis for most of the important initial expressive language for the students. This environment communicates the message immediately that the target language is adequate and appropriate for dealing with the ongoing communication needs of the students in the class.

Many traditional elementary school foreign language activities that emphasize recitation or imitation can be converted to useful experiences with listening comprehension with just a slight shift in emphasis or a minimal change in the procedure. For example, playing cards can be used for comprehension practice instead of in their usual role of motivating speech. Children grouped in circles of three or four lay one suit of cards (1 to 10) face up in the center of the circle. When the teacher calls a number, the first child to place her or his hand over the number keeps the card. The teacher surrounds the entire activity with relevant language, but the children participate fully without being required to speak.

Listening Strategies

Specific strategies for helping students to develop skills in listening follow.

Total Physical Response: TPR

TPR, or Total Physical Response, is a systematized approach to the use of commands developed by the psychologist James Asher in the late 1960s (see Asher 1986). TPR has become a common and effective means of introducing children and adults to a foreign language, and in particular to listening, especially in early stages of instruction.

In TPR, teachers interact with students by delivering commands, and students demonstrate comprehension through physical response. The following sequencing is recommended by Berty Segal (no date):

1. Commands involving the entire body, large-motor skills

   - Point to your ear.
   - Put your left hand on your head and turn around three times.
   - Walk backwards to the front of the class and shake the teacher's hand.
   - Clap your hands for Mary. She did a good job.

2. Commands involving interaction with concrete materials and manipulatives, beginning with classroom objects

   - Take the red circle and place it in the wastebasket.
   - Pick up your green crayon and lay it under your chair.
   - Walk to the chalkboard, take a piece of yellow chalk, and draw a picture of the sun.

3. Commands relating to pictures, maps, numbers, and other indirect materials

   - Go to the map and trace the outline of Paraguay.
   - Go to the picture of the bathroom and (pretend to) brush your teeth.
   - Go to the wall chart and point to a food from the fruit and vegetables group.

Students are not expected to respond orally until they feel ready, and early oral responses involve role reversal (a student takes on the role of the teacher and gives commands to others in the class), and some yes–no and one-word replies to the teacher's questions. This strategy involves little or no pressure to speak in the early stages.

Some very important aspects of the strategy include the creation of novel commands, which encourages careful and creative listening, and the combination of commands so that students perform several actions in sequence. The sequence of commands must never become predictable, and students must be confident that the teacher will never embarrass them.

In its simplest terms, TPR seeks *to teach new concepts through the body*.

Gouin Series

With this strategy, the teacher prepares a series of six to eight short statements describing a logical sequence of actions which takes place in a specific context—getting up in the morning, cooking a meal, using the library, making a phone call. These statements should all include action verbs and use the same tense and the same person throughout. The teacher presents the statements to the class orally, accompanying them with pantomime of the actions involved. The class responds first through pantomime and later by imitating the statements while doing the actions. Here are some examples:

> I get up in the morning.
> I stretch.
> I walk to the bathroom.
> I brush my teeth.
> I comb my hair.
> I walk into the bedroom.
> I make my bed.
> I get dressed.

In preparing a Gouin series, it is useful to have simple props and visuals for at least some of the activities.

In numerous workshops, Constance K. Knop has identified the following values of the Gouin series in language instruction:

1. It links language to action and visuals, providing for greater comprehension.
2. It teaches appropriate verbal and physical behavior, which makes it useful for shaping classroom behavior as well as for teaching culture.
3. The Gouin series is easy to recall because it has significant meaning reinforcers (acting out, visuals, logical sequence), and it appeals to several senses.

Audio–Motor Unit

This strategy incorporates elements of TPR and the Gouin series. The teacher creates a series of commands that evoke a series of actions taking place in a specific context; for example, a French picnic, a visit to a cafe, making a (foreign) telephone call, and so forth. These commands are recorded on an audio tape, preferably by a native speaker. The teacher plays the tape in class and pantomimes the actions in sequence as they are commanded. The class then joins the teacher in the pantomime on subsequent hearings of the tape. Later, the commands can be recombined, and students can proceed to role reversal and other forms of active use of the language (Kalivoda et al. 1971).

The Natural Approach

This approach (Krashen, Terrell 1983) seeks to "bind" new vocabulary by providing experiences and associations with the words in a meaningful context. Extended listening experiences include TPR, use of vivid pictures to illustrate concepts, and active involvement of the students through physical contact with the pictures and objects being discussed—by means of choice–making, yes–no questions, and game situations. The Natural Approach outlines a useful sequencing of teacher questions which moves students from a listening mode to a speaking mode; the first level (except for the use of "yes" and "no") gives a demonstration of listening comprehension only, while the last three levels move the student into speaking:

Level 1.   *Yes-no question*

Students answer with *yes, no,* or a name:
Does Helena have the cheese?
Who has the cheese?
Is Margaret jumping to the door?

Level 2.   *Either-or question, using nouns, verbs, adjectives, adverbs*

The student answer is contained in the question:
Does Helena have the cheese or the bread?
Is the cheese Swiss or cheddar?
Is Margaret running or jumping to the door?
Is the cheese on the bread or under the bread?

Level 3.   *What, when, where, who question*

Students answer with a single word, moving toward a phrase answer:
What does Helena have?
What kind of cheese is this?
Where is the cheese?
Where is Margaret jumping?

Level 4.   *Students answer with the entire sentence or action*

What is Margaret doing?

Descriptions

The teacher describes an object or a picture, preferably one in color, that has high interest and vivid action and/or cultural value, constantly using gestures and elements from the object or the picture to make the meaning clear. Listening comprehension is checked through yes-no, short answer, or either-or questions, or by means of pointing or otherwise identifying information from the picture.

> Point to the cap on Whistler's mother.
> Is the woman standing by the chair?
> Put your thumb on the rocking chair.
> Hold up a picture of your mother.

Demonstrations

The teacher or a guest (or native) speaker gives instructions on how to complete a task or recounts an experience, making heavy use of props, pictures, pantomime, and other visual aids to comprehension. For example, the teacher might demonstrate the steps in setting the table in the foreign culture, or a guest speaker might describe how to tie-dye fabric. There should be frequent rephrasing during the presentation, just as it might occur in real conversation, and regular comprehension checks throughout. The following steps are recommended.

1. Make the presentation.
2. Rephrase the presentation.
3. Check student comprehension.
   - yes-no (true-false, logical-absurd)
   - either-or
   - short answer

Telling or Reading a Story

Storytelling can provide "input" for children at even very early stages of language acquisition when the stories meet the following criteria:

1. The story is familiar to the children from their native culture, or highly predictable, with a large proportion of previously learned vocabulary. In early stages it is especially important to choose stories that include vocabulary representing the home and school environments of the children.
2. The story is repetitive, making use of formulas and patterns that occur regularly and predictably. In the best story choices, these repeated

elements will provide language that children can later use for their own expressive purposes. Storybooks like *Brown Bear, Brown Bear* or *When It Snows, It Snows*, by Bill Martin Jr., written for American children, are good examples of this type of story.

3. The story line lends itself to dramatization and pantomime.

4. The story lends itself to heavy use of visuals and realia to illustrate its content and progress.

"The Three Bears" is an example of a story containing all of the above features.

Stories that meet these criteria can be presented without use of English, relying entirely on visuals, pantomime, and the children's existing knowledge of the story or the situation to make meaning clear. The teacher may check comprehension using physical responses (point to the big bear, hold up the little bowl), yes-no questions, and other levels of the Natural Approach sequence described above.

After the story has been told several times, children may pantomime the story as the teacher tells it again. This "physical story telling" can be carried even further, as the teacher recombines previously learned TPR commands with familiar story material to create a new story which the children act out as the teacher tells it.

Reading stories aloud has the additional benefit of connecting the narrative with the printed page. The teacher can successfully read very familiar stories aloud at an early stage of language acquisition, especially if the book is heavily illustrated.

The emphasis in each of these listening activities is on the development of associations between the language that is heard and the meaning that that language communicates; at this stage students are not expected to imitate the language, just to understand it. In each of the strategies that emphasize listening, there is some provision for speaking, usually as a natural outgrowth of the communication that takes place within the activity. There is no emphasis on the direct teaching of oral skills. Reading and writing skills can be incorporated for many of the strategies as a part of the natural, communicative extension of the activity.

SPEAKING

In the communicative classroom oriented to the principles of second language acquisition, acquiring speaking skills is not viewed as a separate category that receives isolated attention. Students begin to speak when they have acquired sufficient language through exposure to a rich and varied language environment—and when they have something to say. Once students begin to express themselves orally, it becomes the teacher's task to provide them with encouragement and opportunity to communicate with one another and with the teacher in a wide variety of ways. Much of this book, especially chapters 7, 9, and 13, is concerned with this task.

Direct Teaching of Speaking Skills

Within the communicative classroom environment, however, learners may need to be able to express some messages before they have had a chance to fully assimilate the language to the point at which oral language is ready to emerge.

Classroom and School Survival

Teachers often wish to provide children with a number of basic expressions that will enable them to interact sooner during the course of the language class or of the school day. Use of these language patterns allows children to have a certain amount of control over their own environment and the conduct of the classroom. Phrases requesting permission to sharpen a pencil, to go to the bathroom, to get a drink of water, or to borrow a piece of paper and other such items, as well as requests for clarification or questions and comments about homework and schedules, all need to be taught directly if they are to be available early in the language acquisition experience.

Passwords and Language Ladders

One popular and effective approach to teaching classroom expressions is the use of passwords and language ladders.* Passwords are phrases such as "Please may I sharpen my pencil?" which are taught directly and then posted on the wall with some identifying visual to assist students in recalling the meaning connection. Passwords are frequently taught one each day, and students are then required to produce the password before leaving the class for some desired activity such as lunch, recess, passing to another class, or going home for the day. When the student attempts to express the idea contained in a password that has already been learned, the teacher can simply refer the child to the password posted on the wall and thus assist the student in recalling the information they have already learned. These are examples of sample passwords:

> May I go to the bathroom (office, drinking fountain, clockroom, etc.)?
> How do you say that?
> Can you help me?
> I can't find my eraser (paper, book, homework, lunch ticket, etc.).
> Give me a jump rope, please.
> Please leave me alone.
> I have a stomachache (headache, sore throat, etc.).
> Do you know how to play?

*Suggested in workshops by Constance Knop, University of Wisconsin - Madison.

Language ladders are similar to passwords in that they are also phrases taught one per day. They usually represent a series of different ways to express a similar idea or a similar need, often in different registers, degrees of politeness, or social context. For example, a language ladder might include levels of reaction to a homework assignment, or different ways of giving a compliment or encouragement to fellow group members in a cooperative learning situation. Language ladders, like the one which follows, are posted on the wall with accompanying visual cues, and they are usually sequenced or clustered to show their relationship and to assist the student in remembering their meaning.

Some other components of the curriculum are also usually taught directly. The dialog, long a component of elementary school foreign language instruction, can serve as a rehearsal of language that is useful in actual situations. Songs, rhymes, and pattern phrases for games are also usually the object of direct oral teaching and are not acquired by means of a period of exposure. Even elements that are to be taught directly, however, should include a large proportion of language that is already familiar through other communicative activities in the classroom, and the meaning of the language must be very clear to students before any practice is begun.

The language ladder helps children to recall language they can use in managing their lives in the target language.

Specific Teaching Suggestions

While most aspects of audiolingual methodology are inappropriate in today's communicative climate, audiolingualism did lead to the development of several strategies that can be useful even now to assist with the direct teaching of oral skills. While most student speaking should occur naturally, in communicative settings, the teacher may want to use occasional practice activities; the following suggestions will help him or her to do so in an effective manner.

1. Teacher Repetition

During activities calling for a group or whole-class response, the teacher should never repeat a response with the students. It is very tempting for teachers to try to model a quick, clear, vigorous response by playing the role of cheerleader. However, students quickly become dependent on the teacher's leadership. Moreover, teachers who speak with the students are not in a position to evaluate the quality of the student response and the degree to which students may actually have mastered the material.

2. Modeling

Teachers should always model the language with natural speed and intonation, especially in practice settings when they might otherwise tend to emphasize the components of the message which they expect to cause the students problems. When students seem to be having difficulty with a sentence, it is a better strategy to repeat the message several more times, using natural speed and intonation, than to distort the language by slowing it down or giving difficult segments inappropriate emphasis.

3. Backward Buildup

Most language in songs, passwords, rhymes, and dialogs should be simple and direct enough for children to understand and learn it in complete utterances. When an utterance is longer than about seven syllables, however, it is often necessary to teach the utterance part by part instead of in a single stream. Under these circumstances it can be helpful to segment the utterance into meaning units so that, for example, prepositions and their objects are not separated into different practice segments. It is also useful to begin teaching the utterance with the statement closest to the end. In the sentence "I wasn't able to get my homework done yesterday" the teacher might proceed as follows:

> . . . yesterday.
> . . . done yesterday.
> . . . my homework done yesterday.
> . . . to get my homework done yesterday.
> . . . able to get my homework done yesterday.
> I wasn't able to get my homework done yesterday.

Backward buildup should be used only in very specific situations, with language that is *understood by the children* and highly motivating, such as a very important password, a song that is integral to the rest of the lesson, or the language necessary for a game or for expressing a message of considerable importance to the children.

4. Answer Precedes Question

When dealing with question–answer exchanges, it is useful to teach the answer first and then the question. For example, one might teach "It is three o'clock." "Today is Wednesday." "My name is Mary." "I feel terrible." All of these are statements that can stand alone and that clearly communicate information that might have value to the hearer. Once the answer has been learned the statement can be cued with the question, and the question becomes a form of input: "What time is it?" "It is three o'clock." As a final step the question is learned, and the question and the answer can then be used together in natural settings. This is a much more natural approach than teaching the question first, since questions really cannot stand alone without an answer. When the answer is taught first the question is always practiced in combination with an answer, thus creating much more meaningful, realistic practice settings. These experiences lead naturally to awareness of typical adjacency pairs in the target language, typical questions and answers that always occur together.

Teaching Pronunciation

While direct teaching of spoken language may have its place, and while there are useful techniques for accomplishing it, there is probably far less justification for the direct teaching of pronunciation, at least in early stages of language acquisition. As Berty Segal (no date) has pointed out, focusing instruction and correction on pronunciation raises the potential for creating problems and for communicating some inappropriate messages. Segal describes three problems that may arise when pronunciation is taught directly:

1. Students often do not know which sounds to say. They sometimes cannot separate the teacher's command from the word or phrase to be repeated. They frequently cannot determine which part of the phrase is causing difficulty, so they do not know where to focus their attention.

2. If a sound does not exist in the native language, over forty hearings are required before the students even recognize the sound they are trying to imitate. Drilling with a single student who is not able to hear the sound in question is frustrating for both teacher and student.

3. The frustration inherent in premature individual drill work in pronunciation leads to student anxiety and loss of self-confidence in all areas of the language acquisition process.

In addition to the above, and perhaps most important of all, the direct teaching of pronunciation at early stages of language acquisition encourages students to focus attention on the surface features of language rather than on the meaning. It is another way of inviting children to listen for speaking rather than to listen for meaning. As is the case with other errors, early pronunciation problems can effectively be dealt with when teachers restate student messages correctly as a form of reflective listening, rather than in a correction mode. Most children tend to be good imitators, so there is no serious danger of reinforcing poor pronunciation habits.

When students have gained confidence and comfort with the new language, and as the emphasis on communication has been established, attention to pronunciation becomes more appropriate. Teachers can assist students to communicate more effectively and more precisely by guiding improvement in pronunciation as well as in grammar, structure, and vocabulary usage.

READING AND WRITING

In the classrooms and in the methods texts of the 1960s, reading and writing were considered a potential obstacle to the development of speaking because of interference from native language sound symbol association. Some methods texts of the time recommended that children in a FLES program should not be exposed to the written form of the language for three to six years. In the elementary school foreign language classroom that has been influenced by recent second language acquisition research, by the insights gained from communicative competence, and by the experiences of immersion, however, the written language has become one more tool of communication. It takes on a somewhat different and much more natural role in the development of second languages in children.

From both first and second language acquisition theory, we know that languages are acquired in real-life, natural settings through interactions with others. This applies also to reading in both first and second languages. Reading methods are most effective when reading materials are based on real–life, natural settings. Reading comprehension involves communication between the writer and the reader within meaningful contexts (Cook 1986). Once oral language is acquired (understood), the basis for both first and second language reading is established. Meaningful reading experiences in both first and second language classrooms are dependent on the student's oral language mastery and also on the student's existing background knowledge and experience. This existing conceptual framework is referred to as *schemata* in the literature on first language reading.

Meaningful reading experiences occur in second language classrooms that provide appropriate settings for communication—communication that is expressed not just through oral language, but is expanded into reading and writing activities. In a holistic, integrated approach to second language learning, reading and writing activities do not take place in a separate compartment, but flow out of listening and speaking activities. The amount of time devoted to reading and writing experiences will vary according to the grade level of the students and the amount of time available for instruction. Since background experience plays such an important role in reading, it is crucial that the second language teacher keep this experience in mind when providing reading material for the students. Rigg (1986:83) presents criteria for choosing reading material to be used with second language students. She points out that such material should have "content that is familiar enough so that it makes some sense . . . The material should have some recognizable structure, whether it be that of a folktale, of a set of instructions, or whatever. The structure should not shift back and forth; that makes the reader's schemata of little help in predicting."

Second language reading differs from first language reading in that most students (except for those in immersion programs) have already made the connection between meaning and a written symbol for that meaning and transfer the skills they have acquired in one language to another. Usually by the middle of grade two, reading skills are well enough established in the first language that teachers can work systematically with reading in the second language. In first- and second-grade elementary school foreign language classrooms, activities emphasize oral language experiences that build a solid foundation for later reading experiences and for the transfer of first-language reading skills to the second language. Prereading experiences at the first- and second-grade level should focus on teacher story telling and story reading and incidental exposure to the written language.

The report *Becoming a Nation of Readers* (1985) revealed that reading instruction in primary schools consists mostly of students doing exercises in workbooks which focus on isolated reading skills rather than actually reading. Unfortunately, this is sometimes also the case with reading instruction in the second language classroom. Data from standardized reading tests shows that reading programs that focus on isolated skills do not teach students to read. In the same way, focusing on isolated fill-in-the-blank exercises in second language reading does not provide meaningful reading experiences. Focusing on reading subskills rather than on whole language experiences also puts students who are already having difficulty with reading in the first language at a special disadvantage and reduces their chances for success. In a truly communicative second language program, these students can have an opportunity to begin anew with success-building language and reading experiences. In order to insure this success, elementary school foreign language reading experiences that focus on isolated reading skills must be transformed into those which provide for whole-language experience.

Advocates for the whole-language approach to reading lament the fact that many students do not love to read because most of their reading experiences are with ditto sheets and workbooks rather than with real books and exciting, interesting stories. This observation is as insightful and appropriate for second language learning as it is for first language learning.

The writing of Alma Flor Ada and Maria Pilar de Olave is helpful for the teacher who is trying to gain a better understanding of the reading process as it applies to elementary school foreign language. They point out that, "by learning the mechanics of reading, one does not necessarily become a good reader . . . success depends not on specific techniques but on high interest material." They synthesize basic general principles of reading for the second language teacher in the introduction to the primary–level Spanish reading series, *Hagamos Caminos* (1986):

Basic General Principles of Reading—Alma Flor Ada and Maria Pilar de Olave

1. Learning to read and write should be an extension of the process of learning to speak.
2. Children should be motivated. They will grasp more easily what has meaning and interest for them.
3. Reading to children and telling them stories will make them better readers.
4. Reading materials should be written in the clear and simple language children are familiar with.
5. Teaching of reading and writing should be done simultaneously.
6. There is a correlation between children's oral language development and their reading ability.
7. Children learn to read more quickly and easily when there is a reason for doing so:
   - exchanging letters with a friend
   - mailbox in the classroom
   - books authored by peers in the classroom library.

When Should Reading Start?

George Rathmell (1984:43) suggests that for students who are already literate, delaying reading will have "diminishing returns after a dozen or so hours of instruction because students are prone to develop their own covert writing system." Delaying reading in the second language may also be very frustrating to students whose learning styles are more visually oriented. Rathmell goes on to say, "More profitable than an extended period of printless teaching is the limiting of printed versions of language to meaningful elements that students have learned orally." If reading experiences are focused on what the students have been exposed to during other classroom activities, students will encounter success with second language reading.

Reading Aloud

Reading should be approached first of all as a process for deriving meaning from the printed word and not for using the printed word as a stimulus for speaking. Reading aloud and "round robin" reading, often seen in elementary school foreign language classrooms, are rarely appropriate strategies for developing reading skill. Reading aloud tends to encourage students to respond to the surface features of the language and not to the message. Many students master the "trick" of sound-symbol association without developing skill in comprehension or communication. Because reading aloud is a practice with such a long tradition, it gives many teachers a sense of security to use it as a strategy, but current understanding of the reading process does not support its continued use.

The Language–Experience Approach to Reading

An excellent way to move from print to meaning is to use the language–experience approach, which incorporates all the communication skills of speaking, listening, writing, and reading. The language–experience approach to reading is based on the idea that children will be able to read printed words if these words are part of their everyday language and experience. Familiar experiences are translated into oral expression, then recorded and read. When a visual symbol is connected to the spoken word and the word is part of the child's experience, the meaning is readily understood and has immediate relevance. The students are not asked to read material in texts for which they have no background knowledge.

Initially, the teacher elicits language from the students through group discussion of an experience. For example, the class might have prepared crepes in small groups following the directions of the teacher. After the cooking activity is over, the teacher and the class talk together about what they have experienced. The teacher speaks only in the target language, but the students may volunteer some information in their native language.

As the activity progresses, the teacher writes down the students' words and ideas, usually on a large chart or on the chalkboard. The final story might be something like this:

We made crepes.
We stirred the batter.
We baked the crepes.
We filled them with sugar.
We rolled them up.
They tasted good!

The story might be shorter or longer or more or less complex depending on the age and language level of the students.

After the story has been written, the teacher and the students read the story aloud. Then the story can be copied and illustrated by the children and read and reread at school and at home. In later stages of elementary school foreign language programs where there is considerable contact time, children might write their own stories and share them at a class story table or in the library.

Nancy Hansen–Krening (1982) states that the learner's task is made easier and less frustrating when the language–experience approach is used because reading materials match oral language patterns and draw on personal experiences. Learners are not asked to confront the unfamiliar or confusing language of texts that are not yet meaningful.

Eleanor Thonis (1970:140), in her seminal work on reading for second language students, explains the effectiveness of language–experience approach activities for the early language learner: "In spite of his marginal

The language–experience approach to reading builds on the child's knowledge of the world.

control of the oral language, the introduction to print by way of *his* language and *his* experience will insure that he will understand what he is reading. The written symbols represent words and groups of words."

The language–experience approach is used successfully with both first– and second–language learners. In foreign language classes the experiences are often planned by the teacher, since there is a need to maintain control over the vocabulary load. In first language classes this is not the case, and many of the experiences for language–experience stories come from outside of school. While the steps in the process are similar for both groups, the foreign language teacher spends much more time creating the experience and less time with the dictation process. The actual language dictated by the children is usually modified and sometimes translated by the teacher at this step.

The language–experience approach must be adapted somewhat for second language classrooms to allow for firmer direction from the teacher, but the central concept remains the same—use the students' own vocabulary, language patterns, and background of experiences to create the reading text. For more information about using the language–experience approach with students learning a second language, see Dixon and Nessel, 1983 and Cantoni-Harvey, 1987.

Developing Communicative Reading and Writing Activities

Activities that emphasize meaning and the students' background of experiences, instead of discrete subskills and fill-in-the-blank worksheets, are vital for successful integration of reading and writing. The lists below are intended as idea-starters for the teacher developing materials for meaningful reading and writing activities.

Sample Student Reading and Writing Activities

Have students complete these activities:

- Read and write classroom requests, passwords, and language ladders.
- Read and write classroom–centered survival vocabulary.
- Read and write simple pattern stories such as *Brown Bear, Brown Bear* by Bill Martin Jr.
- Read and write songs, rhymes, and poems that have been learned orally.
- Write weather reports and include pictures.
- Write dialog journals (diaries that are written by the student and answered by the teacher).

- Create crossword puzzles.
- Write action (TPR) commands for students to give each other or the teacher.
- Fill in balloons in a comic strip with very simple captions.
- Create pattern stories according to a model that students have heard and seen.
- Write a note to tell someone where you have gone.
- Write a simple Gouin series.
- Fill in cloze versions of familiar stories (To create a cloze exercise, you replace words with blanks at a specified interval, such as every five words, in a reading passage with which the students are familiar).
- Answer true–false questions about familiar stories.
- Write theme books and class experience stories.
- Supply simple dialog for picture books or for soundless filmstrips.
- Write simple captions for pictures in a class or personal album.
- Write down a telephone message from or for a fellow student.
- Describe personal routines.
- Fill out a questionnaire with one– or two–word answers.

Sample Copying/Labeling Activities for Beginning Students

Have students complete these activities:

- Copy expressions that they want to be able to say.
- Copy a language–experience story.
- Label items in a picture.
- Make a list by copying parts of a list:

    Given a list of items sold in a store, students can make a list of things they would like to buy for their mothers.

    Given a restaurant menu, students can list what they would like to order.

    Given the jobs Mother has written in a "job jar", students pick out and list the ones they hope to draw.

- Complete graphs, charts, and maps to give personal information or show preferences.
- Sequence steps in a story, an experiment, an event, or a Gouin series.

- Make a list of items in a picture and categorize them according to type.
- Put a favorite story in the correct sequence.

Sample Student Activities with Authentic Materials

Have students complete these activities:

- Using a target language newspaper, make a TV viewing schedule for the week.
- Pick a movie from the movie page and write down information to share with a friend.
- "Shop" out of a target language catalog, making a list of items to buy and filling out an order form (simplified for beginning students).

Sample Reading and Writing Activities for Learning Centers

Have students complete these activities:

- Read a question card about a pictured activity and put the answer in a yes–no or true–false slot in the learning center.
- Match a sentence or caption to an appropriate picture.
- Read a question and find the answer in an envelope.
- Match a word or sentence to a picture by using a yarn board (see chapter 12 for information about how to make a yarn board).
- Attach a clothespin with a word or phrase written on it to the correct picture on a clothespin matchup (see chapter 12).

SUMMARY

Communication has become the organizing principle for second language teaching at every level of instruction. The central task for the elementary school foreign language teacher is to create a communicative climate within which language acquisition can take place naturally. This climate reflects a holistic approach to language, in which the skills of listening, speaking, reading, and writing are not artificially separated, but are integrated in a meaningful total experience. While initial stages of instruction will stress listening as the foundation for development of all skills, activities will be developed early in the program to incorporate the use of all four skills as tools of communication.

This chapter provides background in the use of communication to organize the curriculum and offers strategies and activities for developing student facility in listening, speaking, reading, and writing.

FOR STUDY
AND DISCUSSION

1. Why is it often so difficult for teachers to make the change from a grammatical to a communicative orientation to language teaching? What kinds of assistance can help them make the transition?

2. Choose a drill–oriented activity that you have observed or used in an elementary school foreign language classroom or have located in a elementary school foreign language teacher's manual. Redesign it so that the same goal is being met in a communicative way.

3. What do you consider to be the most important benefit of providing an extended listening period in early stages of language instruction?

4. Choose a topic that has value either for helping children deal with their classroom environment in the target language or for teaching appropriate cultural behavior. Use it as the basis for a Gouin series of six to eight sentences and demonstrate it to the class.

5. Under what circumstances is the direct teaching of speaking skills necessary or desirable?

6. Identify several experiences appropriate for the elementary school foreign language grade level you know best which would be effective starting points for a language–experience approach to reading. Choose one of the experiences and identify the key vocabulary and sentence structures the students will need to use in creating a language–experience story.

FOR FURTHER READING

The following sources are recommended for additional information about material covered in this chapter. Chapter citations are documented in *Works Cited* at the end of the volume.

General Resources

Ada, Alma Flor, and María del Pilar de Olave. *Hagamos Caminos*. Reading, MA: Addison-Wesley, 1986.

Asher, James J. *Learning Another Language Through Actions: The Complete Teacher's Guidebook*. 3d ed. Los Gatos, CA: Sky Oaks Publications, 1986.

Byrne, Donn. *Teaching Writing Skills*. Burnt Mill, Harlow, Essex, UK: Longman, 1979.

Byrnes, Heidi. "The Role of Listening Comprehension: A Theoretical Base." *Foreign Language Annals* 17 no. 4 (September 1984): 317–348.

Cantoni-Harvey, Gina. *Content-Area Language Instruction: Approaches and Strategies*. Reading, MA: Addison-Wesley, 1987.

Dixon, Carol, and Denise Nessel. *Language–Experience Approach to Reading and Writing: Language–Experience Reading for Second Language Learners*. Hayward, CA: Alemany Press, 1983.

Hansen-Krening, Nancy. *Language Experiences for All Students*. Menlo Park, CA: Addison-Wesley, 1982.

Hudelson, Sarah, ed. *Learning to Read in Different Languages*. Washington, DC: Center for Applied Linguistics, 1981 (Papers in Applied Linguistics: Linguistics and Literacy Series: 1).

Krashen, Stephen D., and Tracy Terrell. *The Natural Approach. Language Acquisition in the Classroom*. Hayward, CA: Alemany Press, 1983.

Met, Myriam. "Listening Comprehension and the Young Second Language Learner." *Foreign Language Annals* 17 no. 5 (October 1984): 519–523.

Morrow, Keith. "Principles of Communicative Methodology." In Keith Johnson and Keith Morrow, eds., *Communication in the Classroom*. Burnt Mill, Harlow, Essex, UK: Longman, 1981.

Phillips, June K. "Practical Implications of Recent Research in Reading." *Foreign Language Annals* 17 no. 4 (September 1984): 285–299.

Raimes, Ann. *Techniques in Teaching Writing*. New York: Oxford Press, 1983.

Rathmell, George. *Benchmarks in Reading*. Hayward, CA: Alemany Press, 1984.

Savignon, Sandra J. *Communicative Competence: Theory and Classroom Practice: Texts and Contexts in Second Language Learning*. Reading, MA: Addison-Wesley, 1983.

Terrell, Tracy. "The Natural Approach to Language Teaching: An Update." *Canadian Modern Language Review* 41 no. 3 (1985): 461–479.

Thonis, Eleanor Wall. *Teaching Reading to Non-English Speakers*. New York: The MacMillan Company, 1970.

Ur, Penny. *Teaching Listening Comprehension*. Cambridge, England: Cambridge University Press, 1984.

Van Ek, J. A. *The Threshold Level for Modern Language Learning in Schools*. The Council of Europe. London: Longman, 1977.

Sources for Activities

Bassano, Sharron and Mary Ann Christison. *Look Who's Talking*. Hayward, CA: Alemany Press, 1987.

Ferrer, Jami, and Patty Werner DePoleo. *Bridge the Gap*. Hayward, CA: Alemany Press, 1983.

García, Ramiro. *Instructor's Notebook: How to Apply TPR for Best Results*. James Asher, ed. Los Gatos, CA: Sky Oaks Productions, 1985.

Klippel, Friederike. *Keep Talking. Communicative Fluency Activities for Language Teaching*. New York: Cambridge University Press, 1984.

Linse, Caroline. *The Children's Response. TPR and Beyond Toward Writing.* Hayward, CA: Alemany Press, 1983.

Malay, Alan and Alan Duff. *Drama Techniques in Language Teaching.* New York: Cambridge University Press, 1978.

Morgan, John, and Mario Rinvolucri. *Once Upon A Time: Using Stories in the Language Classroom.* New York: Cambridge University Press, 1984.

Chapter 9
Experiencing Culture in the Classroom

Learning more about culture, empathy for other people, and global awareness have all been frequently cited as elements of rationale for the teaching of foreign languages at the elementary school level. Culture has been interpreted in a variety of ways: as the important names and places in the history, geography and literature of a people; as great works of art and music; as learning to get along in the day-to-day life of a people. Children have achieved the full potential of extended experience with a second language only if they have also achieved at least some measure of competence in all three cultural areas.

GOALS FOR CULTURAL INSTRUCTION

H. Ned Seelye (1984) has identified the following seven goals as a framework for cultural instruction with all students (p. 49–58). The elementary school foreign language teacher will make the most effective choices and combinations of cultural information and activities if he or she keeps these goals in mind during the planning of the entire curriculum. While not all goals can be met in every lesson or even at every grade level, they must all be addressed if the students are to leave the elementary school foreign language program with a balanced cultural perspective.

Cultural Goal 1: The Sense, or Functionality, of Culturally Conditioned Behavior

The student should demonstrate an understanding that people act the way they do because they are using options the society allows for satisfying basic physical and psychological needs.

Child-appropriate example: When talking with one another, speakers in many Latin American countries stand much closer to one another than is common in the United States.

Cultural Goal 2: Interaction of Language and Social Variables

The student should demonstrate an understanding that such social variables as age, sex, social class, and place of residence affect the way people speak and behave.

Child-appropriate example: In German-speaking countries children address their peers and immediate family members with the familiar form *du*, and all other adults with the formal second-person form *Sie*. In Japan people address one another differently depending on their relationship to one another and their social station.

Cultural Goal 3: Conventional Behavior in Common Situations

The student should indicate an understanding of the role convention plays in shaping behavior by demonstrating how people act in common mundane and crisis situations in the target culture.

Child-appropriate example: Individuals in many European countries habitually shake hands when they meet one another on the street, even if they are pausing only briefly. In Japan a bow is a part of every greeting, and in South America a greeting is often accompanied by an *abrazo*, a hug.

Cultural Goal 4: Cultural Connotations of Words and Phrases

The student should indicate an awareness that culturally conditioned images are associated with even the most common target words and phrases.

Child-appropriate example: Pigs, white horses, storks and chimney sweeps are associated with good luck in Germany—so much so that marzipan pigs are common Christmas and New Year treats.

Cultural Goal 5: Evaluating Statements About a Society

The student should demonstrate the ability to evaluate the relative strength of a generality concerning the target culture in terms of the amount of evidence substantiating the statement.

Child-appropriate example: Americans visiting in a German home sometimes feel their hosts are unfriendly because they keep the doors between rooms closed all the time. Germans, by contrast, feel their American guests are disorderly because they leave doors open.

Cultural Goal 6: Researching Another Culture

The student should show that she or he has developed the skills needed to locate and organize information about the target culture from the library, the mass media, people, and personal observation.

Child-appropriate example: When children begin to ask questions about the target culture that the teacher cannot immediately answer, or that the teacher knows are researchable, they can be encouraged to seek the help of library resources or of willing native speakers who represent the target culture. Children often have questions about house pets, school schedules, allowances, and common aspects of daily life.

Cultural Goal 7: Attitudes Toward Other Cultures

The student should demonstrate intellectual curiosity about the target culture and empathy toward its people.

Child-appropriate example: All activities that bring the child into contact with individuals living in or otherwise representing the target culture provide opportunity for development toward this goal.

MEANINGFUL EXPERIENCES WITH CULTURE

Cultural topics to be included in a communication-based elementary school foreign language program are chosen at least in part on the basis of their potential for enabling students to communicate through the target language and for their inherent ability to motivate students to use the target language. Interest in the culture in which the target language is spoken can motivate language acquisition and practice. In addition, the cultural dimension of the language class can assist the children to better understand their own culture, as they make comparisons and begin to understand a point of view that is based in the target culture and expressed in the target language.

Even more important than the potential for communication, the interests and developmental level of the children in the class must guide the choice of cultural information selected for instruction. It is interesting to consider that there might be parallels between the acquisition of a second language and the acquisition of a second culture. Many similar criteria could be said to apply. Children will not understand or be open to cultural information and practices that are so divorced from their own experiences as to seem funny or even bizarre, any more than they will learn language that is not directed to their interests and built on their own experiences. They are also unlikely to "acquire" cultural information that primarily affects adults in the target culture, since they have yet to penetrate the adult culture of their own world and often find it confusing. Perhaps most importantly, just as children do not acquire a language primarily by being told about it, but rather through meaningful, communicative experiences with the language, so also do children penetrate a new culture through meaningful experiences with cultural practices and cultural phenomena that are appropriate to their age level, their interests, and the classroom setting.

Experience
↗   ↘
Culture ← Language

Experiences with the culture in the target language can begin with the first language class and infuse all classroom activities. For example, children in a German classroom can learn from the first day that a greeting is always accompanied by a hand-shaking ritual (Goal 3). Young students beginning Spanish can learn first the colors of the Mexican flag and then learn to place the flag on Mexico on the North American map (Goal 4). Children beginning French can celebrate April Fool's Day with fish shapes placed on one another's backs (Goal 4). A teacher of Japanese might greet students with a bow and expect them to greet one another in the same way (Goal 3). Children learning any European language can learn to count on their fingers starting with the thumb representing the number one (Goal 3). Children in a German class can learn very early to press their thumbs for good luck, or to knock on their desks instead of applauding to show approval (Goal 1). None of these small cultural items requires elaborate explanation, but each is a step toward identification with another way of thinking and another way of behaving in everyday situations.

Simple crafts and food activities can provide experiences with elements of the target culture which extend over a longer period of time. An activity such as building and later breaking a class piñata, or perhaps individual piñatas made with paper bags, can be both an opportunity to apply language to a new activity and an experience in preparation for a celebration common to the target culture. Mask making can be a prelude to the celebration of an in-class version of a festival specific to the target culture, such as the pre-Lenten carnivals observed in several German-, French-, and Spanish-speaking

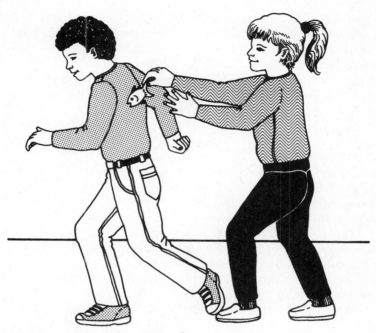

Playing a fish game on April 1 gives children learning French an experience with French culture.

cultures. A food activity such as preparing an open-faced sandwich in a German class, and then eating it with a knife (in the right hand) and a fork (in the left hand) provides an opportunity for experiencing several cultural contrasts in food presentation and eating behavior (Goal 4). A food activity for a Chinese class could include making home-made noodles and then eating them using chopsticks.

These crafts and food activities can later become the focal point for language-experience stories and for writing or copying activities. They can serve as the central feature of simulations or the starting point for student-prepared skits or presentations to parents. Preparations for a festival, including making such crafts as piñatas, paper flowers, or masks, might culminate in a festive celebration, either within the class or as a joint experience with other classes or invited guests.

The use of a variety of visuals representing the target culture can help to relate interests of the children to the wider world in which the target language plays a role. Posters and bulletin boards can create an awareness of the cultural settings in which the target language is spoken. Magazines and comic books from the target culture can be used to illustrate vocabulary items or to communicate a bulletin board message. Coins from the culture used as counters for math activities or as playing pieces in a board game bring a reality to these everyday cultural objects. Board games, puzzles and picture books, when made available to children in a learning center or in a special foreign language corner of the classroom or the library, open doors to the daily life of the child in the target culture and invite the learner to experience a small portion of that culture.

FANTASY EXPERIENCES

It is possible to create more extensive experiences with culture in the classroom, even for students who have very limited language background. By combining fantasy, culture, and elements of Total Physical Response and Suggestopedia the teacher can create a vivid, living connection between the children in the classroom and the target culture. Like simulations, fantasy experiences can place students in a setting that replicates important elements of the target culture and offers the opportunity to experience new feelings, new combinations of circumstances, and new solutions to familiar problems. The fantasy experiences described below are highly structured and teacher controlled, designed to be used for early stages of language instruction, when it is often considered to be very difficult to deal with culture in the target language. Variations and adaptations of this technique can be used at every level of language instruction.

Experience with fantasy can begin as early as the first day of class: With Baroque string music playing softly in the background, the teacher explains to students that they are to imagine themselves as children in the target culture and to choose a name by which they will be called during the course of the class.* They close their eyes and listen as the teacher reads a list of names expressively, then a second time in an angry voice, so students know how a name might sound in case the teacher should ever become angry during class. Finally the students open their eyes and listen as the teacher reads the names a third time, raising their hands when they hear a name they would like to use. When two or more students choose the same name, the teacher goes on, continuing through the list until only one child chooses each name. In the case of very popular names, which several children want, the teacher might either give more than one child the same name, or simply remove the name so that children make other choices.

This activity establishes the connection between background music and use of the imagination. It also gives children an opportunity to take the first step toward identification with a new culture, a new way of thinking, even a new way of being addressed. The following is a plan for a simple fantasy experience which can be used in early stages of instruction. With music in

*Suggested in workshops by David Wolfe, Moorestown Township Public Schools, Moorestown, New Jersey.

the background, the teacher talks about being very tired and directs the children to stretch, to yawn, to lay their heads on their arms, to close their eyes, and to sleep (perhaps even to snore). The teacher counts off the hours of the night, reminding the children to sleep, perhaps to snore (or *not* to snore). At seven o'clock the teacher plays a recording of church bells (reflecting German culture) or sets off an alarm clock, and then directs the children to wake up, to stretch (again), to wash their faces, brush their teeth, dress, make their beds, and sit down for breakfast. The culminating portion of this fantasy might be a small continental breakfast, if the class can include food experiences, or the pantomiming of leaving home to go on to other activities.

Airplane Fantasy

A longer fantasy experience is popular in summer classes for children at Concordia College, Moorhead, Minnesota. Children are issued passports and airline tickets and prepare for a "trip" to Germany, Canada, Colombia, or any other destination appropriate to the language being taught. In addition to the Baroque music in the background, the teacher prepares an "aircraft" with a masking tape outline on the floor. This takes up much of the room, especially in a large class, with chairs placed side by side, in twos or in fours depending on the size of the class, and labeled with letters and numbers, as in a real aircraft. In the Concordia experience there are actual airline ticket folders, luggage tags, and air-sickness bags, as well as some in-flight magzines and other realia typically found in an airplane. Children are directed to show their tickets and their passports to the flight attendant, to find their seats, to buckle their imaginary seatbelts—and of course they are told to refrain from smoking and to participate in all the other activities associated with the beginning of any flight. During the course of the flight, children are directed to look out their imaginary windows at drawings of clouds and of other aircraft. Turbulence comes, and they are led by the teacher in jiggling up and down and back and forth. The teacher exclaims over the unease in the stomach that they all feel, and many children discover an imaginary use for their real air-sickness bags. In an extended fantasy, the teacher might distribute in-flight meals, consisting of a half sandwich, a pickle, fruit, and a mint or a cookie assembled on small trays from a meat department wrapped in plastic food wrap. The children are directed to close their eyes and sleep as the teacher counts off the hours and notes the change of time because of passage through time zones. The children finally arrive at their destination and exclaim over large pictures of the city in which they have landed, as they are directed to look at and point to special landmarks they should note. Classes that have shared this experience often remember a feeling of actually having traveled in an airplane to a distant place. As a follow-up to the

Just a few props can create a fantasy environment with great potential for culture and language acquisition.

airplane trip, classes might write a language-experience story together or draw pictures of the trip on post-card sized tagboard and write messages from their destination to send home.

Steamer Trip Fantasy

Another example of a fantasy, this one taking place in Germany, is a trip on a Rhine steamer, again to the accompaniment of Baroque music, using inexpensive sunglasses and a simple box camera as props, and with the outline of a Rhine steamer taped to the floor. Children are directed to exchange coins for tickets, to give their tickets to a ship attendant, and to board the steamer. As the steamer progresses down the Rhine, the children are directed to go to the left and the right on the deck, to look at and point to castles and other landmarks as they go by, and to pass the camera back and forth to "take pictures" of the special features along the Rhine. If a snack is desired, it might be some kind of finger food, an ice cream bar, or some juice. A day or two after the Rhine trip the students might view slides of an actual Rhine trip, once again point to special landmarks they have seen, and perhaps even pick out themselves and their classmates in pictures of Rhine passengers. (Although of course they are not actually present in the pictures, children usually have no problem in "finding" themselves in a large group of people from an actual Rhine photo.)

Other Fantasies

Other examples of potential fantasy settings might include a bus trip or a walking trip around Paris, with important Paris monuments along the way to look at and point to; or a canoe trip down a river in Canada, during which animals from the woods appear and disappear on either side of the masking-tape river "flowing" through the center of the classroom.

In some fantasies, all children can take part at the same time, as in the airplane trip and the simple morning fantasy. In other fantasies, a few students may take part and the rest of the class serves as observers. There can be several episodes of the same fantasy, involving different members of the class. In each repetition the script might change so that children never know exactly what to expect and thus remain attentive through several repetitions. In a fantasy that takes place in Berlin, for example, several students stand in line, press the call button outside the elevator, choose the correct floor, and press the button to reach the observation tower. Many variations are possible in this fantasy: the door might fail to open or become stuck part way, one student might be left behind, a child (or the teacher) might get a hand or a piece of clothing caught in the door; thus children will be directed to perform different activities in each variation of a similar situation. For the elevator fantasy, only a masking tape elevator, the up-down button on the outside, and the floor buttons on the inside of the elevator are required as props. (The elevator door "opens" when the masking-tape door is temporarily lifted from the floor.) Passengers in the elevator might discover their stomachs growing queasy, as the elevator goes very high very fast.

Planning a Fantasy Experience

Some of the key components to be considered by a teacher wishing to plan a fantasy experience include the following:

1. Precede major culture-bearing fantasies with shorter experiences.
2. Choose background music that is regular and unobtrusive. (Baroque string music works very well.)
3. Set the scene in a physical way, using masking tape, chair arrangement, or other physical means.

Even a school classroom can include an elevator—at least for the purposes of fantasy.

4. Choose cultural features that have dramatic potential.
5. Choose topics that include possibilities for movement, props, and sounds as a part of the dramatic sequence.
6. Plan the sequence to include a beginning, a middle, and an end.
7. Build in elements of humor and surprise.
8. Choose a few appropriate props; do not over-prop.
9. Use familiar commands with new content OR introduce new commands carefully in advance.
10. Plan for natural follow-up during succeeding class periods.

Fantasy activities such as those described here can provide very vivid, memorable experiences with the target culture. Since fantasy requires the suspension of disbelief, it is important that major or extended fantasies not be overused, or they will lose their special quality. Student willingness to suspend reality for extended periods of time will also diminish if elaborate fantasy experiences are planned too frequently.

CLASSROOM EXCHANGES

A "twinned classroom" program is a particularly effective means of combining linguistic and cultural goals, as it offers children the opportunity to experience aspects of the target culture in a very direct and personal way. First described by Jonas (1969), this idea can be used as the core of the foreign language curriculum for a period of time or as an effective supplement to any program model.

The elementary school foreign language teacher establishes a relationship with a teacher, preferably an English teacher, at a comparable grade level in a school in the target culture. Together they set goals for a variety of activities involved in an exchange of class projects. Setting up individual pen-pal relationships is not part of the early stages of this program, since the emphasis is on group work within each class. The program takes place in two phases; during the first phase each school plans and prepares the projects they will send to their partner school, and during the second phase they interpret and respond to the project they have received from their partner school.

A fourth-grade class in a parochial school in Northfield, Minnesota, developed a classroom exchange with a fifth-grade group in Hamburg, West Germany, in a project designed by the author (Pesola). As a first step the two groups exchanged group photographs of class members, class lists, and school schedules. Then the Northfield group discussed the best way to show their partner group what it meant to be a fourth-grade child, in their school, in Northfield, in Minnesota, in the United States. At the same time they began to generate questions about the life of the German children (Goal 7).

The project resulted in the following activities:

1. A questionnaire based on students' questions about life in Hamburg was developed. The questions reflected interest in family and pets, modes of transportation, size of families, hobbies, and favorite film, TV, and pop music stars. The children also took the questionnaire themselves and analyzed the results to gain insight into their own lives. Because these students were beginners, the questionnaire was developed in English and translated by the teacher before it was sent to Germany. With more advanced learners the same activity might be conducted in the target language.

2. Materials containing information about the community and aspects of the children's daily lives were collected. This involved visits to the local chamber of commerce, letters to the state tourist agency, and visits to many local businesses and service organizations. The final collection of materials included these items:

   • TV and movie schedules
   • mail-order catalogs
   • telephone book
   • weekly food ads and coupon pages
   • comic books
   • brochures about the city and the state
   • colorful information about community businesses
   • seed catalogs and packets for favorite garden products
   • circus flyers
   • school student handbooks
   • copies of the school paper and of the local paper

3. Photographs of selected aspects of the children's daily lives were taken. Different children's homes were selected for each room of the house; other children had pets or hobbies photographed. The final slide collection included pictures of the following:

   • all possible rooms in a home
   • a school bus
   • the school, the classroom, the gymnasium
   • stores and businesses familiar to the children
   • pets and children engaged in hobbies
   • the cafeteria

- school athletic, music, and drama events the children like to attend
- individual pictures of the children with a favorite pet or toy

4. Music and information which held meaning for class members were recorded. Some of the recorded material included these items:

    - favorite songs from German class and music classes
    - school song and cheers
    - favorite pop or rock music (determined by class vote)
    - self-introductions by each child in the target language

(The German partner class also made recordings of the material the American children were learning in their German classes, but there was no interest in having the American children return the favor because at the time an American accent was not considered acceptable in the partner school.)

5. To see how the climates compared, the weather was charted day-by-day over a period of several months, and later compared with information sent from Hamburg.

The period of preparation for the exchange lasted about six weeks and was an experience with inquiry and interdisciplinary involvement that resulted in better knowledge of the children's own class and environment and heightened interest in life in German-speaking countries. The activity would have been valuable even if nothing had ever been received from Hamburg. When the Hamburg projects actually arrived, there was considerable excitement throughout the school.

Many of the Hamburg contributions had been prepared by individual children, who enclosed drawings, favorite rhymes and games, family pictures, post cards, maps, and short descriptions of favorite activities. The responses to the questionnaire provided material for investigation and discussion for the rest of the school year: why would so many American film stars appear in the list of favorites? Where were the Saturday-morning cartoons on television? The contact with authentic materials and the awareness of the lives of real children of about their own age provided a context for the study of language and a springboard for a continuing interest in culture.

Teachers wishing to develop a classroom exchange project may find a potential partner teacher in several ways. Several of the professional associations and journals have teacher pen-pal opportunities with fellow teachers abroad, and these contacts can be developed into classroom exchanges. Many colleges and universities have programs of study abroad, and students in these programs are often willing to serve as a liaison in setting up such a program. The best route for developing a program is a personal contact with a teacher or a school during a trip to a country of target culture. The goals of the project should be fully discussed and agreed on before the project begins, and the project should begin in the fall, to allow enough time for materials to be developed, to reach their destination, and to receive a response before the end of the school year.

Many variations on the classroom exchange are possible. A videotape component can be an exciting addition, but it requires a multi-standard player and camera for most countries. Interesting possibilities are suggested by the *TELEclass* project in Hawaii, which uses satellite communications to link students in classrooms all over the world via videotelephones and computers (Wollstein 1987). Developing exchange relationships with several different countries in which the target language is spoken and focusing on a different country each year would help students to appreciate the variety of approaches to daily life which can be discovered through the use of a single language. Exchanges between same-language classrooms in different parts of the same country can be motivating and revealing, as children discover that lifestyles and customs are not identical even where others speak their own native language.

EDUCATION FOR GLOBAL AWARENESS

The elementary school foreign language classroom presents an especially favorable setting for introducing the child to the whole world of cultural diversity. When the language teacher limits the attention of the class to a single country, or even to one region of a country in which the target language is spoken, an important opportunity is being missed. Each of the languages most commonly taught in elementary school in the United States is used in a number of countries that have customs and lifestyles that are very different from one another. The classroom experience will be much richer if this variety is brought into the classroom through activities, visual representation, and specific songs, games, crafts, foods, and other experiences reflecting a variety of cultures.

Global awareness can be further enhanced when teachers use every opportunity to show relationships between countries where the target language is used and other nations around the world. The presence of many Germans in South America, the trade of a local business with Switzerland, the role of French explorers in America and in other parts of the world can all become a part of the information exchanged in an elementary school foreign language classroom. The teacher can invite speakers of the target language who have had experiences in any part of the world to show the class slides and to discuss the countries they have visited. In more advanced classes, the teacher and students together can discuss implications of events in any part of the world for countries in which the target language is spoken and for the children themselves.

ADDITIONAL ACTIVITIES

Elementary school foreign language teachers who are committed to providing cultural experiences for their classes will be constantly in search of authentic games, music, crafts, foods, and customs to share with them. In addition, many of the following activities will contribute to developing the seven cultural goals mentioned above:

1. Invite foreign visitors or target-language speakers to visit the class and share their experiences, using visuals, slides, and as many concrete materials as possible.
2. Learn and perform folk dances and singing games from the target culture.
3. Celebrate holidays and festivals of the target culture in the class, especially those which do not have an American counterpart.
4. Where possible, make field trips to a neighborhood, restaurant, museum, or store that reflects some aspects of the target culture.
5. Invite children to bring to class any items from the target culture or samples of the target language which they may come across in their homes. Many students become very good at finding the target language on directions, store labels, and advertisements. These items can become the stimulus for a great deal of language when the child or the teacher shares them with the class.
6. Identify local or regional place names which may be derived from the target language and investigate the reason for the choice of name. Some communities may have namesakes in the target culture, or sister cities in another country, and these relationships can be the source of many activities.
7. Students can skim target-language newspapers or magazines to find illustrations for concepts they are learning in the foreign language class or in subject content classes.
8. The teacher can read or tell fables, folktales, and legends that come from the target culture or from other cultures around the world (all in the target language).
9. The class or individual students can visit a supermarket or a gourmet shop and list foods that are imported from countries where the target language is spoken.
10. The children can be encouraged to read fiction and nonfiction books about children in the target culture. The school media center director is

often willing to help develop a list or a collection of these books for each grade level.

SUMMARY

The elementary school foreign language classroom is an ideal setting for the development of cultural awareness and understanding. Each of the seven goals identified by Seelye can be addressed through activities and experiences in the target language. Cultural goals can best be met by giving children experiences with the culture rather than by talking about cultural facts and artifacts. Many of these experiences can be a part of daily classroom activity, integrated with the use of language in an authentic, communicative setting. This chapter also describes two types of extended cultural experience—the fantasy and the classroom exchange. The fantasy makes use of a few props and the child's imagination to bring the child together with the culture in a fantasy setting. In the classroom exchange, two cultures actually meet, as a language class exchanges projects and information with a partner class in the target culture. The classroom exchange requires extensive preparation and continues over a period of time.

Global awareness is an additional goal that has special importance in the elementary school foreign language classroom. The target language can be used as a point of departure for making connections with the entire world. The chapter closes with a series of additional activities that can give children experiences with the target culture or with global concepts.

FOR STUDY AND DISCUSSION

1. Identify *five* examples of culturally conditioned behavior (Cultural Goal 1) or conventional behavior (Cultural Goal 3) which are representative of the target culture you teach. Describe how you might build each of them into the experiences of your elementary school foreign language class in the early stages of language acquisition.

2. You have invited a native speaker to speak to your class of fourth graders, who are in their second year of learning the language you teach. Based on what you know about language and culture, what instructions and help will you give your speaker in advance to insure that the experience will be valuable for the children in your class?

3. Choose a feature of the target culture which you feel would be suitable for the development of a classroom fantasy experience. Follow the guidelines in the chapter and plan a fantasy for the grade and language level with which you are the most familiar.

4. You have made contact with a teacher of English in an elementary school

in the target culture, and the teacher is eager to take part in a classroom exchange but has no idea how to begin. Write a letter in which you describe the mechanics and the potential of the idea.

5. List seven ideas for meaningfully linking the target language that you teach with world-wide cultures, beyond the limits of the countries in which the target language is spoken natively.

FOR FURTHER READING

The following sources are recommended for additional information about material covered in this chapter. Chapter citations are documented in *Works Cited* at the end of the volume.

Banks, James A. *Teaching Strategies for Ethnic Studies.* 3d ed. Rockleigh, NJ: Allyn and Bacon, 1983.

Cole, Ann, Carolyn Haas, Elizabeth Heller, and Betty Weinberger. *Children are Children are Children: An Activity Approach to Exploring Brazil, France, Iran, Japan, Nigeria and the U.S.S.R.* Boston: Little, Brown, and Company, 1978.

Collins, H. Thomas, and Sally Banks Zakariya. *Getting Started in Global Education.* Arlington, VA: National Association of Elementary School Principals, 1982.

Crawford-Lange, Linda M., and Dale L. Lange. "Doing the Unthinkable in the Second-Language Classroom: A Process for the Integration of Language and Culture." In Theodore V. Higgs, ed., *Teaching for Proficiency, the Organizing Principle.* Lincolnwood, IL: National Textbook Company, 1984: 139–177.

Damen, Louise. *Culture Learning: The Fifth Dimension in the Language Classroom.* Reading, MA: Addison-Wesley, 1987.

Global Perspectives in Education. *Intercom: Moving Toward a Global Perspective: Social Studies and Second Languages.* New York: Global Perspectives in Education, 1983.

Rosengren, Frank H., Marylee Crofts Wiley, and David S. Wiley. *Internationalizing Your School.* New York: National Council on Foreign Languages and International Studies, 1983.

Seelye, H. Ned. *Teaching Culture.* Lincolnwood, IL: National Textbook Company, 1984.

Strasheim, Lorraine A. "Language is the Medium, Culture is the Message: Globalizing Foreign Languages." In Maurice W. Conner, ed., *A Global Approach to Foreign Language Education.* Skokie, IL: National Textbook Company, 1981: 1–16.

Chapter 10

Making It Happen: Planning for Day-to-Day Instruction

If careful planning of the program and preparation of a community and a school are the most important preliminary factors in the ultimate success of an elementary school foreign language program, planning for each day's instruction is the most important component of the program once it is in place. Each day's lesson fits into a larger framework of planning which makes it a part of long-range goals and unified, sequenced objectives. A planning process organized around communicative principles will develop activities that enable students to function effectively in situations that require them to seek and provide information, to express ideas and opinions, and to control their environment in a variety of ways. Such a planning process will first attempt to give children control over their immediate environment and then move outward, enabling them to discuss interests, needs, and concerns in the school beyond their classroom: in their families and in their community.

PLANNING FOR IMMERSION, BILINGUAL AND SUBJECT–CONTENT INSTRUCTION

Planning in an immersion or a bilingual, content-based classroom will focus on and take its direction from the goals of the subject content area. The difference between the classroom in which a second language is the medium of instruction and the native-language classroom is at least in part the extra dimension of planning, which focuses on language development and on subject content goals at the same time. While the organizing principle for instruction will be the subject matter content, the language skills necessary to progress in communication about subject matter content must also be intentionally developed through the planning process. This suggests that it will sometimes be necessary to do language development activities in preparation for or as a component of a lesson directed toward subject content goals. The teacher of subject content in a second language must always be aware of the language skills demanded by the concepts and the activities involved in the subject content goals. The teacher must also plan carefully for the concrete experiences and the visual reinforcement that will make the academic language of instruction comprehensible to the students and that will help them to develop the linguistic skills necessary for dealing with the subject-content material.

PLANNING FOR FLES AND FLEX INSTRUCTION

In order to achieve and maintain high student interest and motivation in the FLES or FLEX classroom, planners must organize the curriculum and the everyday activities of the classroom around the needs and interests of the children. In the elementary school, perhaps more than at any other level, this is an individual challenge from school to school and from class to class. The elementary school foreign language teacher will no doubt always have to develop a great many materials and will have to adapt existing curriculum to meet the needs of the individual elementary school class. In order to be compatible with the goals and philosophy of the elementary school, planning for foreign language instruction must be thematic and multidisciplinary, addressing the needs and the development of the whole child. Close cooperation with classroom teachers can lead to an effective integration of second languages with the emphases and the goals of other content areas.

PLANNING ACTIVITIES

In planning a daily lesson or unit based on communication, the teacher might begin by asking a series of questions:

1. What communication needs will the student be able to meet through the activities of this unit, and in what kinds of situations should the student be able to meet those needs?
2. What kind of activities will help the student to meet those needs?
3. What can I do as a teacher to motivate the student to feel the need and to want to meet the need?
4. What kind of materials will help clarify the new information and make the experiences come alive for the children?
5. What language will the children need to practice in order to experience success in meeting their goals?
6. What will the payoff be? How will the teacher and the children themselves

know whether the children have developed the skills necessary to meet the communicative goals identified in this unit or for this lesson?

Both a unit plan and a daily plan must include a variety of possible activities for meeting each goal.

Importance of Planning

The importance of a written plan cannot be overemphasized. There is a remarkable correlation between the presence of a detailed written plan and the ability of a teacher to be creative and flexible in the actual class setting. Many FLES and FLEX programs have a very limited amount of class time in which to give children experiences with the target language. Only careful planning can prevent the loss and misuse of time, which is already in very short supply.

The careful formulation of written objectives will help the teacher plan relevant activities and coherent lessons. Effective objectives always describe what students will be able to *do* at the end of the lesson. The statements include action verbs which represent a *student* activity that is *observable*. Verbs such as *teach*, *learn*, and *understand* are not useful because they describe process rather than outcome, and because they are essentially unobservable. It is often helpful to think of each objective as beginning with the phrase "The students will be able to . . ."

Here are some examples of objectives for a beginning elementary school foreign language class.

Students will be able to do the following:

1. Respond to the teacher with an appropriate greeting
2. Point to a day of the week on the calendar when it is named
3. Identify numerals 0 to 5 when they are not in sequence
4. Respond correctly to the following commands, individually and in a group:

   - stand up
   - point to . . .
   - walk
   - sit down
   - touch . . . (color, number, body part)
   - turn around

5. Respond with name when asked "What is your name?" (Some children will also say "My name is . . .")

Actually writing a lesson plan on the board helps children to anticipate the variety of activities they will experience and to feel a sense of progress through the lesson or through the material. The plan itself can become the object of meaningful communication and language practice, as the teacher asks children to remind her or him of the next activity or invites them to choose an activity from those remaining. Teachers in some advanced classes write the day's schedule in sentences on the chalkboard, and it becomes a class activity at the end of the day to rewrite the sentences in the past tense to show that the activity has been completed. Rather than talking about changing the tense of the verb, the teacher says, "This sentence isn't true any more; how can we change it to make it right?" In some classes the revised daily schedule is written in a class diary, illustrated, and used to maintain a class history.

Warm-up

Each elementary school foreign language class period, regardless of its length, should begin with a brief warm-up. This is a time for communicative use of completely familiar language. The warm-up has several purposes:

1. It provides a review and a basis for new material to be introduced.

2. It provides a transition from the instructional time the students have just experienced in their native language to an intensive experience of learning and thinking in the target language.

3. Because of the relatively easy level at which the warm-up is conducted, it helps students to build or regain confidence in their ability to work with the target language. At some point in the warm-up every child should have the opportunity to say something in the target language, either individually, in a small group, or in the larger group.

4. It provides a time during which teachers and students alike can share dimensions of their personality and their interests—as they talk about likes and dislikes, families, weather (and how they deal with it)—and personalize applications of material they have learned earlier, in a more structured setting.

The warm-up does not "just happen." It must be carefully planned to include different material and strategies each day.

Balance of Old and New Material

Children need a great deal of practice with new material before they are able to appropriate it for their own functional, communicative purposes. Every class period should contain some new and some familiar material; the exact balance will vary from day to day. One of the teacher's tasks is to make the old material seem new and the new material seem familiar. The teacher must plan for many different contexts within which to practice, in order to prevent boredom with the practice and to provide the children with a sense of progress—the old always seems new, because the message to be communicated has a new context and the need to communicate that message is also new. For example, when children are first introduced to numbers, they might count objects, participate in a count-out rhyme, guess which number the teacher has hidden in her or his hand, participate in a concentration game with numbers, play a Go Fish game with number cards, roll giant dice and call out the numbers, sing a song based on numbers, and so forth. Each activity presents a new context and a new challenge, but in the process the children have practiced the numbers vocabulary enough so for it to have become "automatic."

Introducing New Material

When introducing new material, the teacher tries to build on what students have already learned so they have maximum security and reason for self confidence. For example, on the first day of class, the teacher might point out, if appropriate, some relationships and cognates between the native language and the target language, and show how many of the target-language words the student may already be familiar with without realizing it. When the class hears a new song, poem, story, or another message for the first time, the teacher may invite the students to identify familiar words and phrases. In order to facilitate this task, making the new seem familiar, the teacher will consciously "seed" or plant material in the lesson for Monday which will appear in a larger context on Wednesday or Thursday, so that the later, longer message will not seem entirely new: familiar material is already present.

For example, the German teacher has decided to introduce a birthday song because one of the students has a birthday on Thursday:

Zum Geburtstag viel Glück! (Good luck/happiness on your birthday!)

Zum Geburtstag viel Glück! (Good luck/happiness on your birthday!)

Langes Leben und Gesundheit! (Long life and good health!)

Zum Geburtstag viel Glück! (Good luck/happiness on your birthday!)

On Monday, the teacher introduces the exclamation "Good luck!" in the course of a game, demonstrating the contrast between the American gesture of crossed fingers and the German gesture of pressing thumbs to symbolize a good luck wish. The exclamation is reentered at every opportunity during the course of the week. On Tuesday, the lesson includes the opposites *kurz* and *lang* (short and long), applied during a TPR exercise at the chalkboard in which children draw monsters with long and short hair, long and short arms and legs, long and short ears and noses. On Wednesday, the teacher pretends to have a cold, sneezing frequently, and the children are taught to wish the teacher and one another *Gesundheit*, which is already somewhat familiar to them. By Thursday, the only new words in the birthday song are the word for birthday itself, *Geburtstag*, which the teacher explains by means of a visual showing a birthday cake and presents, and the word for life, *Leben*, which the teacher may explain by contrasting a *long* life of someone who is ninety-six years old with a *short* life of someone who is two years old. After listening to the song one or two times (and with a minimum of repetition) the children are ready to sing the birthday song.

Planning from day to day should incorporate these linkages. The teacher should constantly be helping students to recognize these links, so that students discover language learning as a cumulative process—in contrast to what seems so often to be the case in other classes, where learning for the test (and later forgetting) seems somehow to be acceptable and inevitable.

Variety

Every class period, especially in the primary grades, should include a certain number of regular, predictable classroom routines which make heavy use of language repetition and patterned teacher-student interaction. Show-and-tell and the calendar activities that begin the day in many primary classrooms are examples of such routines. These routines provide children with a sense of security, and they also help to give meaning clues to the content discussed in the course of the activity. Special routines are common for lineups to leave for another classroom, or for changing activities within the classroom. Passing out or turning in papers becomes an opportunity for routine use of language for many teachers.

Each class period should also include a number and variety of activities. In general, the younger the children in a class, the greater the number of different activities planned for each class period. The attention span increases with the age of the child, but even in the middle school/junior high, activities should rarely last longer than ten minutes, and they should usually be planned to last from five to eight minutes.

Activities should be developed with attention to high and low energy requirements on the part of both the teacher and the students. The teacher might think in terms of planning for peaks and valleys of excitement, of movement, or of physical and verbal involvement. The FLES or FLEX teacher who visits a classroom for a period of time during a day, or whose children return to another classroom at the end of the language period, would do well to plan activities at the end of the class period which leave the children ready to go on to work in other classes. Closing a class period with a game that leaves the children excited, unmanageable, or noisy will not earn the appreciation or the future cooperation of their next teacher.

Each lesson should include a balance of active and passive activities, of listening and speaking, of one-way and two-way communication. It is very important that children have the opportunity to ask questions as well as to answer them and, especially in the TPR-oriented classroom, to give directions as well as to respond to them. It is also wise to plan for change of pace. Songs, games, and rhymes with actions can change the tempo and the emphasis of a class period, while continuing to further communicative goals.

CLASSROOM STRUCTURES

In the elementary school foreign language classroom that is oriented toward communication, the traditional large-group, teacher-led structure has severe limitations. Communication flows primarily in one direction, from teacher to students, and children have few opportunities to test their own use of the language for personal communication. Yet both cognitive learning theory and second language acquisition theory tell us that for children to learn, it is important for them to express themselves orally. Expressing concepts, putting them in our own words, explaining them to others and speculating about them aloud, making applications of concepts to new situations, and finding creative and personalized ways to remember new concepts or language materials all contribute to genuine, successful learning.

When children learn to work cooperatively in small groups or in pairs, their opportunities for language use are multiplied many times over. Many teachers have little experience with small group and pair work and are reluctant to place children in a situation of relatively greater independence than is usually the case with large-group work. Teachers may also have anxiety about classroom noise and the potential for off-task behavior and disruption.

Cooperative Learning

Pair and small-group work, when they take place under the umbrella of cooperative learning, can be the most natural and effective means of helping students to communicate in a second language. However, children need just as much guidance in developing cooperative skills as they do in developing communication. The elementary school foreign language classroom is a natural setting for this growth.

Small groups and pairs, in order to function successfully, require that the following elements of cooperative learning be in place (Johnson and Johnson 1987):

1. *Positive interdependence* means that everyone depends on one another and that no one feels exploited, unnecessary, or left out.
2. *Face-to-face interaction* is possible only when children are in a physical setting in which they can talk with one another and work together easily, without raising their voices.

3. *Individual accountability* is in effect when each child knows that she or he may bear full responsibility for the information or the skills being learned by the group. There are no hitchhikers, only full participants.

4. *Social skills training* is an integral component of all the work in the cooperative classroom. The teacher helps children to understand the skills they will need to work successfully together and helps them to practice and monitor them. As is the case with language skills, a few specific cooperative skills will be highlighted at the beginning, such as making sure everyone has a turn to speak, giving encouragement, and listening when other group members are talking. Additional skills can be added after practice of the first skills has become habitual. Only development of the skills of working and living cooperatively can make communication possible, in either the target language or in the native language.

5. *Group processing* of the cooperative skills is just as important to the classroom routine as are quizzes and other strategies for determining progress in the subject content. The teacher helps children analyze what is working well in their group and what can be improved, offers suggestions when individual groups are having specific problems, and focuses the attention of the entire class on a limited, manageable number of skills at a time. Much of the group processing can take place in the target language, providing an additional area for meaningful communication within the classroom.

Many potential activities for small groups in the foreign language classroom are described by Gunderson and Johnson (1980), who structured a junior high French class around the principles of cooperative learning. A number of their ideas are immediately transferrable to elementary school foreign language classrooms at any level.

The special value of activities for pairs of students is noted by Nerenz and Knop (1982). Their research shows evidence that pair work offers the best balance of on-task behavior, percentage of student time spent in communicative use of the target language, and ratio of teacher talk to student talk.

Pair Activities

A typical pair activity for elementary school children is based on the idea that each partner has different information or must perform a different task in order for the pair to reach a common goal. For example, each partner might have a sheet of paper with pictures arranged in the following order: Partner A begins the activity, because Partner A has a "Pac Man" symbol on the first set of pictures. Partner A names the pictures in number 1 in order,

Children develop both language and human-relations skills when they work in cooperative groups.

and Partner B compares what Partner A reads with what is found on her or his sheet of paper. If they match, Partner B says "It's the same." If they don't match, Partner B says "It's different." Just to be sure, Partner B might name the animals in the order found on her or his sheet. When the partners decide they have a match, they place a __+__ on the line following the item. If they decide they don't have a match, they place a __0__ on the line. Then Partner B names the animals in order as they are found in item number 2 on her or his sheet, because Partner B has a "Pac Man" beside that item. The activity continues until the students have made decisions on all six items. Only then do the partners compare sheets to see if all their decisions are correct.

The type of matching activity described above can have endless variations, depending on the language skills of the students and on the goals of the activity. Students working on reading skills might match a picture with a word, or a more complex picture with a written description. Single pictures with small differences might be compared, eliciting descriptive language and questions as the partners try to determine if their pictures are identical or only similar.

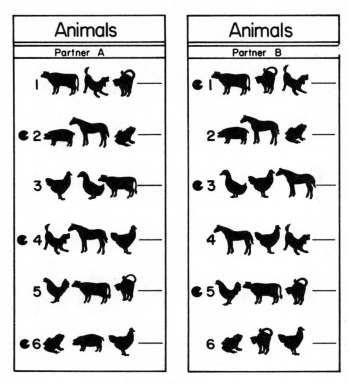

Pair Activity

In another common type of pair activity, one partner gives instructions and the other partner carries them out. For example, Partner A has a picture showing an arrangement of colored blocks. Partner B has actual colored blocks, which she or he must arrange to match the picture, based on instructions given by Partner A. If the instructions are not clear, Partner B can ask questions to clarify the task. After the task is successfully completed, the partners switch roles and build an arrangement based on a new picture. Variations of this activity include giving directions for placing furniture in a room, moving a token on a map, or arranging a variety of shapes to form a picture.

A third type of activity involves attitudes and opinions. Each partner receives an identical sheet of paper on which various foods are listed or pictured, as well as target-language phrases that express degree of liking or dislike. At the bottom of the sheet is a series of possible responses. Partner A begins by telling Partner B something that she or he loves, and Partner B draws a line connecting *I love* with the item mentioned, to help her or him

Not all pair activities have to involve reading or paper-and-pencil tasks. These children are helping each other to arrange blocks in a predetermined pattern.

remember what was said. Then Partner B responds using one of the phrases listed at the bottom of the page. Partner A goes on to give an item for each degree of like or dislike, and Partner B records the statement each time and responds to it. Then Partner B goes through her or his likes and dislikes while Partner A records and responds. At the end of the activity the teacher asks individuals from several of the groups to tell about their partners, to compare their results with other groups, to indicate foods that they both liked. As a homework activity, students might write about the food likes and dislikes of their partners. (This activity is adapted from Dr. Constance K. Knop, University of Wisconsin-Madison.)

I love	asparagus
	beans
	corn
I like (a little)	peas
	potatoes
	chicken

I don't mind eating	hamburger
	lamb
	pork
	roast beef
	ice cream
I don't like	chocolate cake
	frozen yoghurt
	strawberry shortcake
I really hate	fresh fruit
	prunes

| I agree! | I disagree! | Really? |
| Me, too! | Not me! | |

The above activity might be adapted for use with any set of vocabulary or for a variety of other purposes.

Many additional ideas for pair activities can be found in Byrne (1980), Dreke and Lind (1986), Klippel (1984), Wright, Betteridge and Buckby (1984), and Yorkey (1985), all listed among *Works Cited*. Most teachers will find it useful to prepare pair activities designed specifically for the interests and curriculum of a specific group of children. The following guidelines will help you to develop successful activities and to choose appropriate activities from a variety of sources.

Checklist for Creating Pair Activities

Not all of these criteria will be applicable to every pair activity, but each of the items should be considered as the activity is developed.

1. What is the source of the message to be exchanged?

   • Is there an information gap?

   • Is there an opinion gap?

2. What language will be required to complete the activity? How much of it will need to be practiced or reviewed?

3. How is the language to be used guided or controlled?

   • Is there a natural limitation because of the task itself?

   • Is most of the language provided in written form?

4. What provision is made for clearly defined turn-taking?

   • Is there a built-in indicator for taking turns, like an asterisk in front of the item for the partner who is to ask the questions?

- Does each partner have an opportunity to participate approximately equally?
- Is there a means to prevent either partner from dominating the conversation?

5. Is the activity self-correcting?

- Can the partners find out immediately if they been successful?
- Is there a way for the partners to monitor their own accuracy?

6. How can the teacher follow up on the activity in a communicative way?

- Can the teacher ask questions about the activity to which the answers are not already known? For example, can she or he ask, "What did you find out about your partner that you didn't know before?" or "Which of the problems did you have the most trouble with?"
- Will the follow-up to the activity be interesting to the students as well as holding them accountable?
- What potential exists for oral or written follow-up or homework?

How to Conduct Small-Group and Pair Activities

Although one of the advantages of small-group work is that it takes the spotlight off of the teacher for a period of time, it can only be effective if it is carefully organized and consistently monitored. Especially for the first few times, preparing and conducting pair activities may actually require more teacher effort than the traditional teacher-centered classroom style. But the many benefits make pair work more than worth the extra effort. The following guidelines, adapted from Dr. Constance K. Knop (1986), will help the teacher plan effectively for pair or small-group activity in the classroom.

1. Limit the size of the group.

   It is easiest to start with small groups, perhaps with pairs, for the first experience with group activities. Cooperative groups are usually most effective when they are no larger than five, and they should never be larger than seven.

2. Motivate the activity.

   When the teacher sets the context for the activity dramatically, using actions and visuals, motivation is enhanced. Also, giving the activity a name makes it easier for students to ask to do it again and to recall the rules for the activity the next time it is introduced.

3. Set clear goals; describe the outcomes clearly for the students.

4. Prime the students with the target language they need to accomplish the activity so they will know exactly how to say what they need to say.

5. Give directions.

Give the sequence of the activity in precise steps, so students know exactly what is expected of them at every step of the way. Then *model* the steps in the activity:

Teacher: Partner A says "I love asparagus."
Partner B draws a line from *I love* to *asparagus.*
Then Partner B says "Not me!" or maybe "I agree!"
Then Partner A says "I like ice cream a little."
Partner B draws a line from *I like* to *ice cream.*
Then Partner B says . . .

Get student feedback on all the steps to be sure students know how the activity will proceed and will not waste time during the activity itself:

Teacher: Who begins the activity?
What does Partner A start with?
What does Partner B do?
What else does Partner B do?
What if Partner B doesn't agree?
What does Partner A do next?

6. Set a time limit.

Set a time limit to help students feel accountable and to make the best possible use of the time available to them. It is effective to use a kitchen timer with a loud bell or buzzer to provide a neutral timekeeper and a clear signal for the end of the activity. Adjust the time limit if necessary during the activity, to allow for less time if children are finishing early or more time if the activity takes longer than expected.

7. Circulate among the students throughout the activity.

This makes it possible for the teacher to respond to questions and problems on the spot, where they occur. The teacher can also give suggestions to students who need help and show interest in the conversations they are having. While moving around, the teacher can monitor use of the target language, language problems the students are having, and success or failure in the use of cooperative skills. Moving among the students, especially if the teacher has a clipboard in hand, is also a form of external control for on-task behavior.

8. Elicit feedback at the end of the drill.

Not every pair or every student needs be reached after every drill, but checking should be at random so students always feel accountable. The teacher should use communicative feedback techniques that are interesting to the whole group, rather than simply checking for recitation of facts or formulas. Also, regularly use the feedback period also to assist students in evaluating the effectiveness of their groups.

Learning Centers

Learning centers are independent study areas designed for use by one or two students at a time. Many elementary school classrooms have a variety of learning centers arranged around the classroom to permit children to work at projects of their choice during independent study time or special learning center time. Some learning centers have magnetic card readers, filmstrip or tape players, microcomputers, and cassette tape players; others provide for

This listening center provides an opportunity for individual work for the interested student. *Signs and activities should be in the target language.*

individual or small-group work that uses visuals, games, or paper-and-pencil activities. (On several occasions activities in this book have been identified as being good for learning centers.)

The learning center provides a series of options for students who have varying interests and who are at differing levels of language ability. Directions for each activity in the center are carefully presented in a step-by-step manner, and most tasks are self-checking, so constant teacher monitoring is not required. A listening center might give students the opportunity to listen to a taped story in the target language while following the story in a picture book. As a follow-up activity, the child might arrange pictures in sequence to recall the order of the story as the story is summarized on the tape. A vocabulary center might include many self-checking vocabulary games, like a clothespin chart or a yarn board, which give children the opportunity to match words with pictures, find synonyms or opposites, or work with vocabulary in another way.

FLES and FLEX teachers with their own classrooms have an ideal setting for the development of learning centers. If enough space is available, they might plan a learning center activity time for part of the class while doing small-group work with another part of the class, an arrangement that makes it possible to do either ability- or interest-grouping very effectively. FLES and FLEX teachers who must travel to a number of classrooms might consider developing one learning station for each classroom, to be used by children during free or elective time throughout the day. These learning centers might be rotated during the school year, so that a new learning center is available in each classroom several times during the year. The presence of a target language learning center in the regular classroom extends both the visibility of and the child's access to the language well beyond the time available in the language class itself.

SUMMARY

Careful planning can help the elementary school foreign language teacher to make the most of the limited time available for instruction in the target language. The careful preparation of student-oriented objectives and a written plan can free the teacher to be flexible and creative during the class period, responding to the needs and interests of the children as they develop without losing the direction and focus of the lesson. Each plan should be organized around the needs and development of the whole child and take into account the child's need for both variety and routine.

The communicative classroom will not focus exclusively on the teacher but will provide opportunities for students to use their language skills in meaningful interaction with one another. Reasons and guidelines for the development of a cooperative environment within the classroom are suggested in this chapter. The use of pair work has special value in the teaching of foreign languages, and examples are given of several types of pair activities that are appropriate for the elementary school foreign language classroom. A checklist for developing these activities and a step-by-step guide to leading group work will help the teacher incorporate these strategies into the daily plan.

Learning centers provide yet another type of structure for accommodating the special needs and interests of individuals in the elementary school foreign language class. They can extend both student interest in and exposure to the foreign language well beyond the limits of the language class itself.

FOR STUDY AND DISCUSSION

1. How can the preparation of student-oriented objectives and a careful written plan free the teacher to be creative and flexible during the class period?

2. Choose a song or a game you would like to teach to your class because it reinforces or anticipates basic concepts that are a part of the curriculum. Analyze it for unfamiliar vocabulary, and build a plan for "seeding" that new vocabulary over a period of several days.

3. Write a set of objectives, phrased in student terms, for teaching the song or game in number 2.

4. You have decided to reorganize your class in order to give children more opportunity to work with each other and to help them build cooperative skills. You plan to use both small-group work and pair activities. How would you explain to your class the reasons for your decision and the kinds of cooperative skills they will need to develop? How will you prepare them to make the most of cooperative structure?

5. Choose a topic for a learning center which you feel would be of interest to the children in the grade level and the elementary school setting you know best. Outline five different activities that might be part of that learning center.

FOR FURTHER READING

The following sources are recommended for additional information about material covered in this chapter. Chapter citations are documented in *Works Cited* at the end of the volume.

CALICO. *Applications of Technology: Planning and Using Language Learning Centers.* CALICO Monograph Series (1). Provo, Utah: CALICO in conjunction with IALL, 1986.

Gaies, Stephen J. *Peer Involvement in Language Learning*. Englewood Cliffs, NJ: Prentice Hall, 1985.

Grittner, Frank, ed. *A Guide to Curriculum Planning in Foreign Language*. Madison, WI: Wisconsin Department of Public Instruction, 1985.

Johnson, David W., and Robert T. Johnson. *Learning Together and Alone*. Englewood Cliffs, NJ: Prentice-Hall, Inc., 1987.

Klippel, Friederike. *Keep Talking. Communicative Fluency Activities for Language Teaching*. New York: Cambridge University Press, 1984.

Lafayette, Robert C., and Lorraine A. Strasheim. "The Standard Sequence and the Non-Traditional Methodologies," *Foreign Language Annals* 17 no 6 (December 1984): 567–574.

Masciantonio, Rudolph. "FLES Latin Lesson—Philadelphia Style," *American Foreign Language Teacher* 4 no 3 (Spring 1974): 30–32.

New York State Education Department. *Modern Languages for Communication. New York State Syllabus*. Albany, NY: University of the State of New York, State Education Department, 1987.

Yorkey, Richard. *Talk-A-Tivities*. Reading, MA: Addison-Wesley, 1985.

Chapter 11

Using Evaluation to Help Students and Programs Grow

STUDENT EVALUATION

When elementary school foreign language teachers gather at conferences and in-service meetings, there is a constant flow of good ideas. They exchange games and activities, suggestions for songs, patterns for visuals, recipes for in-class food activities. They don't exchange ideas for testing and evaluation.

The tendency to focus only on ideas and innovations for presenting material and developing activities is not found exclusively at the elementary school level nor exclusively among classroom teachers. The evaluation of student performance receives far less time and attention in many methods classes and methods books, on conference programs, and in teacher in-service sessions than do techniques for motivating students, planning curriculum, and managing the classroom. Methods for measuring student achievement within the communication-oriented classroom have not kept pace with methods for presenting materials and for giving students the opportunity to use language in communicative ways.

The reorganization of the foreign language curriculum around communicative goals faces a major obstacle when the results of communicative programs are evaluated by the same standards and with the same methods as have been used for decades. The popular and familiar discrete-point test, which measures grammar and vocabulary items in isolation, unrelated to meaningful context, is clearly an inappropriate measure for testing the achievement of communicative goals. It may have been somewhat more appropriate for evaluating students' performance in programs with a grammar–translation emphasis or based on the behavioristic principles of the audiolingual method. Yet because this method of testing has both the security of familiarity and the illusion of objectivity, it continues to play a dominant role in most classroom testing.

The discrepancy between what is taught and what is tested threatens both the credibility of communicative goals as they are stated and their chance of being realized. When students and parents perceive a discrepancy between the stated goals of a course and the contents of achievement tests, they invariably—and appropriately—believe the message of the testing. Sandra Savignon (1983) summarizes the problem very effectively:

> The most important implication of the concept of communicative competence is undoubtedly the need for tests that measure an *ability to use language* effectively to attain communicative goals. Discrete-point tests of linguistic structures of the kind developed in the 1960s have not only failed to sufficiently take into account the complexity and dynamic quality of the communicative setting. In some cases, they have also served, in their emphasis on grammatical accuracy, to discourage the strategies needed for communicative competence and thus to hinder the development of more communicative curricula. A language course that sets out to "cover" all the points of grammar presented in a basic textbook, and then tests learners on their "mastery" of these points, has little time left for communication. (p. 246–247)

PROGRAM EVALUATION

Program evaluation is a concern both separate from and related to the development of classroom testing measures. Elementary school foreign language programs, especially when they are new to the curriculum or are experiencing extensive revision, need to provide evidence that program goals are being met. Classroom achievement testing may provide one component of this evidence. There may also be a need or a desire to demonstrate the impact of the program on student performance in other content areas, on self-concept, on attitudes, or on cognitive or social development. This type of evaluation requires careful advance planning and the cooperation of administrators, classroom teachers, and evaluation personnel, where available. In the case of programs established with funding provided by a government agency or by a private foundation, external evaluators may be involved in developing an evaluation plan.

While the topic of program evaluation is beyond the scope of this chapter and this text, it must be taken seriously by every elementary school language teacher. Schinke-Llano (1985) provides a carefully organized format for program evaluation which will provide helpful background for developing an effective evaluation process.

ACHIEVEMENT TESTING

In many FLES and FLEX programs the problem is not so much inappropriate testing as it is an absence of formal evaluation measures altogether. Because of the nature of program goals and the large number of students each teacher sees in a day or in a week, achievement testing receives little priority. Some teachers are concerned that achievement testing will raise anxiety levels and lower motivation in their classes, especially among students who have been unsuccessful in much of the traditional elementary school curriculum. Yet children and their parents tend to take seriously only those subjects for which there is regular evaluation and reporting; any tendency to regard the foreign language class as an "extra," or as a subject area of less than equal status with the rest of the curriculum, is reinforced by the absence of regular, careful student evaluation and reporting.

Student Achievement Testing

The following guidelines are offered for the use of teachers who wish to develop a program of student achievement testing which is congruent with their own goals and with the needs of the children in their classes.

Guideline One: Use the Achievement Test as an Opportunity for Children to Discover How Much They Know, Not How Much They Still Have To Learn

Many teachers, like their students, recall testing experiences in which it seemed clear that the test was designed to trick and confuse them, and to demonstrate that they didn't know as much as they might have thought. No matter what grade may eventually have been awarded on the test, the feeling of frustration and inadequacy lingered long after the test items had been forgotten.

In an elementary school foreign language classroom that has focused on providing students with successful experiences in communication, the testing situation can be an extension of the same principle. Just as the teacher attempts to reduce students' anxiety and to enhance their motivation and self-confidence for language activities in the classroom, so can the teacher reduce anxiety and enhance motivation to help students to achieve success in demonstrating what they have learned. For example, teachers can schedule short testing sessions on a regular basis to prevent children from becoming anxious and to avoid placing unwarranted importance on the role of testing in the class.

Guideline Two: Test What Has Been Taught in the Way It Has Been Taught

There should be no surprises on a test designed to help students discover what they know. All the skills that have been used in activities during class should be included in the test in some way. Skills and specific materials should be tested using the same type of communicative activity by which they were practiced. For example, if a teacher wishes to use a paper-and-pencil test to determine whether students understand commands that have been practiced in the classroom, that teacher can prepare the children to feel comfortable with the test item by introducing a game: the children choose a picture that matches a command given by the teacher or by one of their classmates; in another game, they draw stick figures to represent a command and compare their results with one another. If listening skills have been emphasized in the class, they should be emphasized in the testing situation. If speaking skills have been practiced during class, they should be a part of the test in approximately the same proportion as they have been a part of the class, using similar speaking situations.

The teacher who plans each lesson on the basis of carefully worded, student-oriented objectives has already laid the groundwork for the activities that will be a part of the test. Each objective that appears on the test should bear approximately the same weight of importance that it carried in the development of class activities.

The best source of ideas for test items are the activities used in daily class sessions. Additional suggestions are provided below, most of them especially appropriate for early levels of language acquisition, when evaluation seems to be the most difficult. Types of test items are organized by skills area.

Suggestions for Testing

Listening

1. *True-false tests.* In advance, prepare answer sheets numbered from 1 to 10 (or 1 to 15, or 1 to 20, depending on length desired), with *true* and

1. True	False		1. oui	non
2. True	False		2. oui	non
3. True	False		3. oui	non
4. True	False		4. oui	non
5. True	False	OR	5. oui	non
6. True	False		6. oui	non
7. True	False		7. oui	non
8. True	False		8. oui	non
9. True	False		9. oui	non
10. True	False		10. oui	non

Sample True-False Answer Sheets

false given for each number. With no additional preparation, the answer sheet shown here may be used for any of the test items described below.

a. Show the class a picture that includes more than one item of information (for example, different types of weather and their effects, a scene with individuals performing a variety of actions, and so forth). Then read statements about the picture, and have the students respond with *true* or *false*.

b. Read a short paragraph or dialog to the class. Then make several statements about the content of the selection. The students respond *true* or *false* on the basis of the correctness of each statement.

c. Read a command and perform the action commanded, or show a picture of the action being commanded. Have the students indicate *true* if the command and the action agree; have the students indicate *false* if they do not agree.

He is going to lift the box. T F

Sample True-False Item

d. Base some true-and-false statements on reasonableness or logic. For example, if you read, "The turtle says bow-wow," the students would mark *false*.

(CAUTION! *Never* include a negative in a statement used for a true-false item.)

2. *Listening/picture stimuli tests.* In advance, prepare answer sheets with 1 to 10 questions (or more) and the choices of (a), (b), (c), (d), or (e) for each question.

1. (a) ——	(b) ——	(c) ——	(d) ——	(e) ——
2. (a) ——	(b) ——	(c) ——	(d) ——	(e) ——
3. (a) ——	(b) ——	(c) ——	(d) ——	(e) ——
4. (a) ——	(b) ——	(c) ——	(d) ——	(e) ——
5. (a) ——	(b) ——	(c) ——	(d) ——	(e) ——
6. (a) ——	(b) ——	(c) ——	(d) ——	(e) ——
7. (a) ——	(b) ——	(c) ——	(d) ——	(e) ——
8. (a) ——	(b) ——	(c) ——	(d) ——	(e) ——
9. (a) ——	(b) ——	(c) ——	(d) ——	(e) ——
10. (a) ——	(b) ——	(c) ——	(d) ——	(e) ——

Sample Answer Sheet

This type of answer sheet lends itself to a variety of question techniques, which are described below.

a. Show students several pictures, each of them numbered. When the students hear a statement, have them place the number of the appropriate picture next to the letter for that statement.

b. Give the students a picture showing several activities. Read sentences describing each of the activities, and have the students place the number of the sentence on the part of the picture that depicts the activity described. As an alternative, show a picture that has numbers on it, and have the students place the number of the activity next to the letter of the sentence read.

c. Present classroom objects or other learned vocabulary in individual pictures, either on the students' papers or on cards in the front of

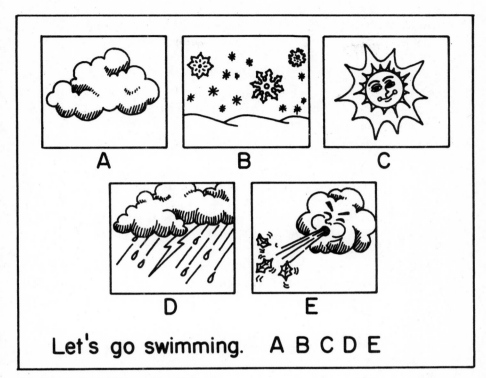

Sample Multiple-Choice Test Item

the class. Read statements containing the individual vocabulary items, and have the students number the items to correspond to the sentences (or place the number of the object beside the letter of the sentence that you read). This tests (and encourages) the students' ability to perceive known language embedded in unfamiliar language.

d. Give a "labeling" exercise: have students place numbers corresponding to the correct identification of a part of a picture (body parts, table setting, countries, and so forth) when they hear you read the identification, *or* when they hear you read a statement containing the label.

e. For more advanced students, prepare a short connected story using sentences that the students have learned, but in a different context. Place a collection of large pictures on the chalkboard tray, flannelboard, pocket chart; or display pictures on the overhead projector. Have the students look at the pictures while listening a second (or third) time to the narrative. Then ask the children to write on their papers the letters of any pictures which represent a part of the story, or perhaps to list the letters in order to show the sequence of the story.

3. *Carrying out commands.* For a classroom in which TPR is an important tool, carrying out commands is one of the most natural of all types of evaluation techniques. Berty Segal suggests establishing a list of commands that incorporate the key learning elements for each unit of instruction. While other students are working at their seats, working at learning stations, or developing group projects, Segal tests students in groups of three by giving the commands and having the students carry them out. She uses the same list of commands for all student groups, varying the order in which they are given. The teacher uses a grid to check students who do *not* perform the command accurately. Other options include the following:

   a. Make a picture test containing balloons, either in numbered squares or in a picture format on which each balloon itself is numbered. Ask students to color the balloons according to instructions. You can construct other tests in which you ask students to identify some elements of a picture with numbers or colors, or in which students draw a picture or construct figures on command (for example, the monster drawings).

   b. Have individual students carry out your commands, either orally or by writing on slips or cards. You can devise these commands to show comprehension of other vocabulary in addition to the verbs involved.

Speaking

If all instruction in speaking has been in context and communicative, the evaluation function should also be contextual and communicative. The scheme of evaluation should reflect the ongoing goals of the program rather than focusing on detail and grammar (which often seem easier to evaluate). Evaluative speaking activities include the following:

1. *Personal question-answer.* Have students discuss a familiar topic, something often discussed in class in the same manner, with you or with one another.

2. *Dialog.* Two (or several) children may perform a dialog.

3. *Rejoinder.* Make a statement to which students respond appropriately: for example, if you say, "I feel terrible today" the student says, "That's too bad."

4. *Picture reaction.* Give students a picture; have them respond either by telling about it, or perhaps by giving the command suggested by the picture (at an earlier stage).

5. *Narrative or dialog completion.* Give the students part of a familiar narrative or dialog, and ask them to complete it, either by choosing the completion learned in class or by providing a new one created for the occasion.

6. *Role reversal.* You may use role reversal as a means of evaluating the individual student's development of speaking skills, but neither the teacher nor the student should view it primarily as an evaluation tool. When role reversal has become a standard and comfortable part of class procedure, you may begin to incorporate some elements from this activity into the evaluation format.

7. *Oral identification and/or description of familiar objects.* Have students draw familiar objects from a sack or from a "magic box" and identify or describe

Sample Picture Item
Teacher says: "Tell me something about this picture."
  OR   "Give a command that would fit the action."

them aloud. (This may also be a good opportunity to work with requests, politeness vocabulary, and other components of the rituals that have been established in class.)

8. *Puppet shows.* Have children work in pairs or in small groups to develop puppet shows that may serve as a demonstration of what they have learned.

Reading

Creating means of testing reading as a communicative function can be challenging, but such means are possible. Asking students to perform written commands is a natural first step, and these commands can take on greater complexity as students progress.

1. Adapt items suggested in the listening section to evaluate reading by changing the stimulus from the spoken to the written word. (Many of the listening items are readily adaptable.)

2. Ask students to perform commands delivered in writing, either individually or as paper-pencil responses done by the entire class at one time.

3. Have students read parts of stories written by the group and react to them in some way—true-false items, multiple choice items, and so forth. They may fill in blanks with words chosen from a list at the end of or on the side of the reading passage (cloze procedure).

4. Have students match labels with pictures or parts of pictures.

Writing

Most writing will be copying in the early years of an elementary school program, but some evaluation of writing, in addition to listening, speaking, and reading, will leave students with a sense of achievement in all four skills.

1. *Labeling.* Have students label pictures or parts of pictures with the appropriate foreign language term.

3. *Cloze or completion.* Have students fill in blanks in a passage, or complete an anecdote without an immediate model.

3. *Commands.* Have students write commands to be performed by the teacher or by a classmate.

TEACHER EVALUATION

The teacher is the most important part of any classroom, in any subject area. Teachers who are committed to personal and professional growth and to providing the finest possible learning environment for their students can be

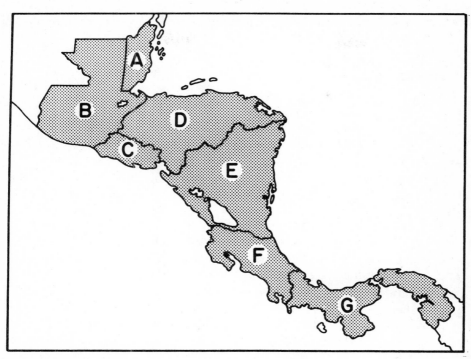

Sample Label Item
Teacher says: "Label the countries on this map from which we have had guests in
class."

the best evaluators of the teaching and learning that take place in their own
classrooms. The assistance of supportive peers and administrators can also
help teachers to achieve new goals and to develop new dimensions of their
teaching skills. In addition to following the program evaluation discussed in
chapter 4, teachers can work together to give one another feedback and
support as they experiment with new approaches and techniques. The
reorientation of language teaching toward communication is a major step
away from the traditions within which most language teachers have themselves learned languages and within which they have been trained to teach
them. Ongoing support and encouragement from peers will play an essential
role in making this significant reorientation.

The checklist of teaching behaviors which follows is oriented toward
communicative language teaching in the elementary school. It is intended to
assist teachers who wish to evaluate their own teaching and to be helpful
observers of one another. It will also assist administrators in giving support
and feedback to foreign language teachers working in their schools. The

observation guide can be used most successfully over an extended period of time, for a series of observations.

Elementary School Foreign Language
Teacher Observation Guide

_____ 1. Teacher uses target language for all classroom purposes
       _____ uses natural speed and intonation
       _____ uses gestures, facial expressions and body language
       _____ uses concrete referents such as props, realia, manipulatives, and visuals (especially with entry-level students)

_____ 2. Teacher uses linguistic modifications when necessary to make the target language more comprehensible for the students
       _____ uses controlled, standardized vocabulary
       _____ uses controlled sentence length and complexity
       _____ uses restatements, expansions, and repetitions

_____ 3. Teacher keeps use of the native language clearly separated from use of the target language

_____ 4. Teacher provides students with opportunities for extended listening

_____ 5. Teacher uses authentic communication to motivate all language use

_____ 6. Teacher maintains a pace with momentum and a sense of direction

_____ 7. Teacher changes activities frequently and logically

_____ 8. Students are active throughout the class period
       _____ individually
       _____ as part of groups

_____ 9. Teacher introduces and tests structures and vocabulary in meaningful contexts

_____ 10. Teachers and students use visuals and realia effectively

_____ 11. There is evidence of detailed planning

_____ 12. Discipline is positive, prompt, nondisruptive

_____ 13. Environment is attractive and reflects the target culture

_____ 14. There is evidence of cultural content in activities
       _____ stereotypes are not reinforced
       _____ global and multicultural awareness is encouraged

_____ 15. Classroom routines provide students with clear clues to meaning

_____ 16. Lessons contain elements of subject-content instruction

_____ 17. Teacher practices sensitive error correction with primary focus on errors of meaning rather than on errors of form

_____ 18. Teacher provides hands-on experiences for students, accompanied by oral and written language use

_____ 19. Teacher accelerates student communication by teaching functional chunks of language

_____ 20. Teacher constantly monitors student comprehension through interactive means such as

    _____ comprehension checks

    _____ clarification requests

    _____ personalization

    _____ using a variety of questioning types

_____ 21. There are varied groupings of students and varied interaction patterns

    _____ teacher/student

    _____ student/teacher

    _____ student/student

_____ 22. There is careful introduction to second language literacy

_____ 23. Reading is based on student-centered, previously mastered oral language

_____ 24. Teacher shows patience with student attempts to communicate

_____ 25. Teacher plans activities that provide students with successful learning experiences

_____ 26. Teacher appears enthusiastic and motivated

_____ 27. Questions and activities provide for a real exchange of information and opinions

_____ 28. Teacher incorporates activities from a variety of cognitive levels

_____ 29. Students ask as well as answer questions

_____ 30. Teacher uses a variety of classroom techniques

_____ 31. Lessons incorporate both new and familiar material

_____ 32. Teacher includes several skills in each lesson

_____ 33. Teacher gives clear directions and examples

_____ 34. Teacher uses varied and appropriate rewards

_____ 35. Teacher allows ample wait–time after asking questions

SUMMARY

Careful and systematic evaluation is an essential component of the elementary school foreign language program. Students will benefit from achievement testing that gives them the opportunity to demonstrate what they have learned, in a supportive, positive atmosphere designed to help them succeed.

The most effective evaluation tools will test what has been taught in the way it has been taught. Only when the means of testing appropriately reflect the goals of the curriculum can those goals most effectively be achieved.

Evaluation of teacher performance is a second important component of the effective elementary school program. It is most valuable when the teacher is a critical self-evaluator who receives support and encouragement from colleagues and administrators. The communicative reorientation of language teaching is a dramatic change in approach that requires a cooperative effort from all members of the teaching team.

FOR STUDY AND DISCUSSION

1. In your department meeting a discussion has developed about the current policy of giving children in the elementary school foreign language program a grade of "satisfactory/unsatisfactory" and basing the evaluation on observation of the degree of each child's participation and enthusiasm. You have been in the department only a few weeks, but you have some insight to add. What suggestions would you make to the department, and why?

2. You and your fellow teacher have decided to develop some of your tests together in order to be able to write more effective evaluations. However, now she is complaining about the tests you write. She claims that if you give the children only material that you are sure they can succeed with, and test them in the same way you taught them, then the results of your tests aren't worth anything. How do you respond to her?

3. Choose a series of lessons from a FLES textbook that you know, from observations you have made, or from the lessons in the Appendix of this book. Design a short test for one or two of the objectives covered in the lessons, no more than five questions, keeping in mind the testing principles identified in this chapter. What activities in the lessons have prepared the children to be tested in this way? Or what activities would you have to incorporate in the lessons in order to use the testing items you have written?

4. Use the teacher checklist in this chapter to evaluate your own teaching performance in the class setting with which you are most familiar. Write a goals statement in which you set objectives for your continued growth as a teacher. Use that personal goals statement to list four things you would like to have your favorite colleague watch for and give you feedback about on her or his next visit to your class (make them very specific).

FOR FURTHER READING

The following sources are recommended for additional information about material covered in this chapter. Chapter citations are documented in *Works Cited* at the end of the volume.

Alexander, Loren, and Maria H. John. "Testing Oral Skills in a FLES Short Course." *Foreign Language Annals* 18 no 3 (May 1985): 235–239.

Cohen, Andrew D. *Testing Language Ability in the Classroom*. Rowley, MA: Newbury House, 1980.

Edwards, Viviane. "Assessment of Core French: The New Brunswick Experience." *The Canadian Modern Language Review* 42 (1985): 440–51.

Madsen, Harold S. *Techniques in Testing*. New York: Oxford University Press, 1983.

Oller, John W. Jr. *Language Tests at School: A Pragmatic Approach*. London: Longman, 1979.

Savignon, Sandra J. *Communicative Competence: Theory and Classroom Practice: Texts and Contexts in Second Language Learning*. Reading, MA: Addison-Wesley, 1983.

Seelye, H. Ned. *Teaching Culture*. Lincolnwood, IL: National Textbook Company, 1984.

Valette, Rebecca M. *Modern Language Testing*. 2d ed. New York: Harcourt Brace Jovanovich, 1977.

Chapter 12

Stocking the Elementary School Foreign Language Classroom with Materials and Resources

USEFUL SUPPLIES, MATERIALS, AND EQUIPMENT

Materials represent a significant portion of the time and resources invested in an elementary school foreign language program, no matter what program model has been chosen. This chapter describes materials that will provide the means for creating the concrete context that is so necessary for meaningful communication. Because children require hands-on learning experiences with concrete objects, the elementary school foreign language classroom must have a wide variety of objects and materials available, as many of them as possible from the target culture. Such materials offer a richness and texture not available even in the most carefully designed textbook. This need for a wide range of materials is one of the most marked differences between teaching elementary or middle school/junior high school children and older students. While high school and university teachers often emphasize the written word and writen homework early in the learning experience, the elementary school foreign language teacher works with the development of oral language skills over an extended period of time.

The need for a wealth of materials creates special problems for the traveling teacher, who must devise practical ways of transporting props and realia, which are often bulky and unwieldy. Some teachers have devised a traveling cart especially for this purpose, and many other elementary school foreign language teachers have become well known for the large bags and satchels they carry with them. Some types of materials, especially those used for crafts and projects, are already present in the regular classroom; but they must be specially ordered and stored in a classroom that is being equipped for elementary school foreign language instruction.

You can tap many sources in the process of stocking the elementary school foreign language classroom. You can arrange for the short-term loan of some items with preschool and primary teachers, or teachers in the ESL or the bilingual program. Some types of visuals and media resources are available through the school media center, especially films, filmstrips, slides, and equipment. School supply houses are good sources of most basic classroom supplies, and many other materials listed in this section are available from distributors of curriculum materials, supplies, and equipment for early-childhood and primary education. Elementary school foreign language teachers will find it useful to be on mailing lists for as many of these catalogs as possible (see list of suppliers in appendix C). Browsing through such catalogs often suggests new activities and new uses for materials already present in the classroom.

Locating authentic materials from the target culture is usually more difficult and more time consuming. A number of companies specialize in importing realia and materials for foreign language teachers, but these materials are often chosen to appeal to older students. The elementary school foreign language teacher traveling in a country where the target language is spoken can find many teaching materials in toy stores, bookstores, record stores, and novelty and souvenir shops. Cassette tapes of children's stories, songs and rhymes, and simple picture books for storytelling are especially valuable "finds" for the classroom. Elementary school foreign language teachers who travel abroad collect items ranging from empty packaging for candy and soft drinks to menus, coins, and ticket stubs. Those who do not have regular opportunities to travel must find other sources for child-appropriate authentic materials and realia.

One of the best ways to obtain teaching materials from the target culture is to correspond with an elementary school English teacher in one of the countries where the target language is spoken. This type of relationship can make it possible for teachers to exchange slides, tapes, and realia spontaneously, either to complement a theme of interest or to serve as a focus for an entire unit of instruction. Such an exchange program provides the opportunity for both teachers to obtain meaningful materials at a reasonable cost, although there is usually considerable delay between making a request and receiving the material.

You can often obtain posters and travel brochures without cost from embassies, consulates, or tourist agencies representing countries in which the target language is spoken. As a starting point for contacting such agencies, consult a telephone directory for New York City (Manhattan) and Washington, D.C., and write letters requesting materials to all possible sources. The Center for Applied Linguistics (see Appendix B for address) has developed a *Directory of Foreign Language Service Organizations: 3*, which lists contact agencies for many languages. A letter requesting posters and city information from the visitors' bureau in capital cities or other cities in the country where the foreign language is spoken can also yield valuable resources. Multinational businesses sometimes make materials developed for another country available to teachers; posters and travel brochures can also be obtained from travel agencies and airline companies who are sometimes willing to provide such material to foreign language teachers.

There are also less formal sources for obtaining materials and resources for classroom use. Garage sales and rummage sales are often good places to find plastic fruit, flowers, and other replicas, as well as toys, costumes, puppets, and other realia. Children themselves enjoy sharing favorite toys or helping to create a visual or a device that will bring classroom instruction to life. Always on the lookout for a new way to make a concept or a communicative situation more vivid, many elementary school foreign language teachers are regular customers at toy stores, variety stores, and souvenir shops.

The time and the budget devoted to developing the materials and resources available to the elementary school foreign language teacher will have a significant impact on the quality and the success of the elementary school language program. Some of the items that are essential to the elementary school foreign language classroom teacher include the following:

Butcher/Chart Paper (1,000-ft. roll)

This can be used for classroom collages, art projects, tracing body shapes, and making life-size paper dolls.

Chart Paper (precut), Chart Tablets, Flip Charts

These are used for language-experience stories, developing charts and graphs, demonstrations and explanations.

Construction Paper, in At Least 12 Colors, and in At Least Two Different Sizes (9" × 12" and 12" × 18")

red	blue	white
black	green	yellow
brown	gold	purple
pink	orange	grey

This is for craft projects, visuals, and games.

Tagboard, Oaktag, Posterboard (9" × 12", 12" × 18" and larger pieces)

These are useful for mounting pictures and for making flashcards, posters, signs (such as passwords), language ladders, and classroom charts.

Self-Adhesive Plastic, in Clear and Assorted Colors and Patterns

This is for preserving visuals, classroom crafts, gameboards, and teacher-prepared materials.

Paper Plates

These are a basic supply for the elementary school foreign language classroom, and they are usually less expensive than tagboard. They can be used as a background for almost any picture and as a basis for crafts, visuals, clocks, masks, displays of meals using food pictures; for mood faces, weather pictures, and mobiles; as well as for serving snacks.

Masking Tape

This can be used for changing the environment by creating shapes and defining spaces on the floor; it also has many commonplace uses such as attaching labels and attaching posters and visuals to walls by making a circle out of masking tape. (When attaching masking tape to pictures and posters, first place a strip or two of tape on the item itself, at each point where the masking-tape circle will be applied. Then, when the masking–tape circle is removed, the picture or poster will not be damaged.)

"Easy-Release" Tape and Notes

This is good for labeling anything on a temporary basis. (This tape sticks but does not remain permanently and does not damage surfaces.)

Spray Adhesive

This is for mounting visuals or for making flashcards. (This adhesive is superior to white glue or rubber cement. It dries quickly, visuals do not buckle, and some types allow for repositioning.)

White Glue

This is especially suitable for adhesive jobs that are similar to model building and for putting a magnet or pin on the back of an object. It is used mainly for crafts.

Glue Stick

This for nonpermanent stickups and paper crafts. (For some tasks, a glue stick is easier for children to handle than white glue.)

Acrylic Spray

This is for protecting visuals; it is one means of preserving nonlaminated visuals. (One advantage is that it can be used at home, where there is no access to a laminating machine.)

Paper Fasteners

These are for making clockfaces and jointed figures and for joining booklets.

Paper Punch

This is for making name tags, clock faces and many crafts.

Colored Chalk

This adds variety to chalkboard activities.

Colored Tissue Paper

This is used for making paper flowers, piñatas, mosaics, papier–mâché figures, mobiles, and many crafts.

Pipe Cleaners

These are for making paper flowers and other crafts.

Yarn in Assorted Colors

This can be used for doing crafts and game activities.

Note Cards (3″ × 5″, 4″ × 6″)

These are used for making games, and for multiple other uses, including activities with flags (cards that are 4″ × 6″ are the same size as silk flags that are commercially available).

Craft Sticks, Tongue Depressors, Dowels

These are for doing craft activities and serve as bases for hand puppets and shadow puppets.

GENERAL RESOURCES

Folk and Fairy Tales (books, filmstrips)

These are good for reading aloud, planning units, or student browsing at a reading table or in a learning center.

Songbooks

A selection of songbooks from the target culture will make it easier for the teacher to choose songs that reinforce specific topics and vocabulary in the curriculum. Teachers should not overlook target language songs in the music series currently being used in the school district.

Coloring Books and Dot-to-Dot Books

These are a good source for visuals and activities, especially when they come from the target culture. Specific suggestions are listed in chapter 13.

Paper Dolls

For individual student use at a learning station with recorded instructions on how to dress the doll, or in a partner activity in which one student tells the other how to dress the doll. Large dolls can be used for whole-class activities.

Books of Simple Rhymes, Finger Plays

Regularly used with preschool and primary–level students, finger plays are rhymes with corresponding actions. Using rhymes from the target culture rather than translations of English rhymes can be a way to provide more cultural experiences in the elementary school foreign language classroom.

Duplicating Master Books

Available from various publishers, these are useful as sources for visuals and student-activity sheets. Activities developed from these sources must be meaningful and must be an integrated part of the curriculum.

Flannel Board Manipulatives

Available from various publishers, they are used as props for telling fairy tales and other stories; they are also available in sets depicting various vocabulary categories such as the house, family, foods, clothing, weather, opposites, and animals.

Rubber Stamps

For creating realia (coin, clock, shape stamps), for incentives and rewards, and for creating pair or partner activities.

Peel-and-Stick Plastic Activity Kits

These are cutout vinyl shapes that adhere to a glossy surface. They are valuable for learning center activities and for physical–response activities with individuals and small groups. The teacher can put together a scene, take a picture of it, and record directions for constructing the scene on an audio cassette. The child re-creates the scene, following the directions, and uses the photograph to check for accuracy. If the vinyl pictures are large enough, they can be used for physical-response activities with the whole class.

Board Games

Some board games from the target culture are useful for small–group and learning center work. Certain native-language board games can be adapted to activities conducted entirely in the target language.

Bingo and Lotto Games

Many commercial games are available to reinforce vocabulary of all kinds. Games specifically keyed to vocabulary and concepts of an individual lesson can be made by the teacher, often with student help in a class project, and laminated.

REALIA

Plastic Fillable Eggs in 4 Sizes

Eggs can be hidden one inside the other for discovery activities. They can also be used to hide various objects, to hold scrambled sentence parts, pictures for sequencing, or objects for guessing games. The largest size is sold as a hosiery container; the smaller, graduated sizes are often available at Easter time.

Magnetic Numbers, Letters

These are used on the magnet board or chalkboard for manipulating number concepts or creating words.

Foam Numbers, Letters

These provide a different texture and an alternative way of dealing with the same vocabulary. Children love to touch soft letters and numbers.

Magnetic Mirror

Useful as a prop on a magnetized chalkboard for pantomime and action chain activities. For example, the teacher might draw a sink on the board and have students go there individually to pretend to comb their hair and wash their faces, looking in the mirror while performing the actions. The simple prop of the mirror makes the activity more meaningful.

Oversized Combs, Toothbrushes, Sunglasses, and Other Props

The use of exaggerated sizes for props dealing with any relevant vocabulary adds to the feeling of play and fun and incorporates an element of surprise.

Inflatable Figures (dolls, animals, skeletons, globes)

Inflatable figures can be foils in classroom activities or serve as giant-sized manipulatives.

Clocks with Movable Hands

This is a necessary prop for activities dealing with time. These are available commercially in both individual student and large teacher sizes, or students can make their own as a crafts activity.

Jump Ropes

Jump ropes are useful for physical–response activities such as jumping a specified number of times, jumping forward, backward, sideways, fast, slow, high, low.

Balls

Sponge balls can be thrown around the classroom with no danger of injury or breakage. They can be thrown to the person who will respond to a question, provide the next question, or be the partner in some kind of exchange. The ball can also be used for various games and for a number of New Games activities (Fluegelman 1976).

Bouncing balls can be used for physical–response activities that are similar to the jump rope activities described above. The balls can be bounced high and low, fast and slow, a specified number of times.

Puppets, Stuffed Animals, Dolls

Puppets, stuffed animals, and dolls can be partners in modeling a conversational exchange. Puppets can be the stimulus for getting information: they can have a secret, speak for a shy child, or be part of an impromptu skit in which the puppets themselves are the characters. Puppets can be the desired objects in a classroom activity in which students ask to hold or to play with certain things. If they are of the right size and design, a large number of them can be placed in the "magic box" to surprise everyone when all the puppets appear.

Puppets can be of various types: hand puppets, stick puppets, paper bag puppets, folded paper puppets, sock puppets, finger puppets, and others. The children can make many types of puppets themselves.

Plastic Fruit, Vegetables, Flowers, Toys

Especially when they are life-sized, plastic models are the next best to the real thing for vocabulary of all kinds.

Suitcase Full of Clothing for Dress-Up, Games

Children enjoy dressing up for games or role plays. Oversized clothing in adult sizes is the easiest to use because students can put it on and take it off quickly and easily. Activities such as relay games and fashion shows are especially effective. The suitcase itself can be a prop in simulations.

Blindfolds

Blindfolds are useful for games, and for changing drill to communicative activities by removing the obvious stimulus from sight.

Portable Electronic Keyboard, Rhythm Box

The teacher can choose a rhythm as a background for practicing rote material like numbers, lists, or rhymes. Providing a background rhythm changes the character of the activity, making it more fun and adding a right-hemisphere dimension.

Silk Flags (4" × 6")

These are a colorful reminder of the variety of places where the target language is spoken; children will learn to identify flags with geographic locations. Flags are also useful for work with colors.

Dollhouse and Furniture

These are useful props for vocabulary dealing with household items and everyday activities.

Sequencing Materials

Pictures and manipulatives designed for sequencing activities in early childhood education can be used as the basis for simple storytelling and vocabulary reinforcement as well as for sequencing practice.

Playing Cards

There are many kinds of commercially available playing cards, including games such as *Go Fish* and *Old Maid,* and many of these can be labeled over for the elementary school foreign language classroom. Target language card games such as the German Quartett games are valuable for small group activities because they put students in physical touch with objects from the culture. Regular playing cards can be used for a variety of games that involve reviewing numbers.

Mathematics and Number Flashcards

Flashcards for addition, subtraction, multiplication, and division facts, as well as for numbers and fractions, reinforce the regular mathematics curriculum while providing practice in the target language.

Individual Chalkboards

These can be used for comprehension checks and for listening comprehension and physical–response activities.

Beads, Blocks, Rods, Counters

These are manipulatives for listening comprehension and communicative language activities. They are useful for dealing with mathematics concepts.

Toy Telephone

This is a prop for skits and simulations. Toy coin telephones in which plastic coins can actually be inserted are available, making them a good prop for an action chain. (Some telephone companies will lend or donate real telephones for classroom purposes.)

Picture Books and Easy Readers in the Second Language

Picture books with very simple texts, if they are well illustrated to provide the necessary visual reinforcement, can be read aloud to a class or a small group or used for beginning reading experiences. It is difficult to find books with the right text-to-picture ratio. Some schools have taken English books and labeled over them in the second language; however this results in a loss of cultural exposure for the children.

Elementary School Second Language (Picture) Dictionaries

These resources help children develop early skills in dictionary use and provide target-language visuals for important concepts.

Toy Money

This is useful for simulations and for reinforcing mathematics concepts. (It is preferable to use toy money from the target culture.)

Toy Cash Register

This is for simulations (making change). (It is preferable to use one from the target culture or one that doesn't have a dollar sign.)

Menus From the Target Culture

These are useful for pair work, for stating preferences, for simulations, for room decorations, and for reinforcing vocabulary.

Thermometer (demonstration)

The classroom demonstration thermometer should have both Fahrenheit and Celsius scale and a movable temperature indicator. It is used for temperature reports and comparisons with temperatures in foreign countries. (Using thermometers reinforces science concepts and knowledge of the metric system.)

Metric Scale

Both a small food scale and a larger scale for weighing people are useful. Scales are especially valuable for cooking activities reflecting cultures in which ingredients are weighed rather than measured with a cup.

Meter Stick or Measuring Tape

There are for measuring activities and reinforcing the mathematics and science curricula.

Postcards, Letters, Stamps

These can serve as classroom decoration, props in simulations and pair work, and cultural inquiry activities.

Newspapers and Magazines

When written in the target language, these provide browsing and early-reading activities, material for art projects, bulletin board backdrops, and props. English language magazines can also be a source of materials for visuals and collages.

Empty Food Containers

Preferably from the target culture, these are useful for simulations and as props and decorations. Some teachers set up a "store" in part of the classroom as a part of the regular classroom environment.

Table Settings

Flatware, dishes, glasses, cups, napkins, and tablecloths are useful for practice in table setting. Real food, food replicas, or pictures for nutrition lessons and simulations provide the finishing touches.

Rhythm and Orff Instruments

These are for developing accompaniments to songs and rhymes and for creating sound effects for simulations and fantasy experiences.

Stamps and Coins from the Target Culture

These are useful for role play and simulations and are a good source of cultural information. Coins can be used to make rubbings, as counters in board games, and for mathematics activities.

Sporting Goods

Sports equipment from the target culture is useful for games and demonstration purposes.

Calendars

These show different customs for formatting the date and the month, and they provide attractive pictures reflecting the culture.

PICTURE VISUALS

Use of Picture Visuals

Pictures provide context and stimuli for various classroom activities. For use with the entire class, they should be mounted and should be large and clear enough (at least 8″ × 10″) so that all students can see them. Smaller pictures are appropriate for small-group and pair work. When used to illustrate a concept, they must not be cluttered or confusing; only one thing should be represented by each picture.

Pictures are very helpful in keeping the classroom in the target language. They should provide the focus for meaningful, communicative activity, and not just be used to elicit one-word responses and naming. For example, students can sort a series of pictures into the four food groups, or arrange them to plan menus. Other pictures might be used to classify types of clothing by appropriate season, color, or degree of formality or informality. In the beginning stages, pictures help the teacher to convey meaning, but later the same or similar pictures can be used as cues for partner activities or group work so that they become communication as well as vocabulary aids.

Picture Files

It is important to have a variety of materials so that students do not become bored. Picture files can be developed from magazines, post cards, calendars, catalogs, brochures, posters, wall charts and commercially available flashcards. Yunus (1981, 49–55) discusses a variety of types of picture material.

Travel Posters and Brochures

Posters and travel brochures provide an especially colorful point of reference for the target culture in the classroom, and they can sometimes be used to set the stage for a fantasy or a culture activity. They should be changed periodically so that they do not lose their appeal for students. Posters, maps, and charts should be laminated before they are displayed if they are to be used for an extended period of time.

Flashcards

Flashcards can either be commercially produced or teacher-prepared. They provide picture or symbol stimulus for a wide range of vocabulary and for sequencing activities. Tagboard, oaktag, or posterboard is a good base for making flashcards. It is helpful to make all flashcards in a series the same size for convenience in storage and in dimensions that can be easily held and manipulated by small hands if they are intended for individual or small-group activities, or viewed by an entire class if they were meant for work with large groups. If the flashcard is rectangular it is also helpful to have each flashcard oriented the same way vertically or horizontally so that the pictures do not have to be constantly rotated from horizontal to vertical when they are shown in a sequence.

Study Prints and Charts

These are commercially available pictures centered around a theme, such as "Children Around the World," or "Community Workers." They are especially useful for content teaching.

CLASSROOM EQUIPMENT

Chalkboard

This is probably the most used classroom aid. Using colored as well as white chalk makes it more effective. Walking up to the chalkboard is a change of pace activity for the students. In some schools, the chalkboard has a steel core, making it possible to use it like a magnet board.

Pocket Chart

Pocket charts are a standard tool for reading instruction in the primary grades. They are made of sturdy cardboard or vinyl and contain pockets that are useful for holding word cards and picture cards. Yunus (32–34) offers a thorough discussion of the uses of pocket charts and how to make various types of charts. A long pocket chart with only one pocket can be placed along the chalkboard.

Flannel Board

Flannel boards are commercially available or can be made by stretching a piece of cotton flannel or felt over a backing such as stiff cardboard or wood.

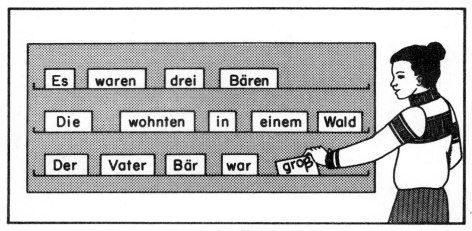

Pocket Chart

They should be about 3' × 2' in size if they are to be used with the entire class, or they may be smaller if they will be used by small groups or individuals.

Lightweight items with a piece of flannel, felt, or sandpaper on the back will stick to the flannel board so that scenes can be put together and changed easily. Pieces of dress–stiffening fabric or interfacing can also be cut out and colored for use on the flannel board. The flannel board provides an excellent device for story telling and manipulation of objects. The board can be divided into rooms of the house, roads, farms, calendars and many other spaces with felt strip dividers. Other materials that adhere easily to the flannel board include paper with flocked backing, yarn, pipe cleaners, string, suede and sponges. Many flannel board manipulative materials are available from school supply stores and catalogs.

Magnet Board

Magnet boards are commercially available in classroom sizes similar to those available for flannel boards, and they can be used in much the same way. Magnets can be placed on top of figures to hold them in place, or they can be glued to the back of objects or figures to be used. Magnetic letters, numbers, pictures, and other magnetized items can also be obtained commercially. Teachers can create their own magnet boards using a large cookie sheet or a piece of sheet metal. Many chalkboards have a steel core and can be used as a magnet board.

Pegboard

The pegboard consists of a sturdy board perforated with a regular pattern of holes and with a series of fixed or movable pegs or hooks that protrude from it. The pegs or hooks can be used to hang flashcards, numbers, pictures, or letters that have a hole punched in them. The items can be moved from peg to peg. Boards with hooks can be used to display three-dimensional items or to mount shelves for storage and display.

Hook-and-Loop Boards and Strips

Hook-and-loop material—commercially known as Velcro®—which is sometimes used for fasteners in sewing, consists of two different types of surfaces which attach very tightly to one another. Hook-and-loop boards can be used for displaying three-dimensional materials because the system creates a very strong bond. Even without a hook-and-loop board the teacher can attach a strip of the hook-and-loop material along the side of a chalkboard or bulletin board and use it to mount various items.

Chart Stand, Easel

These are useful for displaying large visuals and maps and for supporting chart tablets and flip charts.

Globes, World Maps

Frequent reference to globes and world maps will help students to set learning into a global context. Ideally, these resources will be printed in the target language, although first-language maps and globes can also be useful. Inflatable globes are available in English and in some target languages. These can be tossed around the classroom and used in a very personalized way; they are usually less expensive than traditional classroom globes.

AUDIOVISUAL EQUIPMENT

Overhead Projector

The overhead projector allows the teacher to control the focus of class attention by turning the projector off and on and by revealing only one part of the transparency at a time. The overhead projector is especially valuable for the traveling teacher, provided that there is a projector in every classroom the teacher visits. Many instructional materials can be prepared ahead of time and projected when they are needed during the class; this saves class time that would otherwise be spent in writing on the chalkboard.

Transparencies are especially effective when they include color, which may be added even to commercially prepared transparencies with special transparency pens or adhesive transparency film. Figures on transparencies can be cut out and moved around on the glass projector stage to achieve a variety of effects. (A number of additional activities for the overhead projector are listed in chapter 13.)

Videocassette Recorder/Player

Videocassette recorder/players make it possible to view commercially prepared lessons or supplementary materials, many of which provide an image of the target culture which is nearly impossible to achieve in any other way. Some classrooms also exchange videotape "letters" or projects with children studying or speaking the target language in other parts of the country or with children living in the target culture. Multi-standard video recorders are essential for use with videotapes made in foreign countries.

Phonograph

It should be easy to find a portable phonograph to use for playing music, or songs and rhymes recorded by native speakers. The speakers should be of good quality and the recordings themselves should be free of scratches and background noise.

Audiocassette Recorder/Player

These can be used for learning stations as well as in the whole-group setting. Students can read a book and listen to an accompanying tape, or they can listen to a set of instructions for performing activities such as completing a scrambled dot-to-dot puzzle or dressing a paper doll. There are many possibilities for individual listening activities in which there is a product at the end and the opportunity for self-check.

The cassette player is also useful for playing accompaniments to songs, providing background music for a variety of classroom activities, and for recording and playing back special songs or skits done by the class—either for their own enjoyment or for sharing with other classes through a tape exchange.

The cassette player is often more portable and easier to use than the phonograph, especially for the traveling teacher. It should have a good quality speaker that does not distort the sound when played at a volume high enough to be heard by the entire class.

Magnetic Card Reader

Cards of varying lengths with magnetic strips at the bottom are used for short recorded messages which relate the word(s) or picture on the card to the spoken language. Primarily an individual tool at a learning station, this provides both an audio and a visual stimulus for students to help them practice everything from individual vocabulary items to a conversational exchange.

Filmstrip Projector

A number of available sound filmstrips with a target–language sound track are suitable for use with children. English-language filmstrips depicting fairy tales or science and social studies topics can be used in the elementary school foreign language classroom without the sound. It is possible to arrange the frame in such a way that children are not distracted by the English captions.

Slide Projector

Slides can be useful for imparting cultural information. Slides and filmstrips can be hand-prepared by the teacher and the students to illustrate a favorite story or song. Pictures from books or magazines can be photographed on a copy stand to produce slides. Some teachers have children illustrate a play with drawings for each scene, and then photograph the drawings on a copy

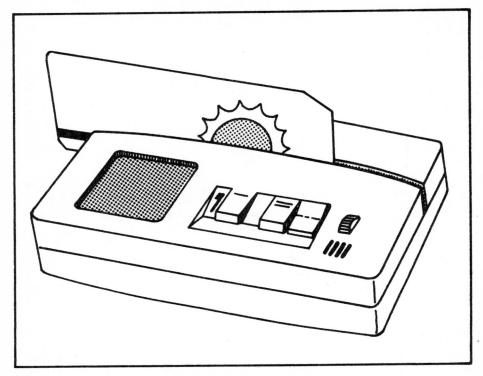

Magnetic Card Reader

stand to create a slide or filmstrip sequence telling the story. Children then record a dramatization of the play and present the slide-tape story to parents or other students.

Microcomputer

The microcomputer has a lot of potential for providing interactive and communicative practice. At the present time, most commercial foreign-language software is grammar-focused and drill- and practice-oriented. Some translations of popular elementary school mathematics and language arts programs are available in French and Spanish, and some word processing programs are also available in a variety of languages. Word processing in the target language offers creative writing opportunities for elementary school foreign language classes. Teachers who have students with computer programming talent might encourage them to develop interesting programs in the target language to share with their classmates.

VISUAL REINFORCEMENT
IN THE CLASSROOM

Labels

All classroom furniture and classroom features can be labeled in the target language (chalkboard, desk, door, erasers, electric outlets). It is also effective to label other parts of the school with target language names—toilets, offices, specialty classrooms, exits, and so forth. Where there is more than one language taught in the school, labels from all languages may be used side by side.

Name Tags

Name tags can be an effective reinforcement of the second language atmosphere if the students have chosen names in the target language. Name tags may be placed on the desks for the language period every day or they may be hung around the neck or pinned on an article of the students' clothing. Some teachers create classroom rituals around the distribution of name tags every day; others prefer to have the students keep the name tags in their desks and take them out as a sign of the beginning of class. Name tags may not be needed beyond the first several weeks of the year; although, for teachers who see many students in a day or in a week, the name tags may be necessary for a much longer period of time. Name tags permit teachers to call students by name, even when a target language name has not been assigned, in a situation where it is otherwise very difficult to learn all the names of the students.

Calendar

Having a calendar in the target language is an easy way to have the target culture present in the classroom at all times.

Signal Indicating Language Being Spoken

This signal can be a sign or a flag or an apron or some other device that indicates whether English or the target language is being used. The teacher changes the signal when the language of the classroom is changed.

Symbols to Hang from Ceiling

Signs with specific vocabulary items, such as weather, months, or time of day, can be hung from the ceiling in various parts of the room. They can be used as a way of organizing children or as a part of physical-response activities.

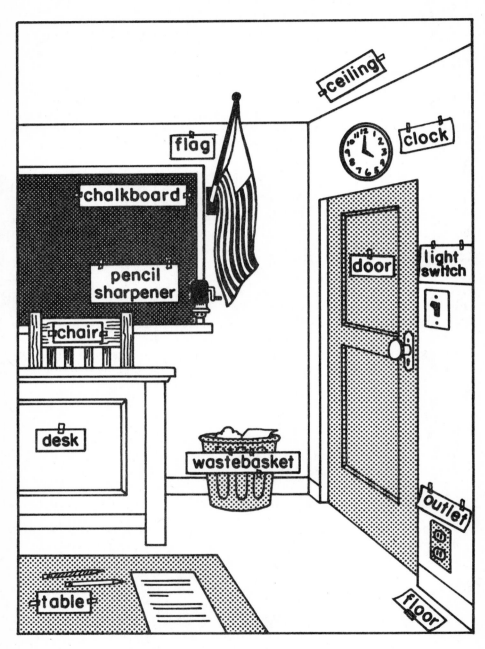

Classroom Labeled (in the Target Language)

Mobiles

Coat hangers are the easiest base for creating classroom mobiles. Directions for making mobiles can be found in many classroom craft books.

Reference Charts

Charts can be student- or teacher-made, or they can be obtained from commercial sources. They visually represent the concepts taught in class. For example, a nutrition chart might be used in conjunction with a food unit.

Other charts are teacher- or student-made and used for the maintenance of classroom routines. Here are some examples:

Day, Date, Weather Chart

Some teachers incorporate weather into the calendar activity and chart the daily weather directly on the calendar. Others post a chart just for this purpose.

Helper Chart

This is a list of classroom jobs performed by students, with visual cues to make the meaning clear.

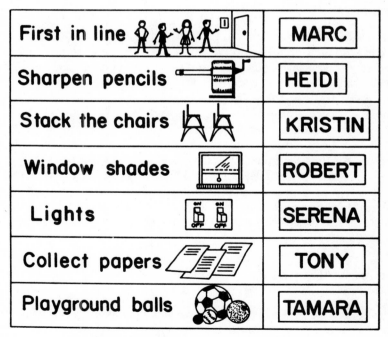

Sample Helper Chart (in the Target Language)

Classroom Rules Chart

Classroom rules should be spelled out in the target language, with a visual cue to make the meaning clear.

Color and Number Charts

In primary and beginning elementary school foreign language classrooms, these are helpful reference points for early activities with colors and numbers.

Bulletin Boards

Bulletin boards captioned in the target language and reflecting the target culture can be a source of cultural stimulation in the classroom, and they can also serve as valuable teaching tools. They should be changed frequently, often with the help of the students themselves, and they should reflect the concepts and the vocabulary being taught in the classroom. Bulletin boards in hallways and entryways of the school provide an opportunity to gain attention for the elementary school foreign language program.

TEACHER-PRODUCED MATERIALS

Teacher-made materials are often most effective in communicating a concept, structuring an activity, or motivating a lesson, because they are usually tailored to the special needs and interests of a specific class and situation. Both the teacher and the students value the extra effort that has gone into making them and use them with special pleasure. Supplementary materials like most of those represented here should contribute to the goals of the lesson and not become a separate entity in themselves.

Many of these items can also be produced by students or with student assistance. All items prepared for the classroom should be of good quality, carefully prepared, durable, and colorful. Edges should be straight and squared, cut with a paper cutter. Pinking shears should be used to cut any cloth with a tendency to ravel, or to provide a decorative edge to paper or fabric. Zamora (1985) provides a detailed discussion of hand-made visuals and materials.

Protecting Teacher–Made Visuals and Game Boards

Three methods for protecting a visual are *binding, mounting,* and *making surface coverings*. Binding (with masking tape or other strong tape) protects the edges and makes for longer wear.

Mounting a visual keeps it flat and makes it easier to handle and file; mounting material must be sturdy so that the pictures are not flimsy and do not become dog-eared. Two effective techniques for mounting involve using the dry-mount heat press and spray adhesive. Visuals should be mounted on backings of similar sizes so that they are easier to store.

The surface of visuals can be protected through lamination, clear self-adhesive plastic, and acrylic spray. Lamination tends to enhance the colors of the visuals and to give a more professional, long-lasting finish. It is frequently no more expensive than other techniques, but it may sometimes be a source of glare, making it difficult for some students to see the visual under certain lighting conditions. With clear self-adhesive plastic there is often a loss of vividness of color, but no machine is necessary, so projects can be completed at home. Do not use permanent ink pens to mark materials that will be laminated or covered with clear contact paper as it will bleed; instead, use water-based pens. Acrylic spray protects visuals adequately when they are not subject to repeated handling by students.

Magic-Mystery Box

This resource can conceal or reveal vocabulary items and can be a recurring source of surprises and motivation in the classroom. Specific suggestions for its use are found in chapter 13.

Here are the directions for making a magic-mystery box:

1. Cover the bottom and sides of a 42 oz. (large) oatmeal box with two layers of self-stick plastic covering. If patterned covering is not used, decorate the box with symbols cut from contrasting plastic.

2. Cut the heel and the foot from a large heavy sock, or use a portion of a leg warmer. Pull the sock over the top of the oatmeal box until the entire sock is stretched around the box.

3. Staple the sock around the top edge to fasten it to the box.

4. Place a strip of plastic around the top edge of the box, covering the staples and the top edge of the sock.

5. Pull the sock up from the bottom, inside out, to form a "handle" for the box.

Laminated Circles and Numbers

Make large and small colored circles (at least one set of each, 12 inches and 6 inches in diameter) out of construction paper for every color to be taught. Make large numbers out of 9" × 12" colored tagboard. Laminate or cover with clear self-stick plastic.

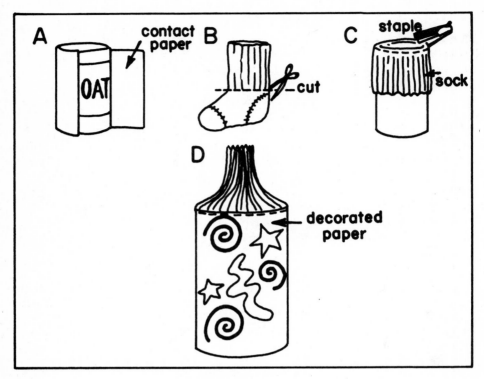

Magic-Mystery Box

Floor Maps and Pattern Games

Use a sheet of heavy-gauge vinyl table covering (preferably without texture) to make a floor map of countries, continents, or cities. (If the vinyl is white on both sides, each side can be used for a different map or activity). Attach the vinyl to the chalkboard or the wall and project a copy of the map using an opaque projector or an overhead projector. Trace the map onto the vinyl using a permanent felt marker or a laundry marker. For additional interest, add colored markers to indicate bodies of water and other features of importance.

This teaching tool can be used for teaching geography concepts by TPR as children step, sit, or jump on a country, a city, or a physical feature. (Additional teaching suggestions are found in chapter 13.)

Use the back of the map or another piece of vinyl to create a game board, a chart, or a geometric grid for use with physical–response activities associated with a variety of concepts.

Laminated Shapes in a Variety of Colors

These are useful for physical–response activities, creative play, and content instruction.

Name Tags

Punch holes in the two top corners of a piece of tagboard, pull yarn through the holes and tie it, write the student's target language name on the tagboard, and hang it around the student's neck. The name tag can be shaped to represent elements of the culture being learned, such as berets, flags, pretzels. (If name tags are laminated, they will last much longer. They must be laminated if they are made out of construction paper.)

Booklets, Theme Books, and Shape Books

Use booklets or theme books as initial, developmental, or culminating activities for just about any topic. When you create a booklet that represents concepts just learned in pictures (and perhaps also in words), the students have something tangible to take home with them and share with their parents, and the second language learning becomes more concrete for them. You can prepare the illustrations for the booklet, or the booklet pages themselves, before class, and have students complete them as a classroom activity. Typical booklet topics include weather, feelings, the alphabet, a group trip, foods, and animals. For variety you can prepare the cover and the pages for a theme book or booklet in the shape of the topic of the booklet, and students assemble the booklet and use it to record information about the topic. For example, an experience with a rabbit might be recorded in a booklet shaped like a rabbit, or a nutrition experience might be described in a book shaped like an apple or an egg. These experiences give students both tactile and verbal reinforcement of the concepts under discussion.

Clothesline

Clotheslines provide an easy way to display visuals or student work in the classroom. For example, the teacher might hang paper or doll clothing on it, use it as a time line, or hang up weather signs or other symbols.

Wheel of Months, Seasons

This teaching tool provides a way of looking at the months of the year and the seasons as a whole and associating them with distinctive characteristics representative of the target culture. The teacher uses heavyweight tagboard or poster board to cut two large half circles that will be hinged together to form a complete circle. The circle is divided into twelve equal segments, each representing a month of the year and identified by a picture reflecting special activities or occasions for that month and with the name or initial of the month. The board can be used for teaching months of the year, locating class birthdays, and for songs and rhymes dealing with months and seasons.

Clothespin Matchups (self-correcting activity)

To create clothespin matchups, use the following materials: a large circle (or other shape if preferred) made of cardboard or tagboard divided into 8 to 12 sections, and wooden clothespins—enough so that there is one pin for each section of the wheel.

There are many varieties of activities with clothespin matchups. The circle can contain pictures of vocabulary words, and the clothespins can have the correct word written on them; the activity can deal with rhyming words, opposites, various tenses, or many other topics; students must match the clothespin with the section of the wheel which has the correct picture. To

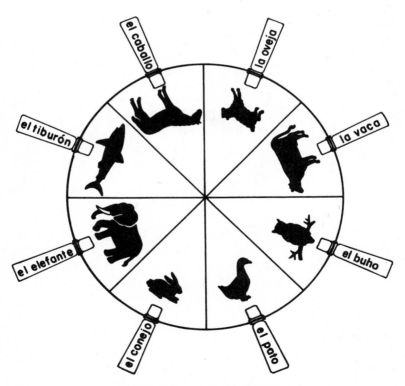

Sample Clothespin Matchup Activity

make the activity self-checking, place a number or symbol on the back of the clothespin and the same number or symbol on the back of the correct section of the wheel.

Dominoes (number or picture)

You can create domino games using colors, numbers, or pictures representing current vocabulary. Use the dominoes for small groups or for whole–class activities on the chalkboard or on the floor. Commercial domino games are also useful for many activities.

Yarn Board (self-correcting activity)

To make a yarn board, use these materials:

- An 8-½" × 11" piece of tagboard divided in half lengthwise, and into 4 to 6 sections horizontally
- Colored yarn (either enough pieces of one color or a different color for each horizontal section)
- Paper fasteners
- A hole puncher
- Reinforcements for 3-hole punched paper.

Arrange various pairs for matching practice so that one member of the pair appears in the left-hand column and the other member of the pair appears in a random position in the right-hand column. Attach one piece of the yarn to each segment on the edge of the left-hand column and punch one hole on the edge of each segment in the right-hand column. The student places the yarn in the hole representing the correct match. Many items can be matched: vocabulary pictures with vocabulary words, opposites, and so forth. This activity can be self-correcting in the following ways:

Variation 1:   Cut the yarn various lengths so that each piece can fit into only the hole with the correct answer.

Variation 2:   Use multicolored yarn strands all of the same length, and color-code the correct answers on the back of the hole by placing a round reinforcement for 3-hole punched paper over the hole; color-code the reinforcement the same color as the yarn.

Game Boards

You can make simple game boards similar to those popular with children and create games to reinforce concepts that you are teaching. Game boards can be of any shape and design.

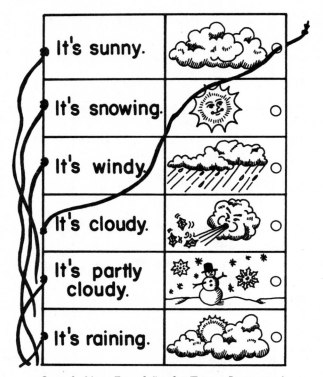

Sample Yarn Board (in the Target Language)

Felt Beanbags in 12 Colors

Here are instructions for making beanbags:

1. Cut two pieces of felt in a circle shape with a 5″ diameter.
2. Stitch them together with a ⅜″ seam around the edge, leaving about a 1-½″ opening for filling the bag.
3. Use light cardboard to make a funnel for beans.
4. Fill bag with a rounded ¼ cup of navy beans.
5. Sew shut.

Beanbags can be used for physical–response activities, in games involving a floor map or gameboard, and in other common children's games.

Milk Carton "Computer"

This is how to make a milk-carton "computer":

1. Open a half-gallon milk carton at the top and wash.

2. Cut a narrow slit opening for "input" at the top and for "output" at the bottom (see illustration).
3. Put in partitions to make a chute for "computer cards." (Slick paper works best.)
4. Cover the box with patterned self-adhesive plastic and decorate it with contrasting plastic to look like a machine or a computer.
5. Staple the top.

This is how to make "computer cards":

1. Use stiff paper for cards so they slide through the chute.
2. Place word, problem, or point value on one side of the card. Turn the card upside down before placing the clue, answer, or game problem into the computer.
3. Make cards for mathematics, vocabulary, singulars and plurals, vocabulary recognition, and so forth.

Students can use the "computer" as an individual activity to review concepts or vocabulary, or groups can play in teams.

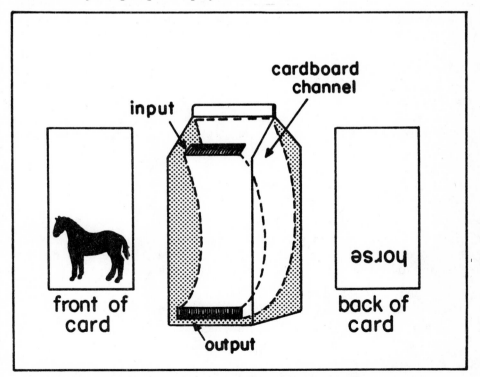

Milk Carton Computer (in the Target Language)

Lotto Color Board

Out of a piece of white or beige 9″ × 12″ construction paper, make a lotto or bingo grid divided into nine squares or rectangles with the title "Colors!". Next, cut out squares of construction paper in the colors that the students will learn, probably twelve or thirteen in all, including white. Arrange the squares systematically so that each of the game boards is different from the others, and affix the squares to the boards using a spray adhesive or a glue stick. Laminate each of the game boards for permanence. Using a water-based transparency pen or a wax pencil, write in the numbers 1, 2, 3 above each of the columns. (These numbers may be changed for more advanced students.) Prepare game pieces to be drawn out of a hat, a magic box, or another device, three of each color, marked 1, 2, and 3 respectively.

Play the game by having the teacher draw game pieces and call out the color and the location, as in Bingo: "1 blue, 3 red," and so forth. The game may be played in any of the usual Bingo ways, including filling the whole board. This can become a more speaking-oriented game if the students call back the numbers to the leader when they have won a round. When students are ready to begin speaking, they will volunteer the number. With only nine squares in the grid, the game does not go on endlessly, and many different children have a chance for success.

Scrolls

Scrolls can be used for telling a story or presenting a sequence of events or steps, and they are often student-produced. They are made by rolling a long strip of paper from one stick or dowel to another. They can also be used as a way of keeping a class or individual record of language learned or experiences shared.

CRITERIA FOR EVALUATING NONTEXT MATERIALS AND REALIA

Whether they have been prepared by hand, commercially produced, or obtained directly from the target culture, materials will be most effective when the following questions can be answered affirmatively:

- Are the materials durable? Can they stand up to repeated, ungentle handling?
- Are the materials culturally authentic? (Some items, such as balls, numbers, shapes, models of food, are culture-free.)
- Are they free of nonessential detail?
- Are they brightly-colored? Are they safe for use by children?

- Is their size appropriate to their intended use?
- Are they appealing to the intended age and developmental level?
- Do they have a versatility that lends itself to multiple use?
- Are they free of gender and racial bias?
- Do they collectively incorporate a variety of textures (soft, hard, rough, smooth)?
- Are the materials functional and simple to use?
- Are they easy to keep clean?
- Are they esthetically pleasing?
- Do they reflect quality workmanship?
- Is the cost within the budget?

CHOOSING A TEXTBOOK AND OTHER PRINTED MATERIALS

Choosing a textbook is one of the most important tasks for the foreign language teacher at any level. In the elementary school the process is made much more difficult by the fact that there are few text series from which to choose. A number of programs that are still available were written in the 1960s or soon after and do not reflect the insights about communication and language acquisition which have been achieved since then. Other materials have been developed for specific purposes and are not completely transferrable to the elementary school foreign language classroom. Spanish materials from bilingual education, for example, are designed for children who already speak Spanish, at least to some extent, and who function at least some of the time in a Spanish-speaking environment. Thus, the linguistic level of these materials is inappropriate for English-speaking children who live in an all-English setting. Materials developed for French immersion and core programs in Canada are often too advanced and proceed too rapidly for many program settings in the United States. German materials developed for the children of guest workers in Germany or the children of German-speaking families living abroad present similar problems when they are used with American speakers of English.

Many elementary school foreign language programs develop a curriculum that is not dependent on the use of a text series for at least the first year or two, but it is extremely difficult to maintain a well-articulated local curriculum over a long period of time without reference to a professionally developed text series. In the absence of a satisfactory commercial text series, some school systems have invested the funding and the effort necessary to create successful locally developed materials for an entire elementary school sequence. Short-term FLEX programs, designed to offer an experience with a language that lasts no more than a year, usually work with a locally produced curriculum, since textbook publishers have produced very little material appropriate for this type of program. Current curricula and program descriptions can be located using the ERIC data base and the resources of the National Network for Early Language Learning (see appendix B).

As the interest in elementary school foreign language programs continues to grow, publishers are producing textbook materials to add to the small number of contemporary elementary school foreign language text series already developed for the American market. Many of these will be welcome resources which can provide a useful core for the elementary school foreign language program.

Even when a satisfactory text series is available, it represents only a starting point for the curriculum. Supplementary materials and activities chosen or devised by the teacher respond to the interests and needs of children in each specific school setting, and they constitute the most dynamic part of elementary school foreign language instruction. The materials described in this chapter and the sample activities discussed in chapter 13 are intended to serve as useful components of both those programs built around a text series and those which have been developed locally.

CRITERIA FOR EVALUATING TEXTBOOKS AND OTHER PRINTED MATERIAL

As elementary school foreign language teachers evaluate text series or curriculum materials developed in other districts, the following questions are recommended for the screening process:

Goals

- Are the goals of the program or authors clearly stated? Are these goals compatible with local program goals?
- Is the scope and sequence for the entire series carefully developed and clearly presented?
- Do the materials reflect authentic use of language? Is this the way people in the target culture *really* express themselves?
- What is the intended grade level for the materials? Are the materials suitable for the interests and maturity level of the proposed audience?

Communication

- Does *communication* rather than *grammar* serve as the organizing principle? Does work with grammar concentrate on functional use rather than analysis? Do the activities focus on meaning rather than on form?

- Is the use of English avoided in student materials and discouraged in the activities described in the teacher's manual?
- Do the materials reflect an understanding of the use of physical-response strategies and of immersion methodology?
- Is the material oriented to activity and experience rather than to exercise and drill?
- Do the materials provide opportunities for meaningful, purposeful language use?
- Are the materials designed to develop a solid oral language base upon which to build reading and writing skills?

Culture

- Is culture integrated into the program materials? Is there emphasis on *experiencing* culture rather than on learning *about* culture?
- Is culture presented from a global perspective rather than focusing on a single country, region, or ethnic group?
- Are the situations and language presented culturally authentic?
- Do the materials promote an appreciation of the value and richness of cultural diversity?

Subject-Content and Thinking Skills

- Is there provision for the teaching of grade-appropriate subject content in the target language? Are there suggestions for *interdisciplinary* content and activities?
- Are the materials conducive to the development of higher-order thinking skills, and not restricted to rote learning?

Bias

- Are the illustrations and text free of racial, gender, and cultural bias?

Flexibility

- Are the materials adaptable to different program models and time allocations?
- Do the materials provide options for a variety of student learning styles— visual, auditory, kinesthetic?

Physical Characteristics

- Are the student materials visually oriented and colorful?

- Are photographs and other pictures clearly linked to the printed material?
- Is the size of print in student materials the same as that used in subject-content textbooks used at the same grade level?
- Are the materials durable? Can they withstand handling by many children over the period of time covered by a textbook adoption?

Support Materials

- Is there a teacher's manual with abundant suggestions for the teacher? Does the teacher receive adequate guidance in the use of the materials?
- Are there relevant and effective charts, transparencies, filmstrips, flashcards, pictures, tapes and other support materials available in addition to the basic program?
- If taped materials are available, do they feature native-speaker voices speaking naturally in the presentation of songs, rhymes and stories? Are there tapes available which include program-relevant sound effects and background music?

Budget

- Are the materials affordable?

SUMMARY

The elementary school foreign language teacher works with the whole child in the whole classroom learning environment. Every aspect of the classroom and all of the materials and realia have potential for contributing to the language experiences from which language acquisition develops. An ample inventory of supplies will encourage the development of craft and other activities and will make it easier for teachers to prepare materials tailored to classroom communication needs. A good selection of manipulatives and realia makes it possible to vary the contexts within which students communicate, giving them the practice that they need while maintaining high motivation. A variety of picture visuals to supplement the realia helps students to stretch the concepts they have learned to include a variety of occurrences. A classroom that is well equipped with display boards and equipment makes it easier for the teacher to draw on all the resources available to create a target-language "island." Audiovisual equipment can make it possible for children to have a direct visual or auditory experience with the foreign culture and with speakers of the language, and it can also facilitate many types of individual instruction. The classroom environment can illustrate that a foreign language is an important part of the curriculum, through bulletin boards, charts, calendars, and other vivid evidence. Even when the elementary school foreign language teacher must travel to several rooms in a day, each classroom should be able to find a place for some evidence of the new language and its culture. Teacher-produced materials and visuals add a personal quality and investment to any lesson, and they are often the most effective of all teaching tools. Equipment and materials necessary to conduct in-class food activities provide for some of the most motivating and memorable of all classroom activities.

Textbook series appropriate for American elementary school foreign language programs are more difficult to find than are locally produced curriculum materials, but they are of great assistance in developing an integrated and articulated program that spans several grade levels. All materials must be carefully chosen and evaluated, with the goals and philosophy of the local program serving as the main criteria. The guidelines suggested in this chapter will assist teachers and supervisors in making choices of materials and curriculum and in communicating with textbook publishers.

FOR STUDY AND DISCUSSION

1. What special advantages might be expected from the use of teacher-made visuals and realia? What are the drawbacks of their use?

2. Choose an item from one of the materials lists and describe four different ways in which you could use it in the elementary school foreign language classroom. Identify the grade and language level of the children for whom you plan the activities.

3. Choose a textbook series or a teacher-developed curriculum designed for an elementary school foreign language program and evaluate it in terms of the criteria questions found at the end of the textbook section of this chapter.

4. How do the criteria for choosing and evaluating materials for elementary school foreign language classes differ from criteria used in other content areas?

5. One of the exhibitors at a foreign language conference has announced the publication of a new textbook in your language for children in kindergarten through grade 6. Write down seven questions you would ask the publisher's representative to help you determine if the series is worth a closer look.

FOR FURTHER READING

The following sources are recommended for additional information about material covered in this chapter. Chapter citations are documented in *Works Cited* at the end of the volume.

Yunus, Noor Azlina. *Preparing and Using Aids for English Language Teachers*. Kuala Lumpur, Malaysia: Oxford University Press, 1981.

Zamora, Gloria Rodriguez, and Rebecca Maria Barrera. *Nuevo Amanecer Teacher's Reference Book*. Lincolnwood, IL: National Textbook Company, 1985.

Chapter 13

Bringing Language to Life: Choosing and Creating Classroom Activities

Games and game-like activities are among the most natural means available for developing a context for communication with children. Play is often described as a child's work, and games form a natural part of the child's most important work setting, the classroom. Games and game-like activities might be credited with carrying the largest role in the acquisition of language in the elementary school foreign language classroom. While some educators make a distinction between games and activities, it is often very difficult to draw a clear line, and the differences between them are far less important than is the impact they have on the motivation and the language acquisition of the children in the class. Many elementary school foreign language teachers have discovered that students regard any well–designed, successful activity that they enjoy as a "game." This chapter treats activities and games as a single category and makes no distinction between them. The suggestions and guidelines presented are applicable to all classroom activities.

The most successful games are very simple, requiring a minimum of explanation and rules. The simple addition of a competitive factor, or an element of mystery or surprise, can convert a meaningless but necessary practice activity into a game. Most games should flow naturally within the class period from the topics and vocabulary being worked on, and only rarely will they be set apart as major events in themselves.

The most important requirement for a game is that it should be fun for the children to play! Before planning a game activity, the teacher should consider whether the children would enjoy the topic and the game in the real world outside of the classroom. Some additional guidelines for choosing and using games in the language classroom follow.

GUIDELINES FOR GAMES
AND ACTIVITIES

Here are some guidelines for games and activities:

1. Choose games or adjust them so that the children need to understand the language and express themselves in it. Then they will realize that the language is useful and they will be motivated to communicate. It is to be expected that the teacher will produce most of the language during the early stages of language acquisition; this is perfectly natural and acceptable but the language must play an important part in every game. Some games, such as dominoes and certain board games, include important concepts being covered in class, but they can be played successfully with virtually no use of the target language. These games need not be abandoned, however, if the teacher can devise a playing routine or a variation that will necessitate language use in them.

2. Provide maximum opportunity for students to participate. All children should be engaged in the activity all of the time. Some activities, like "Simon Says," are designed so that children who miss are "out," which leaves many children inactive for most of the game. These games can be redesigned to allow for students who are "out" to contribute to the game in a new way, such as by taking turns at giving commands to other children, or give them a method for reentry into the competition by paying close attention or by completing a special performance of some kind.

3. Organize and score the game so that most of the playing time can be spent communicating in the target language.

4. Add an appealing element of suspense or competition, but structure the game to avoid intense individual competition that could carry over into bad feelings outside the classroom. The healthiest type of competition takes place when teams or groups are evenly matched and have equal opportunity for success. It often works well, when a higher level of competition is desired, to pit the class against the teacher or against an imaginary villain, like the ghost in some computer games. That way the entire class works together to "win," and when the class wins, so does the teacher.

5. Choose a game that is easy to play so that it will move quickly. In most cases short games that can be repeated in several rounds during one class period are preferable to longer games, which may not be completed by the time the language class is over.

6. Stop the game or the activity at a point when the class still wants more, rather than continuing it until interest begins to flag.

7. Do not repeat successful activities, except those designed to be played with several rounds, during the same class or on the following day, even when children request them. Using any specific game sparingly helps to keep it fresh and motivating.

8. Structure activities when possible in the spirit of New Games (Fluegelman 1976), in which *everybody* plays to the level of her or his ability: "Play Hard, Play Fair, Nobody Hurt!" (p. 13)

9. Give games a name, especially if they are likely to be used again in a similar form. Children regard the game as something special if it has a name, and a name makes it easier for them to talk about the game outside of class or to request it at a future time.

10. Incorporate games played in the target culture or in other cultures around the world whenever possible. Several sources for games with global roots are listed at the end of this chapter. The physical education teacher may have suggestions for references on international games and may also be willing to include such games in the physical education curriculum at your suggestion. Other possibilities for locating games include the following:

    - Games books for elementary school teachers, especially those with a theme of games around the world
    - Teacher's manuals for elementary school foreign language textbook series, even in languages other than the ones taught in your school
    - The ERIC data base, under the descriptors *FLES Programs and Materials* or *Games*
    - *FLES News*, published by the National Network for Early Language Learning
    - Professional journals for early childhood and elementary school teachers, as well as those for language teachers

The games and activities that follow have been gleaned from many sources; they represent only a sampling of the kinds of activities that are possible in an elementary school foreign language classroom. Two types of activities with special value for the elementary school foreign language classroom receive specific attention and suggestions within the chapter: the role of puppets and stuffed animals, and the use of songs.

This collection emphasizes activities for which a minimum of spoken language is required of students, although a number of games and activities in which children play an active speaking role are also included. This emphasis on comprehension is deliberate, because most traditional language games have been designed to encourage children to speak. Awareness of the importance of a listening stage is a recent development in the teaching of foreign and second languages, and materials for the early stages of language acquisition are often difficult to find. In games and activities in which children do a minimum of speaking or do not speak at all, it is important for the teacher to surround the activity with meaningful, communicative language. Every game in the elementary school foreign language classroom is a language game; every activity is a setting for language acquisition.

IDEAS FOR GAMES AND ACTIVITIES

Name Games

Names or Numbers Concentration

Sit with the students in a circle, if possible, and set up a rhythm, slowly at first, as follows:

> slap, slap (knees)
> clap, clap (hands)
> snap, snap (left hand)
> snap, snap (right hand)

On the left–hand snaps call your own name, and on the right–hand snaps call the name of one of the students. On the next left–hand snaps, have the student call her or his own name and on the right–hand snaps the name of another student. The chain continues until someone misses a turn or loses the rhythm, at which point the teacher begins the game again. When this game is introduced, it is often helpful if you tell students to practice by always responding with the teacher's name on the right–hand snaps for the first few times, until the rhythm and the name-calling have become coordinated. As students increase their confidence and ability and begin to call on one another, you can speed up the rhythm. You can also play with numbers, letters of the alphabet, or any other vocabulary by placing the visual representing each child on the floor in front of her or him.

Spin the Plate

With children sitting in a circle, if possible, set a metal pie plate on its edge in the center of the group. Spin the plate and call the name of one of the children. If the child reaches the plate and catches it before it stops spinning, the child takes your place. If the child does not reach the plate in time, you take another turn spinning the plate. The game continues, with each successful child taking the role of plate-spinner and calling another child's name, until most or all names have been called at least once.

Seven-Up

Here is a variation of a favorite primary-school game: call seven children to the front of the room, and have the rest of the children in the class place heads down on their desks with their eyes closed. The seven children move around the room and each touch one child on the shoulder, after which they return to the front of the room. You can recite (or have the seven children recite in chorus) a routine such as "1, 2, 3, eyes open!" The children whose shoulders were touched take turns guessing which child touched them. If they guess correctly in a single try, they trade places with the child in the front of the room. Children who are not correctly guessed stay in the front of the room for another round.

Chalkboard Activities

Total Physical Response with Chalk

Using colored chalk, ask children to do as follows:

- Walk (jump, run, crawl, walk backwards) to the board
- Write _____
- Circle _____
- Pick up the _____
- Make an *x* on _____
- Draw (part of a face, body, and so forth)
- Take the eraser and erase _____

(This is an especially good activity for giving children practice in remembering a series of commands.)

Chalkboard Monster

Have a child or two children go to the chalkboard and create a monster by following your directions, preferably using colored chalk. In more advanced situations, the monster might develop from the joint commands of the class. For example, you might say, "Draw a big head; draw an ear," and then ask the class, "Do you want large ears or small ears?" so that students can contribute to the development of the monster in various ways, depending on their language level. If more than one child is at the chalkboard at the same time, it is interesting to compare the efforts of each child in a class discussion, always being careful to avoid comparative judgments.

What's the Weather?

Draw a window on the chalkboard. Direct the children to go to the board and draw the weather in the window as you describe it. (Variation: Use a felt or magnet board and have children choose elements to place in the window.) To activate the language, you might lead a discussion about what time of year this weather represents, whether children like or dislike this kind of weather, and what kinds of activities they enjoy in this weather.

Activities with a Magic-Mystery Box

(See directions for making the box, pages 221–222.)

1. Draw items from the box, describe them, and have students ask for them.
2. Draw familiar items from the box, revealing a little bit at a time, and have children take turns guessing the items or describing it.
3. Have students describe and/or guess an item in the box from touch alone.
4. Stuff the box with a number of items; have each student draw out one item and use it as a speech stimulus.
5. Use the box and the items it contains with physical-response activities such as *take, put, give, throw.*
6. Have students draw out words or phrases and string them together into a narrative or combine them into a command.
7. Play "I'm going on a trip and I'm taking . . ." with items (or pictures of items) pulled from the box.
8. Stuff food items—real or artificial—into the box. Have students draw out three to five items, construct a menu, and identify the meal.
9. Play *Twenty Questions* about an item or group of items in the box.
10. Place items in the box that suggest a specific person and have students guess who it is as each item is revealed.
11. Have students bring items for the box to "quiz" the teacher or the class.
12. Seat children in a circle. Place a number of familiar items in the magic box and pass it around the circle until a bell rings, the music stops, or some other prearranged signal is given. Have the student holding the box draw out one of the items and identify it. The game proceeds until all the items have been removed. Variation: Place items that were incorrectly identified in the center of the circle. When the box stops, the child holding it has the option of drawing an object from the box or choosing one from the center of the circle. The reward for correct identification is the opportunity to hold the object (and perhaps to play with it) during the course of the game.

Activities with Laminated Circles and Numbers

(See page 221 for directions.)

Total Physical Response Commands

For giving commands at the beginning stages of learning, use short specific directions such as

Take red!
Touch red!
Give me red!
Sit down on red!
Jump over red!
Jump from red to blue!
Lay red on Mary's head, arm, leg, knee, hand, stomach, etc.
Lay red under the chair, in front of the chair, beside, behind, left of, right of etc.
Take the colors of the German, United States, Puerto Rican etc., flag, and lay them on the flag.
Make the numbers 19, 21, etc. (by placing two numerals together)

Clockface

Lay numbers out in a circle to make a clock face; have children move large, laminated hands to tell time or lie down and make their own arms tell the time.

Number Match

Pass out a set of numbers from 0 to 9 to each of two teams (or more, as class size suggests). Call (or have another leader call) a number; the first team whose "number" stands up gets a point; if more than one child stands, the team cannot win a point.

Who Has It?

Use this at the end of an activity, when each child has either a number or a color. Tell the children to lay their number or color in front of them on the floor or hold them up so everyone can see. Set rhythm as for concentration: slap knees, clap hands, snap left fingers, snap right fingers. Ask a question in rhythm; have students answer in rhythm. If they cannot answer, either repeat the question or give the answer.

Teacher:	Who-	has-	sev-	en?
Student:	(slap)	(clap)	Sus-	an.
Teacher:	Loud-	er	(snap)	(snap)
Student:	(slap)	(clap)	Sus-	an!

Activities with Floor Map or Game Board

(See page 222 for directions.)

1. Using the floor map, direct children to do the following:

   - Step from country to country or area to area or lay various parts of their own bodies on different countries
   - Lay flags on the appropriate countries
   - "Swim" in rivers, lakes, or oceans; "ski" in the mountains, etc.
   - Jump over rivers or borders
   - Locate capitals
   - Lay maps of political subdivisions on the larger map (as in a jigsaw puzzle)
   - Place geographical features such as mountains or major cities on the map
   - Place products on the region where they originate
   - Trace routes from place to place using a toy car, boat, or train

   This kind of activity can make geographical and cultural concepts very concrete.

2. Using a geometric grid or randomly placed numbers, children can be directed to:

   - Step from number to number or shape to shape
   - Toss beanbags or lay objects on various parts of the board
   - Perform on the board in response to commands
   - Lay vocabulary flashcards on various parts of the board
   - Perform other activities similar to those described for the floor map.

Paper and Pencil Activities

Paperfolds

Direct the children to fold paper in specific ways, either to form a shape or to create a type of Japanese paperfold. You can make simple paperfolding activities more complex by adding the step of writing a figure on some section of the paper.

Dot-To-Dot Puzzle

Modify a simple dot-to-dot puzzle by renumbering the dots randomly. Call out the numbers in the prearranged order for students to connect the dots

Floor Map Activity

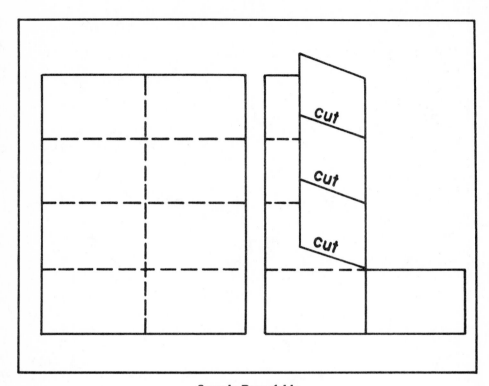

Sample Paperfolds

to complete the puzzle. (Note: Be sure you have solved a copy of the puzzle for yourself, so you do not forget which numbers to call and in which order!) Success is measured by whether the completed puzzle looks as it is supposed to look! You can make this activity more challenging by adding several numbered dots to the puzzle that are not used in the completion of the picture.

Variation: As a reading and writing exercise, write out the numbers in the target language, e.g. *uno, tres, ocho*. Students can then solve the puzzle as an independent reading activity.

Monsters

Give the children each a blank piece of paper and have them take out their crayons, pencils or markers. Direct the children to write their names on one corner of the page and then to draw a head *only*. Then have the children pass their papers a specified number of times to the left or right (or front or back) and tell them to draw another part of the body (or of the face). Keep adding face and body parts and move the papers around after each new part has been drawn. The result is the product of listening comprehension and a series of works of "group art."

Variation: Have the children take turns telling the class which parts of the anatomy to draw.

List Bingo Game

Have the students choose five to six words from a list of eight to twelve previously learned vocabulary written on the chalkboad or overhead projector, or on a handout. Have the students write the words they have chosen in a list on a piece of paper. Then call out words from the large list in random order and have students cross off the words on their own lists as they are called. The first student to cross out all the words on her or his list is the winner.

Activities with Playing Cards or Small Flashcards

Playing Card Coverup

(Use numbers 1 to 10 only, no jack, queen, or king.)

Group children in circles of three to four. Lay one suit of cards with numbers from 1 to 10 face up in the center of each group. Call a number—the first child to *cover* the number with an open hand keeps it. If two or more children touch the number at the same time, no one gets to take it. The successful child holds the number up for all to see (and for you to check comprehension). Identify who has the most at the end of each round, asking in the target language: "Who has three?" "Who has four?" and give congratulations. As a variation, you can have each group work with two suits of cards, one black and one red. You can then call both numbers and colors. This game can also be played with cards from any other number or color game.

Colors and Shapes Variation

Glue shapes in various colors on playing cards or note cards, approximately ten to twelve cards for each small group. Lay them face up in the center of each group of three to five children. Call a color and a shape (it works best if there are at least two colors per shape and at least two shapes per color). The first child to cover the number gets to take it and hold it up (so you can check for comprehension). At the end of the game, count who has the most cards and give congratulations.

Concentration

(Can also be played on pegboard, transparency, chalkboard, pocket chart, or masking taped grid.)

Use one red suit and one black suit, each numbered from 1 to 10. With masking tape, attach matching pictures, flags, numbers, or other information to the *back* of each card—being sure that every card has a match. (It could be a flag and its country name or two of the same flags.) Place cards in 4 × 5 rows, number side up, in the center of the circle. Have the children take turns around the circle: each child calls for two cards to be turned over, one at a time (one-red, five-black). If the cards match, the child keeps the cards and takes another turn. If not, the cards are turned over again and play goes on to next player. This game can be played with any set of vocabulary items, synonyms, matching words and pictures, opposites, or mathematics operations.

Variation: The child must name the item on the first card in order to call a second card.

Go Fish

Have children play in groups of three or four. Each child receives five cards, and the remainder are placed in a pile in the middle of the group. The child to the left of the dealer begins by asking for a card from any other player, in the hope of finding a matching card to one in her or his hand. If the player has the card, she or he must give it to the player requesting it, and that player places the pair on the table (or floor) in front of her or him and receives another turn. If not, the player says "Go fish!" (an equivalent phrase in the target language), and the first player draws a card from the pile. If the first player draws the card for which he or she asked, that player lays down the pair and receives another turn. The winner is the player who completes the most pairs.

Variation: The children seek to accumulate groups of four rather than two.

Ugly Monster

This is played like *Old Maid* but with an "ugly monster" as the extra card. Any category of vocabulary sets can be used.

Changing the Classroom Environment with Masking Tape

Masking tape can be used to create shapes, games, and imaginary settings on the classroom floor. Children might respond to such commands as "Jump backwards from the triangle to the square!" or "Sit down in the middle of the rectangle!" Human tic-tac-toe, hopscotch, and many other play environments can be created. Masking tape will peel off most floor surfaces, including carpet, without damaging them, *provided the tape is removed promptly*.

You might lead the class on an imaginary trip with the help of a large airplane (or boat or train) taped in outline to the floor. Other fantasy environments might include the floor plan of a house, an elevator with "up" and "down" and floor buttons, a map with rivers and mountains indicated. (See chapter 9 for more details.)

Tic-tac-toe

Use masking tape to create a large tic-tac-toe board on the floor. Make large Xs and Os out of laminated tagboard, about the same size as the giant numbers described above.

Variations: Many variations are possible. Place different colors or numbers in the squares, and hand out smaller versions to the class. Call a color or number; the child who has it chooses the X or the O to place in the square, or sits on the square holding the symbol.

Variations on "Safe Tag"

In an open area of the classroom or the gymnasium, outline several rectangles on the floor using masking tape. Within each of these possible "safe zones" place a different color. The person who is IT must begin and return to a designated spot. The game begins when you (or a child, later) call out "Go to ___(a color)___!" As of that moment, the IT is free to tag anyone not touching the indicated safe zone. The first person tagged becomes the new IT. As soon as every player is touching the correct safe zone or there is a new IT, call a different color, creating a new "safe zone." The beauty of this fast-paced game is that it demands immediate recognition of vocabulary items.

Variations include: (1) taping different geometric shapes instead of just rectangles to the floor; (2) giving more complex commands, such as "Everyone wearing tennis shoes go to the blue!" or "Hop backwards to red!"; (3) substituting numbers for colors and indicating the "safe zone" with numbers or with simple equations; (4) using features of the classroom environment as "safe zones," such as the chalkboard, the door, and so forth.

Games Focusing on Body Parts

Life-Sized Paper Dolls

You will need these materials: butcher paper; crayons or markers.

1. Working with one child at a time, instruct each child to lie down on her or his back on a piece of butcher paper and to shut her or his eyes.

2. Trace around the child's body using a marker.

3. Have the children write their names at the top of their outlines.

4. If children are at the prewriting or prereading stage, instruct them with commands such as—"Take your red crayon and write a number five in the thumb." or "Take your black crayon and write a seven in the foot."

5. Use these giant paper dolls later for clothing lotto:

   - Provide each child with an identical number of pieces of clothing, including, for example, pants, socks, hats, shoes.
   - Call out random commands: "If you have a skirt, put the skirt on your paper doll."

See who can be the first child to put all of the clothing on her or his doll by following commands.

Variation: Have one child lie down on butcher paper and direct others to trace around her or him, using various colors. Then have them color in the outline, using body parts or clothing vocabulary.

Living Statues

Give commands to one child at a time such as "Put your left hand on John's right elbow and kneel on your right knee." Use a number of children (in a small class the entire group) and build a "living statue" of class members connected to one another. As a final, interesting, and dramatic gesture, take a photograph with an instant camera and display it on the bulletin board. (Be careful to avoid "connections" that are potentially embarrassing, and avoid placing children together who have a strong antipathy for one another.)

Shell Game from Cameroun

Have one student leave the room and another student lie down while classmates outline the student's shape with shells or stones (large uncooked pasta shells work very well). Direct the activity with such suggestions as "Put the shells around the left arm, the right leg, the head." The returning student must guess which student is outlined by the shells or the rocks. If you desire more language use, give the student the opportunity to ask a limited number of questions in order to improve the chances of a correct guess.

Dressing the Bear

On tagboard draw a large outline of a bear (or other figure appropriate to your class's interests). Hang the picture on the chalkboard. Cut items of clothing to fit the bear's form: pants, shirt, hat, shoes. Students can pick up the items of clothing and hang them on the figure, following your directions in the target language. They can attach clothing with masking tape, hook-and-loop strips, or easy-release magic tape.

Body Collage

Cut individual arms, legs, eyes, noses, mouths, ears from magazines so there are many options for each child. Have children ask for their choice of individual body parts in the target language. They then glue them to construction paper and draw in their own heads, hair, torsos, and clothing. You or the students may label the creations; or give the students captions written on self-stick labels and have them select the appropriate label for each body part.

Variation: As an alternative version for a comprehension emphasis, direct children to choose different body parts one at a time.

Balloon Bounce

Give each child a balloon; for younger children the balloon should be already blown up, while for older children blowing up the balloon could be part of the chain of commands used. Have the children toss the ball into the air on command, then continue to bounce it in the air, using various parts of the body as you direct: "Hit the balloon with the head, with the knee, with the elbow, with the back, with the little finger of the right hand." There is almost no sound from the children, so the listening opportunity is excellent. There is no winner or loser—the challenge of keeping the balloons in the air is sufficient.

Action Games

Command Chairs

Give many commands in a row, sending children as a group all over the room touching doors, walls, jumping, and so forth. In the meantime remove one chair, so there is one less chair than there are students. When the command comes, "Sit down on your chair," the students scramble for a chair and the one left standing is "out." The game goes on until the last person is "out." After the students are "out," they can assist you in giving commands to the rest of the class.

Clothing Race

Have the children form two (or more) teams. Give each team a pile of clothing, the names of which have been learned in the class. Command the first person on each team to put on selected items of clothing. The list and

order of clothing changes each time. The team members can help by reminding
the contestant of items they have forgotten, but *only* in the target language.
The first contestant to put on all the right clothing (and only the right
clothing) wins a point for the team. (It is helpful if all the clothing is a little
too large for the participants, so it can be easily put on and removed.) Lists
of clothing can grow longer with successive rotations, to stretch the listening
memory.

Story in Third Person

As a variation on a fantasy (chapter 9), give each person a role in a narrative,
preferably with a prop for each character. As you read the story, the students
act out their parts. If there is dialog, the characters simply repeat their lines.
This is most effective if there is considerable action and emotion involved,
such as laughing or crying. (This technique can also be used with a familiar
story, but it is perhaps most effective when only the teacher knows what
will happen next, so everyone has to listen carefully.)

Color Walk, Number Walk

This is an adaptation of the old carnival cake walk. Place laminated colored
circles or numbers in a circular pattern on the floor and have one student
stand on each circle or number. Turn on the cassette player or record player
(or music keyboard) and have the students walk around the circle until
the music stops, when they will stop on the circle or number nearest them.
Draw a color or a number out of a box and ask the class, "Who is standing
on _____?" The student standing by that color or number wins and receives
applause. You can set up more than one "cake walk" in the room so that all
of the children can play at one time.

Numbers Game from Austria

The children form a circle around a child chosen as IT. That child is blindfolded
and stands; the other children are seated. Give each child a number, beginning
with *one*. When IT calls out two of the numbers, the children who have these
numbers must trade places immediately and silently. Should their movements
be detected by IT, IT must try to catch one of the children and exchange
places. If their movements go undetected and the two reach their new places
safely, everyone in the circle claps hands (or calls out a predetermined phrase
in the target language), and IT tries once again by calling two other numbers.

　　　　Variation: Instead of numbers, use names of animals, colors, foods, or
other current vocabulary.

Going Fishing

Place numbers, colors, or pictures of vocabulary on small paper fish with paper clips attached to them. Children "catch" their fish with a fishing pole that has a string and a magnet attached to the end. If the child names the number, color or picture, that child may keep the fish; if not, the fish goes back into the "pond."

Variation: Attach individual words or familiar commands to the fish. If the child can label the correct object with the word or perform the command, that child may keep the fish. Or, if reading and speaking are well established, the child may repeat the word or give the command to another child in order to keep the fish.

Follow the Foot Path

Place footprints in a variety of colors and sizes around the room, forming a path that the children can follow. Have the children proceed along the path by placing their own feet on one print at a time, naming the color, and then proceeding to the next print. The goal is to follow the path to its destination.

Variations: 1. Place pictures or symbols for familiar vocabulary on the footprints and tell the children they must name the vocabulary before proceeding further. 2. Point out prints of various sizes and have the children respond with their guesses as to who might have left such a print: the principal, a bear, a well-known young sibling of one of the children, and so forth. The teacher might ask: "Do you think this print was made by the principal? By a bear? By Mr. Jacobson or by Tommy? By a lion or by a mouse?"

Typewriter

Have students holding letter flash cards arrange themselves to spell words, or have students holding numeral flash cards arrange themselves to form several-digit numbers. Distribute the flash cards to a group of students and then call out the word or the number they are to form.

Poor Pierre

Have several children stand in front of the class, each of them holding a picture from a group of related vocabulary items. Begin the game by saying "Poor Pierre is going to school, but he doesn't have any cap." The child holding the cap responds by saying "Oh, yes, he has a cap, but he doesn't have any shoes (picture held by another child in the group)." The child holding the shoes continues the game using the same pattern, and the game continues until one child misses after being called on or until a player mentions an item that no one has a picture of. If a child misses, he or she names another child from the class to take her or his place in the group in the front. The class may play this game with any type of vocabulary by changing the situation established in the "frame" sentence.

Calesthenics and Fitness Path

Use commands to lead children in regular calesthenic movements, using many of the same exercises that they perform in physical education classes, if possible. This makes a good change of pace when children become restless, and as they become more verbal they may wish to lead the exercises themselves.

On the playground, in the gymnasium, or in a nearby park, if available, prepare exercise stations at various points around a walking path, using illustrations to help students understand what they are to do in each case. For the first several times, lead the class around the course, directing the students to perform the activity for a specified number of times at each station. The stations need not all be typical of an authentic fitness path. Some possible stations might include the following:

- Do ten jumping-jacks.
- Touch your toes six times.
- Do four windmills.
- Join hands and form a circle.
- Take four large steps forward.
- Raise your hands high.
- Take six small steps backwards.

Variation: Students may wish to prepare stations themselves, in small groups, and take responsibility for giving the directions when the class arrives at their station.

Aerobic Dance

Obtain an aerobic dance record or tape in the target language, preferably one with directions that are clearly pronounced and easy to understand. First teach the children the actions without music, and then spend a few minutes every few days doing the aerobic dance exercises with the music.

Ducks Fly/Birds Fly

Have the players stand in aisles or beside their chairs. Have the person who is IT (you may be IT) stand in front, facing the group, and call out "Ducks fly!" "Birds fly!" "Horses fly!" and so forth. When IT names an animal that *does* fly, the players go through the motions of flying, raising their arms high above their heads and lowering them to their sides. When IT names an animal that does *not* fly, they must not "fly." Anyone who "flies" when a nonflying animal is named, or anyone who does not fly when a flying animal is named, becomes IT (or gives a forfeit).

Yarn Games

Hang very long strands of yarn in a variety of colors from a hook in a corner to be used when there are a few minutes to spare or as a central activity. Have children work individually or in small groups on the floor to make figures such as these:

- a circle, square, triangle
- a figure 5, 8, 9
- a dog, horse, lion (or "make an animal" and students can guess which animal was made)
- a map of a familiar place
- a boy, girl, man, woman

Use these figures for physical–response activities such as "Jump into the circle"; "Put your left foot in the triangle"; and "Jump backwards over the 8."

Variation: You can make similar figures on the floor or have students use jump ropes as well as yarn. The same types of activities can be performed.

Bear Hunt

Sit in front of the class and narrate the following sequence in the target language, accompanying each statement with an appropriate motion. Have children copy the motions throughout. With each retelling, you might change the order or add new complications, in order to maintain suspense and surprise. Eventually the children will want to repeat the statements, echoing you, and some may even volunteer to lead the bear hunt.

"Let's go on a BEAR HUNT!"
"Everybody ready?" (Class responds "Yes!" or "Yes, ready!")
"Let's go!"
"Look at the *big* woods!" (Make hand gesture for *big*, point to visual of woods.)
"We can't go *around* it!" (Make hand gesture for *around*.)
"We can't go *over* it!" (Make hand gesture for *over*.)
"We have to go *through* it!" (Make hand gesture for *through*, or straight ahead.)

(Slap hands on legs rhythmically to represent *walking* through the woods.)
"Look at the *tall* grass!" (Make hand gesture for *tall*; point to visual.)
"We can't go *around* it!" (Make hand gesture.)
"We can't go *over* it!" (Make hand gesture.)
"We have to go *through* it!" (Make hand gesture.)
(Rub hands together rhythmically, fingers pointing forward, to represent
  walking through the tall grass.)
"Look at the *big* lake!" (Make hand gesture for *big*, point to visual.)
"We can't go *around* it!" (Make hand gesture.)
"We can't go *over* it!" (Make hand gesture.)
"We have to go *through* it!" (Make hand gesture.)
(Move arms rhythmically in a swimming motion.)
"Look at that *tall* tree!" (Make hand gesture; point to visual.)
"Let's climb it!" (Pantomime hand-over-hand climbing motion.)
"Look for the bear!"
(Pantomime looking, hand over eyes and moving head slowly from side
  to side.)
"Do you see a bear?" (Class responds "No!" or "No, no bear!")
"Climb down the tree!" (Pantomime.)
"Look at the thick vines (bushes)!" (Make hand gesture; point to visual.)
"We can't go around them!" (Make hand gesture.)
"We can't go over them!" (Make hand gesture.)
"We have to go *through* them!" (Make hand gesture.)
(Do rhythmic motion with arms, pushing vines or bushes aside.)
"Look! I see a cave!" (Make dramatic pointing motion.)
"Let's go inside!" (Pat cheeks with mouth open to get hollow sound.)
"It's cold (hug arms and shiver) and dark." (Pass hands over eyes.)
"Let's feel around with our hands." (Make groping motions with hands
  in all directions.)
"I feel something!" (Touch tentatively, withdraw hand, touch again.)
"It's furry!" (Stroke as with an animal.)
"And wet!" (Withdraw hand quickly.)
"IT'S A BEAR!" (Pantomime shock and horror.)
(Pantomime each of the actions from above in the reverse order, *quickly*,
  as the narration proceeds.)
"Run out of the cave!"
"Run through the vines (bushes)!"
"Climb up the tree!"
"Look around!"
"Is that the BEAR?"
"Climb down the tree!"
"Swim the lake—fast!"
"Run through the tall grass!"

"Run through the woods!"
"We're home!" (Relax and slouch in the chair.)
"Lock the door!"

Reading Action Chain

This activity provides silent reading practice in a communicative setting. Give each student a card describing an action they are to perform and the action they will observe that triggers their response. (An example of a series of such cards follows.) Instruct students not to show their card to anyone else, to listen and watch very carefully, and to wait to start their action until at least two seconds after the preceding action has been completed. The object of the game is to proceed through the entire series without making mistakes and without leaving anyone out.

You will need to have a list of the actions in the correct order so that if the chain is broken, you will know what went wrong. (For lists of actions, see Linse, 1983, and Romijn and Seely, 1983.) If the chain breaks, the entire sequence starts over from the beginning, and the suspense grows.

This activity is easy to create, although it appears complicated; and it can be tailored to the personalities and special characteristics of each individual class and classroom. Write commands on three-by-five-inch note cards, one command on the bottom half of each card; make enough cards so that there is one card for each member of the class. Place the cards in an interesting sequence, including a beginning, an end, and surprises. Then write the first half of each card in the form of a subordinate clause referring to the card just preceding it (see below). Type out the directions for reference during the game and for future use, mix the cards, and distribute them for the game. You can make the game more complicated and longer if you make two cards for each student in the class.

If students have good writing skills, they often enjoy working in groups to create their own games. Group one might write the first five commands for the game and give a copy of their final command to group two. Group two uses that command as the cue for the first command in their series. They give a copy of their final command to group three, and so on, until the commands of all the groups are linked into a complete chain.

This is an example of a master plan for a reading action chain:

- After the teacher says "Begin," stand up and say "Good morning."
- After someone says "Good morning," go to the chalkboard and draw a triangle.
- After someone draws a triangle on the board, clap your hands slowly four times.
- After someone claps her or his hands four times, jump to the teacher's desk and back to your seat.

- After someone jumps to the teacher's desk and back to her or his seat, count backwards from 5 to 1.
- After someone counts backwards from 5 to 1, say "Blast-off" (appropriate target language equivalent) very loudly.
- After someone says "Blast-off," stand up, turn around two times and sit down.
- After someone stands up, turns around two times and sits down, turn *off* the lights.
- After someone turns *off* the lights say "It's dark in here."
- After someone says "It's dark in here," turn *on* the lights.
- After someone turns *on* the lights, go to the teacher and shake hands.
- After someone shakes hands with the teacher, go to the chalkboard and write the numbers 1 to 10 under the triangle.
- After someone writes the numbers 1 to 10 on the chalkboard, jump four times beside your desk.
- After someone jumps four times beside her or his desk, get up go to the pencil sharpener and sharpen your pencil.
- After someone sharpens her or his pencil, go to the board and erase numbers 1 to 5.
- After someone erases numbers 1 to 5 from the board, meow like a cat.
- After someone meows like a cat, say "Stop that!"
- After someone says "Stop that!" erase the triangle and numbers 6 to 10 from the board.
- After someone erases the triangle and numbers 6 to 10 from the board, say "That's all—good job!"

Guessing Games

What's Missing?

Place any number of objects, animals, colors, and so forth on a tray and make sure that all the students have a chance to clearly see the contents of the tray. Let them study what is there and explain that you will remove something and that they must guess what it is. Remove one item and hide it while the children's eyes are closed. Use a cover cloth for "peekers" (and to add a touch of drama). Repeat with a different item. Adapt the game to desired vocabulary.

Variation: Place small items with a clearly identifiable silhouette on the overhead projector. Turn off the projector, remove an item, and turn it on again. Have the children guess what is missing.

Hot and Cold

One student leaves the room and something is hidden in the classroom. The student returns and must find the hidden object. The rest of the class gives clues as to the location of the object. When the student is near the object they say "hot" and when the student is far away from the object they say "cold" (or anything else your decide).

Variation: Have the children count slowly or repeat a rhyme or other memorized material as a group. When IT comes nearer the hidden object they recite louder; when IT moves away from the object they recite more softly.

I'm Thinking of . . .

Begin the game by saying, in the target language, "I'm thinking of a child in the third row." The children guess the names of children in that row, saying in the target language "Is it Juan? Is it Marie? Is it Fritz?" until they guess the correct child. Continue with another child. (The game can include more language if you choose from the whole class and describe a student a little at a time until the class guesses who it is. Of course, you will start with details that many students share and withhold the clear identifiers until the end.)

You may play this game with clock times, numbers, objects in the classroom, cities in the target culture, or other suitable vocabulary. These are examples of starter statements: "I'm thinking of a time to meet my friend. What time is it?"; "I'm thinking of a number between 7 and 30. What number is it?"; "I'm thinking of a city in South America to visit on my vacation. What city is it?"

Variation: The student who makes the correct guess becomes the leader for the next round.

How Many Do I Have in My Hand?

Play this game with beans, buttons, seeds, marbles, candy-covered chocolates, coins from the target culture, or any other object that comes in handfuls. Reach into a container and take a number of the objects into your hand (not the one you write with), asking "How many _____s do I have in my hand?" The children guess the number and you write the guesses on the chalkboard. After the children have guessed ten to twelve numbers, you and the students count the objects together and determine if anyone guessed the exact number—or who made the closest guess.

Shoe Guessing Game

Blindfold one child who is IT (or simply have her or him close eyes). Then individual children from the class come up to IT and allow IT to feel their shoes. After feeling each shoe, IT guesses who the person is by asking, in the target language, "Is your name _____?". Variations include having children switch shoes or having them bring in a big, funny pair of shoes.

"New Games" Activities

People–to–People

1. Establish a rhythm and have the students clap the beat, as you say four times, "People to people" (translate into desired language).
2. Call out "Hand to hand" four times.
3. Have each student find a partner and place one hand on the partner's hand, repeating the action four times in the rhythm you set.
4. Return to "People to people" and have the students clap and move around four more times.
5. Call out another body parts combination (elbow to elbow, nose to nose, knee to knee) and have the students match up with a new partner. The game continues until all the body parts have been practiced, in a variety of combinations. Be careful not to suggest combinations that will embarrass the students.

Quick Lineups

Have the children line up by month of birthday, height, color of shirt, pants, shoes, hair, and so forth.

Animal Calls

Give the children the name of an animal whose "call" they have learned, two children for each animal. They try to find their partners by making the animal sound.

In-Class Food Activities

Experiences with food customs and with preparing food reflecting the target culture provide vivid context and motivation for language use. An ideal elementary school foreign language setting will offer access to a kitchen, in which food can be prepared with maximum involvement of the students. If no kitchen is available, many food activities can take place in the classroom itself with a minimum of equipment; for example, making sugar popcorn for students in French and German classes or making a French breakfast with French bread and unsalted butter or with a croissant and hot chocolate drunk out of bowls. German or French language classes might make cheese fondue

New Games—*People-to-People*

with buttermilk and Swiss cheese in an electric fondue pot. Spanish classes might prepare tacos, tostadas, or fried plantains.

Food activities add real spark to classes and do not have to require a great deal of class time. For example, crepes for an entire French class can be made ahead of time; you can prepare just a few during the actual class itself. You can demonstrate all the steps while the students pantomime the actions. (Valuable class time is saved because the students do not have to wait while each individual crepe is fried.)

Materials Needed for Food Activities

Paper plates
Plastic cutlery
Plastic or paper bowls, cups
Napkins
Electric fry pan
Popcorn popper

Electric fondue pot
Electric coffee maker or hot pot (for heating water)
Crepe maker

A Potpourri of Additional Games and Activities

Common Games

Relay Races
Charades
Spelling Bee
Hangman
Mystery Guest
Twenty Questions
Auction
Simon Says

Miscellaneous Activities

Go on a treasure hunt, scavenger hunt
Tour the school
Draw favorite foods on paper plates
Draw and cut out items for "store"
Draw family members
Draw community map and label it
Participate in a play with stick puppets or props
Do folk dancing
Make simulated target country currency
Make rubbings of coins from the target culture
Make murals
Make picture dictionaries
Plan a menu
Collect stamps or coins
Collect simple recipes
Cook
Go on field trip
Write a class poem
Dress dolls in native costumes
Model animals or other figures with clay
Make clocks
Make paper bag puppets, dolls, masks
Draw faces on paper plates to show feelings
Make mobiles on many topics: five senses, food groups, pets, family

Make home or school floor plan
Pantomime feelings, illnesses
Make or wear costumes from other countries to learn clothing
Make dioramas in a shoebox
"Shop" from a target language catalogue

USING PUPPETS IN THE CLASSROOM

There are few teaching aids in the elementary school as versatile and appealing as puppets, stuffed animals, and toys. Puppets can take on the role of personalities otherwise not present in the classroom, such as an adult male if the teacher is female, a person who is much older or younger than members of the class, a foreign visitor, a pet, or a special friend to all. A puppet can serve as an alter ego for the teacher, performing exaggerated or foolish actions that the teacher can react to or build on. Puppets can become the second fluent speaker in a conversational exchange, modeling the kind of interaction which the children can someday hope to achieve. Sometimes a puppet becomes the "difficult student" who can't do anything right, or who repeatedly gets into trouble by forgetting to obey the rules. These personalities make every class member feel proud of what they know and how they behave, and the puppet misbehavior gives the teacher a chance to model the rules in a very effective way—and the consequences of breaking them.

Because puppets can be so colorful and often have such distinctive personalities, they provide the ideal subject for descriptions that go beyond simple clothing, size, and colors to include disposition, family, and imagined background. The puppet can also take on the role of teacher, modeling the process of role reversal for the class and encouraging the students to try being the teacher. While the puppet is the teacher, the actual teacher can demonstrate actions or behaviors that will later be expected from the class.

A puppet is an ideal foil for many minidramas that help to create a meaningful classroom context. One favorite puppet character, a colorful frog with a tongue that can be made to pop out of its opened mouth, helps to teach a class to say "please" in the following situation:

Teacher: (holds up frog as if talking very seriously to it) "Show us your tongue, Mr. Frog!"

Frog: (shakes its head)

Teacher: (pleadingly) "Please?"

Frog: (shakes head)

Teacher: (more emphatically) "Please?"

Frog: (shakes head vehemently)

Puppets are a useful tool.

Teacher: (even more urgently) "Please? PLEASE?"

Frog: (shakes head almost violently)

Teacher: (conspiratorially to class) "*You* say please." (implying, "Maybe he'll listen to *you*.")

Class: "Please!"

Frog: (shakes head less emphatically)

Teacher: (to class, in a stage whisper) "Say please—louder."

Class: "Please!"

Frog: (shakes head again)

Teacher: (to class, stage whisper) "Say please twice."

Class: "Please, please!"

Frog: (pauses, looks at the class, shows the tongue)

Teacher: (to frog, beaming) "Thank you, Mr. Frog!"

In any such exchange it is always important for the teacher to play the "ham," overacting from beginning to end.

Students, as well as teachers, enjoy working with puppets and bringing their personalities to life. In early stages, the desire to hold a puppet or a stuffed animal can motivate even a very shy student to tell the teacher or a classmate, "Please give me the frog." In one popular activity, the teacher draws puppets, stuffed animals, and other items from a magic box or from a large bag and hands them to students who volunteer to hold them. When it turns out that there are not enough items to go around, the children are invited to request them from one another, using the phrase the teacher has already used dozens of times in class to collect objects after a circle activity: "Please give me the _____." A lively exchange of puppets and animals inevitably results, all triggered by language use.

In certain activities the puppet can "take the place" of the student, just as sometimes a puppet takes the teacher's place. Many students who are very hesitant about speaking in class will do so much more easily if they are speaking through the new personality of a puppet, especially if the puppet has an established classroom personality to maintain and if all class members are familiar with the routines in which the puppets take part. Some class periods might begin with the call for volunteers: "Who would like to be Mr. Frog today? Who would like to be Schnick-Schnack, the witch?" As children develop more speaking skills and come to know their puppet friends well, they may wish to work together to plan conversations between the puppets, or even short puppet plays.

Puppets can be obtained from commercial sources; or they can be teacher-made or made by the children in the class. A few puppets that specifically reflect elements of the target culture are especially precious participants in the class, but any puppet with personality is a good choice. It is wise to avoid choosing puppets with high commercial visibility, such as those representing popular cartoon characters, so that children are free from prior associations and can participate fully in the imaginary lives of their friends in the language class.

USING EXAGGERATION

A very small comb or tiny sunglasses might be hidden in an egg or in a magic box or somewhere else in the room. The exaggeration lends a sense of excitement and enjoyment to a "seek-and-find" activity. In an action chain in which a child goes to the mirror to comb her or his hair, using a huge comb adds humor to the activity. A regular comb or an imaginary comb do not have the same appeal. When an activity is repeated with the added factor of exaggeration, it becomes a new activity for the class and they will participate with enthusiasm.

SONGS IN THE CURRICULUM

Music is one of the most appealing and effective entry points into a new language and culture. When used for background or listening experiences, music from the target culture adds to the authenticity of the language setting. Songs learned in the target language have the double benefit of giving children experience with an important dimension of the target culture and helping them to internalize the vocabulary, rhythms, and structures of the new language.

Songs can play an important role in every unit and every class period. They are most effective when they are an integrated part of the curriculum, selected for their relationship to all of the activities and vocabulary in a class period and not regarded as an add-on, or filler, should there be extra time available.

Choosing Songs

Choose songs with a vocabulary that is limited and compatible with the language being used in the classroom so that the words and concepts in the song reinforce or introduce material used for many other activities in the curriculum. Some children's songs from the target culture have a greater vocabulary load than children in the first several years of an elementary school foreign language program can manage with understanding and enjoyment.

Choose songs with a limited musical challenge, especially in the primary grades. A song that is musically very difficult will require considerable time just for learning the music, and the language objectives will be overshadowed. Consult with the music teacher about the skills of a specific class, but in general be aware that a simple song moves stepwise from note to note, rather than including wide melodic leaps, and it should have a limited range of notes from low to high. The rhythm should be straightforward and repetitive. Even when they are very simple, songs should be *interesting* in both melody and rhythm. Also, the topics for songs should be within the experiences of the children in the class and of real interest to them.

Choose songs with a potential for actions, dramatization, rhythm accompaniment, or performance (such as a round or canon). Children in primary grades have great difficulty singing rounds, but they participate enthusiastically in songs accompanied by actions, and the actions help children to remember the words and their meanings.

Especially in the early stages of instruction choose songs that are highly repetitive in their text, rhythm, and melody; it is very helpful to use songs that have a refrain.

The best song choices are those that are popular in the cultures of the target language because they reflect the target culture and provide children with an experience in common with native speakers. Songs translated from English have the advantage of familiarity, but they lack cultural authenticity.

Teaching a Song

Teachers do not have to be solo singers to be effective in presenting a song to their students. If teachers know a song they can present it to the class. A less than perfect voice can be an especially good model for children, because it is easier for them to identify with, and even shy singers may feel that they can safely participate.

The teaching of a song will proceed much more smoothly if a careful sequence is followed:

Step 1—Prepare the Students

Prepare the students by telling them what the song is about, preferably in the target language, making heavy use of visuals and gestures. Motivate the students to learn the song by sharing something about the setting of the song, the possibilities for actions or dramatization, or when or how it is sung in another country. Play a recording or sing the entire song so that students know what they are working toward. Note that some recordings made by children's choirs in the target culture are pitched so high that they cannot comfortably be used to provide an accompaniment for classroom singing, even though they may be very successful in motivating the activity.

Step 2—Go Through the Words

Go through the words to make sure the students understand them, or at least that they understand the key words necessary for singing the song meaningfully and with enjoyment. Have the class listen for vocabulary they already know, and ask them to recall the context in which they have used it before. For example, if there is a vocabulary item they know, they can recall a song, game, or situation in which they used it and perhaps some of the things they know about the item. This helps children to appreciate the cumulative nature of language acquisition and to listen for known vocabulary and meanings even in new material. Place new vocabulary in context and illustrate with gestures and visuals, using English only as a last resort. There should be very little new vocabulary in any new song, as most of it should have been introduced in other contexts several days before you introduce the song.

Step 3—Speak the Song Line by Line

Speak the song line by line and have the students repeat the words.

Step 4—Sing a Line at a Time

Sing the song a line at a time and have the students sing it back. Practice each line several times, until the children can sing it independently. Then practice it two lines at a time (for a song that has about 4 lines), and then put the entire song together.

Four lines of a song is a good amount to teach during a single class period. If the song is longer and if it has a refrain, teach the refrain first, so that there is a sense of closure even though the entire song cannot be completed in one day.

Step 5—Add Rhythmic Accompaniment

After the students have learned the song and enjoy it, begin to add rhythmic accompaniment such as clapping, finger snapping, foot stamping, or hand shuffling. Use Orff and rhythm instruments to make the background even more sophisticated. Consult the music teacher for additional suggestions.

If the song includes motions, teach them together with the words and the music; learning each part of the song will reinforce learning the others. If the song can be used for a game or dramatic play, the students can use it for its real purpose as soon as they have learned the words and music thoroughly.

If the song is a round, perform it first with the class taking one part and the teacher the other. Then divide the class into two parts, then three or more, as the round dictates. Rounds are especially satisfying when they end on a chord rather than just by having groups drop out at the end. If the first group holds the final note and the second group holds the note at the end of the next-to-last phrase, and so on, then the final sound is sometimes very impressive.

Step 6—Enjoy Singing!

Enjoy singing a growing repertoire of lively, interesting songs with children in your classes!

Here are some suggestions if you consider yourself to be a nonsinger:

- Ask a friend or an advanced student in your language to record the song for you, line by line, just as you will teach it.
- Use an electronic keyboard; program the melody or have someone do it for you; play the melody line by line in class.
- Use a tape that comes with a song book and play the song line by line during the teaching phase.
- Play the melody on a recorder or another instrument.

OVERHEAD PROJECTOR ACTIVITIES

You may project visuals on the screen using a variety of techniques:

- Cover the transparency with a piece of paper and gradually reveal the entire transparency.

- Use a "peep show" technique to show selected parts of the transparency. Make a mask with "windows" by cutting and hinging doors in an overlay made of stiff paper or card stock. Open the windows to reveal parts of the picture, and allow the students to guess what the picture is or what story lies behind the picture. As an alternative, make a single hole in an overlay mask and move it around the transparency at the request of class members, so that they can see various small parts of the picture and come to conclusions as to what the picture is about.

- Use overlays to put together a picture in various stages or to uncover or reveal various parts of a transparency in a step-by-step sequence.

- Project the outlines of three dimensional objects by laying them on the glass stage.

- Make shadows on the screen using hand motions. This is especially effective when the projector is placed behind a sheet or translucent screen and the shadow play takes place between the projector and the screen.

- Make silhouette stories by cutting out shapes and moving the shapes around to animate a story or dramatize a point in a lesson.

- Play *What's Missing?* games by putting a collection of physical objects or pictures of objects on the overhead projector. Turn off the projector and take away one object at a time; then turn on the projector and have the students recognize which object is missing.

- Draw simple maps and add paper cutout figures to indicate streets, houses, landmarks, people, and so forth.

SUMMARY

Games and activities are the classroom means by which the communicative goals of the elementary school foreign language program are achieved. They involve the students and the teacher in meaningful, motivating situations within which real information is exchanged. Guidelines are presented to assist the teacher in choosing and devising games and activities which will be both successful and communicative, and a selection of classroom tested games illustrates principles from the guidelines. Among the most important of these guidelines are the requirements that a game or activity should be enjoyable, that the use of language must play an important role in the activity, and that all students should be involved or engaged at all times.

FOR STUDY AND DISCUSSION

1. Choose a game recommended in a teacher's manual, or one you have actually used or observed in an elementary school foreign language classroom. Evaluate it according to the guidelines for games discussed in this chapter.

2. Choose a game from among those described in this chapter which call for little or no spoken language to be used by the children. Write a script for the teacher role in introducing and conducting this game, demonstrating how the teacher surrounds the activity with language and provides the class with comprehensible input.

3. Respond to a secondary-school language teacher who complains, "All you do in the elementary school is give them fun and games. When they get to our program and find out that really learning languages requires some work, they are disillusioned and they drop out. I'd rather just wait and start them out when they get to high school."

4. Choose a song for children that meets the guidelines suggested in this chapter. Explain how it might fit into a specific unit of instruction; describe the vocabulary and concepts it can be used to teach or reinforce; and discuss the preparation that would take place before you began to teach the song. Then demonstrate actually teaching the song to the class, using the target language.

5. Plan a lesson in which you use a puppet to introduce an important concept or a portion of a common conversational exchange. Refer to the conversation with the frog in this chapter as an idea-starter. Demonstrate the lesson to your class. Caution: Keep it simple!

FOR FURTHER READING

The following sources are recommended for additional information about material covered in this chapter. Chapter citations are documented in *Works Cited* at the end of the volume.

Ashworth, Mary, and Patricia Wakefield. *Teaching the Non-English Speaking Child: Grades K-2*. Washington DC: Center for Applied Linguistics, 1982.

Fluegelman, Andrew, ed. *The New Games Book*. Garden City, NY: Dolphin Books, Doubleday, 1976.

Hassall, Peter John. *English by Magic. A Resource Book*. Oxford, England: Pergamon Press, 1985.

Holden, Susan, ed. *Teaching Children*. London: Modern English Publications, 1980.

Hubp, Loretta Burke. *Let's Play Games in Spanish, Book I*. Skokie, IL: National Textbook Company, 1968.

Klippel, Friederike. *Keep Talking. Communicative Fluency Activities for Language Teaching*. New York: Cambridge University Press, 1984.

Lee, W.R. *Language Teaching Games and Contests*. 2d ed. Oxford: Oxford University Press, 1984.

Lohfert, Walter. *Kommunikative Spiele für Deutsch als Fremdsprache*. Munich: Max Hueber Verlag, 1983.

MacDonald, Marion, and Sue Rogers-Gordon. *Action Plans: 80 Student–Centered Language Activities*. Rowley, MA: Newbury House, 1984.

Malay, Alan, and Alan Duff. *Drama Techniques in Language Teaching*. New York: Cambridge University Press, 1978.

Malay, Alan, and Alan Duff. *Sounds Interesting*. New York: Cambridge University Press, 1975. Accompanied by cassette tape.

Omaggio, Alice C. *Games and Simulations in the Foreign Language Classroom*. Arlington, VA: Center for Applied Linguistics, 1978.

Smith, Stephen. *The Theater Arts and the Teaching of Second Languages*. Reading, MA: Addison–Wesley, 1984.

Spencer, Zane A. *150 Plus! Games and Activities for Early Childhood*. Belmont, CA: Fearon, 1976.

Wright, Andrew, D. Betteridge, and M. Buckby. *Games for Language Learning*. 2d ed. New York: Cambridge University Press, 1984.

Zamora, Gloria Rodriguez, and Rebecca Maria Barrera. *Nuevo Amanecer Circle Time Activity Book*. Lincolnwood, IL: National Textbook Company, 1985.

Zamora, Gloria Rodriguez, and Rebecca Maria Barrera. *Nuevo Amanecer Learning Center Idea Book*. Lincolnwood, IL: National Textbook Company, 1985.

Chapter 14

Looking at Related Issues: Language Proficiency and Teacher Preparation

THE PROFICIENCY MOVEMENT AND ELEMENTARY SCHOOL FOREIGN LANGUAGES

Previous attempts to emphasize communication have been undermined by the fact that academic expectations and measures of achievement have been based on grammar as an organizing principle and on the teaching of discrete points as a standard practice. This is one reason for the poor articulation in the past between elementary school foreign language programs and the secondary school programs into which they fed.

Fortunately for the prospects of the new orientation toward communication, the climate of academic expectations and evaluation is being changed by the proficiency movement and the *ACTFL Proficiency Guidelines* (Byrnes and Canale 1987). Emphasis is now shifting from grammar and discrete-item testing to global evaluation of listening and speaking, reading and writing. Teachers can permit themselves to evaluate for communication of meaning as well as, though not to the total exclusion of, degree of accuracy, and students can be rewarded for a much broader range of language ability and performance.

The American Council on the Teaching of Foreign Languages (ACTFL) turned to the experiences of the Interagency Language Roundtable (ILR) of the United States government in an effort to describe the outcomes of communicative language teaching and learning in a manner that would be understood across the profession and by interested individuals and agencies outside the field. The ILR had developed an oral proficiency interview to screen candidates for foreign service and other government positions that require a high degree of language fluency. This interview, developed for highly motivated adults operating in a sophisticated target-language setting, had to be adapted for the secondary school and college student population. Considerably finer discrimination was required at the lower levels of proficiency because those are the levels at which most secondary school and college students are likely to perform.

Descriptions of performance at four broad levels of proficiency for listening, speaking, reading, and writing were published by ACTFL in the fall of 1986, after several years of discussion and revision. These guidelines describe student language performance in terms of function, content, and accuracy of the message being delivered or received. They are intended to assist teachers in setting realistic goals for their programs at the secondary school and college levels.

Most elementary school foreign language teachers find that the ACTFL guidelines in their present form are difficult to apply directly to the curriculum of the elementary school program. Many of the functions and much of the content described are not closely related to the interests and needs of children. Yet the principle of purposeful language use is clearly held in common at all levels of communicative language teaching. Until more work has been done with adaptation of the guidelines to the needs of the elementary school program, they can serve the elementary school foreign language teacher very well as a guide to the future uses to which the language taught in the elementary school will be put. This can make the guidelines an important tool for bridging the gap between elementary school and secondary school programs.

The Wisconsin *Guide to Curriculum Planning in Foreign Languages* (Grittner 1985) identifies levels of proficiency that are typically attainable at Level One (150 hours of instruction), Level Two (300 hours of instruction), Level Three (450 hours of instruction) and Level Four (600 hours of instruction) in the secondary school curriculum. Most elementary school foreign language programs can expect to achieve the goals of Level One or Level Two, given the typical amount of time available in programs that are from one to six years long. The 1986 generic proficiency guidelines are provided here for listening, speaking, reading, and writing at the end of Level One, Level Two, and Level Three. Elementary school teachers will find it interesting to note what high school students typically can achieve at these levels, and they can keep these expectations in mind as they plan their own lessons and curricula.

The ACTFL Guidelines (Figure 5) give us a new tool for looking at the outcomes of instruction. This tool can help elementary school foreign language teachers to be both more realistic in their goals for instruction *and* more realistic in their claims for their programs.

PREPARATION OF TEACHERS

The elementary school foreign language teacher situation at the end of the 1980s is similar to that of the 1960s: demand overwhelms supply and many programs are being staffed by teachers without specific preparation in teaching foreign languages to children, and sometimes even by teachers who have limited language skills themselves. Few states have addressed the issue of special licensure or certification for foreign language teachers at the elementary school level, so there is little by way of a standard for schools to use in evaluating and employing a potential teacher. Few institutions of higher education have staff and programs in place to prepare teachers for this emerging field.

Much of the burden of elementary school foreign language teacher preparation has been laid on workshops, summer institutes, and teacher in-service work. Although this "bandage" approach cannot be expected to replace a profession-wide commitment to quality teacher preparation, a number of priorities in teacher background and skills have begun to emerge. These priorities were effectively summarized by Myriam Met at a language conference in Raleigh, North Carolina, on March 17, 1987:

The effective elementary school foreign language teacher has been prepared to do the following:

1. Understand and like children

2. Be skilled in the management of the elementary school classroom

   - Create an affective and physical environment in which learning happens
   - Understand and apply the research on school and teacher effectiveness

3. Know the elementary school curriculum

   - Approach instruction from a holistic, integrated, content-based perspective
   - Select and sequence activities that are appropriate to the developmental needs of the child

4. Teach second language reading and writing to learners who are developing first language literacy skills, so that the foreign language program can build on these skills rather than fighting with what is going on in the first language curriculum

5. Understand the precepts of communicative language teaching and draw from a repertoire of strategies to implement these precepts

6. Use the target language fluently, with a high degree of cultural appropriateness

7. Draw on an excellent understanding of the target culture, especially as it relates to children, including children's literature

A 1987 grant to the National Council for Foreign Languages and International Studies (NCFLIS) was intended to facilitate the development of guidelines and recommendations for the preparation of teachers of all types of elementary school foreign language programs. The working papers resulting from this grant, available from NCFLIS in 1989, when combined with the efforts of the professional foreign language education organizations and the National Network for Early Language Learning, will be of great assistance in the development of standards and teacher preparation programs throughout the United States.

SUMMARY

The preparation and licensure of teachers for elementary school foreign language programs is of the highest priority if foreign language programs are to become an important part of the elementary school curriculum. An elementary school foreign language teacher needs to have the qualities of both an excellent foreign language teacher and an excellent elementary school teacher. As these qualities are clearly identified and defined, programs can be developed to prepare the best possible teachers for these programs.

One of the most promising movements with potential for genuine change and growth within foreign language education may well be the proficiency movement, spearheaded by ACTFL and the ACTFL Proficiency Guidelines. While the guidelines themselves may be of less direct usefulness to the elementary school teacher, it is important that elementary school foreign language instruction take place in a manner that prepares students for programs in which these guidelines have an important role.

As elementary school foreign language programs emerge to play an important role in the education of every child, the challenges of defining goals clearly and of preparing teachers effectively take on considerable significance. There is every evidence that these challenges are being met and that foreign languages for elementary school children will continue to develop as a secure and well-grounded part of the curriculum, unshaken by fad and respected throughout the education community.

FOR STUDY AND DISCUSSION

1. Discuss why it is important that states develop licensure standards for teachers of foreign languages at the elementary school level.
2. Using the elementary school foreign language setting you know best, apply the descriptions in the proficiency guidelines cited in this chapter

and identify which of them are appropriate for the children you have seen.

FOR FURTHER READING

The following sources are recommended for additional information about material covered in this chapter. Chapter citations are documented in *Works Cited* at the end of the volume.

ACTFL. *Guidelines for Foreign Language Teacher Education Programs*. Hastings-On-Hudson, NY: American Council on the Teaching of Foreign Languages. In press.

Byrnes, Heidi, and Michael Canale, eds. *Defining and Developing Proficiency: Guidelines, Implementations, and Concepts*. Lincolnwood, IL: National Textbook Company, 1987.

Level	Minimal Contact Hours	Proficiency Descriptor	Examples from ACTFL 1986 Generic Listening Proficiency Descriptions	Examples From ACTFL 1986 Generic Speaking Proficiency Descriptions
I	150	Novice-High	Able to understand short, learned utterances and some sentence-length utterances, particularly where content strongly supports understanding and speech is clearly audible. Comprehends words and phrases from simple questions, statements, high-frequency commands and courtesy formulae. May require repetition, rephrasing and/or a slowed rate of speech for comprehension.	Able to satisfy partially the requirements of basic communicative exchanges by relying heavily on learned utterances but occasionally expanding these through simple recombinations of their elements. Can ask questions or make statements involving learned material. Shows signs of spontaneity although this falls short of real autonomy of expression. Speech continues to consist of learned utterances rather than of personalized situationally adapted ones. Vocabulary centers on areas such as basic objects, places, and most common kinship terms. Pronunciation may still be strongly influenced by first language. Errors are frequent and, in spite of repetition, some Novice-High speakers will have difficulty being understood even by sympathetic interlocutors.
II	300	Intermediate-Low	Able to understand sentence-length utterances which consist of recombinations of learned elements in a limited number of content areas, particularly if strongly supported by the situational context. Content refers to basic personal background and needs, social conventions and routine tasks, such as getting meals and receiving simple instructions and directions. Listening tasks pertain primarily to spontaneous face-to-face conversations. Understanding	Able to handle successfully a limited number of interactive, task-oriented and social situations. Can ask and answer questions, initiate and respond to simple statements and maintain face-to-face conversation, although in a highly restricted manner and with much linguistic inaccuracy. Within these limitations, can perform such tasks as introducing self, ordering a meal, asking directions, and making purchases. Vocabulary is adequate to express only the

			most elementary needs. Strong interference from the native language may occur. Misunderstandings frequently arise, but with repetition, the Intermediate-Low speaker can generally be understood by sympathetic interlocutors.	is often uneven; repetition and rewording may be necessary. Misunderstanding in both main ideas and details arises frequently.
III	450	Intermediate-Mid	Able to handle successfully a variety of uncomplicated, basic and communicative tasks and social situations. Can talk simply about self and family members. Can ask and answer questions and participate in simple conversations on topics beyond the most immediate needs; e.g., personal history and leisure time activities. Utterance length increases slightly, but speech may continue to be characterized by frequent long pauses, since the smooth incorporation of even basic conversational strategies is often hindered as the speaker struggles to create appropriate language forms. Pronunciation may continue to be strongly influenced by first language and fluency may still be strained. Although misunderstandings still arise, the Intermediate-Mid speaker can generally be understood by sympathetic interlocutors.	Able to understand sentence-length utterances which consist of recombinations of learned utterances on a variety of topics. Content continues to refer primarily to basic personal background and needs, social conventions, and somewhat more complex tasks, such as lodging, transportation, and shopping. Additional content areas include some personal interests and activities, and a greater diversity of instructions and directions. Listening tasks not only pertain to spontaneous face-to-face conversations but also to short routine telephone conversations and some deliberate speech, such as simple announcements and reports over the media. Understanding continues to be uneven.

(Continued on pages 278–279.)

Level	Minimal Contact Hours	Proficiency Descriptor	Examples from ACTFL 1986 Generic Reading Proficiency Descriptions	Examples From ACTFL 1986 Generic Writing Proficiency Descriptions
I	150	Novice-High	Has sufficient control of the writing system to interpret written language in areas of practical need. Where vocabulary has been learned, can read for instruction and directional purposes standardized messages, phrases or expressions, such as some items on menus, schedules, timetables, maps, and signs. At times, but not on a consistent basis, the Novice-High level reader may be able to derive meaning from material at a slightly higher level where context and/or extralinguistic background knowledge are supportive.	Able to write simple fixed expressions and limited memorized material and some combinations thereof. Can supply information on simple forms and documents. Can write names, numbers, dates, own nationality, and other simple autobiographical information as well as some short phrases and simple lists. Can write all the symbols in an alphabet or syllabic system or 50–100 characters or compounds in a character writing system. Spelling and representation of symbols (letters, syllables, characters) may be partially correct.
II	300	Intermediate-Low	Able to understand main ideas and/or some facts from the simplest connected texts dealing with basic personal and social needs. Such texts are linguistically noncomplex and have a clear underlying internal structure, for example, chronological sequencing. They impart basic information about which the reader has to make only minimal suppositions or to which the reader brings personal interest and/or information. Examples include messages with social purposes or information for the widest possible audience, such as public announcements and short, straightforward instructions dealing with public life. Some misunderstandings will occur.	Able to meet limited practical writing needs. Can write short messages, postcards, and take down simple notes, such as telephone messages. Can create statements or questions within the scope of limited language experience. Material produced consists of recombinations of learned vocabulary and structures into simple sentences on very familiar topics. Language is inadequate to express in writing anything but elementary needs. Frequent errors in grammar, vocabulary, punctuation, spelling and in formation of nonalphabetic symbols, but writing can be understood by natives used to the writing of nonnatives.

III	450	Intermediate-Mid	Able to read consistently with increased understanding simple connected texts dealing with a variety of basic and social needs. Such texts are still linguistically noncomplex and have a clear underlying internal structure. They impart basic information about which the reader has to make minimal suppositions and to which the reader brings personal interest and/or knowledge. Examples may include short, straightforward descriptions of persons, places, and things written for a wide audience.	Able to meet a number of practical writing needs. Can write short, simple letters. Content involves personal preferences, daily routine, everyday events, and other topics grounded in personal experience. Can express present time or at least one other time frame or aspect consistently, e.g., nonpast, habitual, imperfective. Evidence of control of the syntax of noncomplex sentences and basic inflectional morphology, such as declensions and conjugation. Writing tends to be a loose collection of sentences or sentence fragments on a given topic and provides little evidence of conscious organization. Can be understood by natives used to the writing of nonnatives.

Figure 5. ACTFL Proficiency Guidelines

Source: Excerpted from Byrnes, Heidi, and Michael Canale, eds. *Defining and Developing Proficiency: Guidelines, Implementations, and Concepts.* Lincolnwood IL: National Textbook Company, 1987:15–24. Used by permission.

Appendixes

Appendix A

Sample Lesson Plans

German Demonstration Class
8 Days / 90 Minutes Per Day

SUMMER ELEMENTARY SCHOOL
FOREIGN LANGUAGE METHODS CLASS
CONCORDIA COLLEGE
MOORHEAD, MINNESOTA

The materials that follow represent the first half of the lesson plans developed for a fifteen-day class that meets for 90 minutes per day in a summer session at Concordia College. Each class has approximately fifteen children, ranging in age from seven to eleven. The summer classes incorporate craft and food activities on a regular basis, but otherwise most materials and activities are typical of what might take place in a regular classroom during the school year. Except where specifically indicated, all activities are conducted *in the target language*. The material presented in these eight days of lessons could be used over a period of *five to eight weeks in a typical FLES or FLEX setting*.

These are not intended to be "model" lessons. They are offered in the same spirit of sharing that has guided the rest of this book. We hope that they will serve as idea-starters for elementary school foreign language teachers of *every* language.

Day 1
Objectives

Children will be able to do the following:

- Identify words in English which are related to German
- Pronounce their own German names so they are recognizable
- Explain how they are going to learn German (through listening and acting out responses, speaking later)

- Identify places where German is spoken as a first language
- Participate in group response to greetings
- Respond to the following commands, in a group and individually:

English	Plural	Singular
(Stand up.)	Steht auf!	Steh auf!
(Sit down.)	Setzt euch!	Setz dich!
(Turn around.)	Dreht euch um!	Dreh dich um!
(Come here.)	Kommt her!	Komm her!
(Point to __.)	Zeigt auf __!	Zeig auf __!
(Take __.)	Nehmt __!	Nimm __!
(Give me __.)	Gebt mir __!	Gib mir __!

- Choose the five colors of the flags of German-speaking countries: *rot* (red), *weiß* (white), *gold* (gold), *schwarz* (black), *blau* (blue)

Materials

- Name tags on tagboard (with yarn long enough to hang around neck), two options for each child—placed in pocket chart
- Pocket chart
- Cassette player, cassette of baroque string music
- Globe, map, floor map
- Flags of *DDR* (German Democratic Republic), *BRD* (Federal Republic of Germany), *die Schweiz* (Switzerland), *Liechtenstein*, *Österreich* (Austria)
- Glue, paper strips, 4" × 6" cards, 3" × 5" cards, felt pens, flag symbols
- Colored circles: *rot* (red), *weiß* (white), *schwarz* (black), *gold* (gold), *blau* (blue)
- Very large blank calendar outline for 5-day week (approximately 24" by 36", with squares drawn for each day of the week), initialed for days (*Mo* = *Montag*, *Di* = *Dienstag*, *Mi* = *Mittwoch*, *Do* = *Donnerstag*, F = *Freitag*)

Introduction

The following could be presented by the teacher in English:

- Children's relatives who are German
- German words that have "relatives" in English words:

Gesundheit	Winter	Kindergarten	Sommer
Ball	Schiff	kaputt	Arm
Hand	Elefant	Finger	Auto
braun	Volkswagen		kalt, warm

- Places where German is spoken—point out on map
- Importance of German as a *second* language
- Special advantages of the child learner
- Goals—using German, mostly listening and responding at first
- Listening habits (listen with ears, eyes, mouth, sometimes hands and feet)
- Explanation of use of German names: how they will be chosen; options for changing names later if they wish

Activities

1. Greet class with "Guten Morgen, Klasse!" Use gestures to call for imitation of "Guten Morgen, Frau/Fräulein/Herr _____!"
2. Introduce the course, as above.
3. Play music (baroque string music is very effective) in the background and read all the names (that have been prepared in advance as name tags and placed in the pocket chart). The second time through, children will raise hands for the names they would like to adopt for the duration of the class. In the case of a tie, move on and have the children choose again on the next round of names.
4. Go around class introducing each child by her or his new name. Pronounce each name several times, call for several group imitations of the names, then individual imitation from child whose name is being practiced. Intersperse with rapid group imitations of names already given, double imitations, changes of voice to indicate surprise, anger, and so forth.
5. Repeat commands with gestures, to entire group: "Steht auf! Setzt euch! Dreht euch um!" (Stand up. Sit down. Turn around.)
6. Repeat to assistant or puppet (or child, with appropriate teacher cueing): "Steh auf! Komm her! Nimm rot! Gib mir rot! Gib Michael rot! Setz dich!" and so forth. (Stand up. Come here. Take [the] red. Give me [the] red. Give Michael [the] red. Sit down.)

   Place colors on floor in center of circle. Have children point to and take colors as directed, giving them to the teacher or to one another. Add colors gradually and mix up the commands to add surprise and variety. Have children sit down on the floor after they have performed, until all children are sitting on the floor. Add colors until all five for the flags have been learned. (Note: Children do not repeat commands—they simply follow them!) At the end of the activity, collect all the colors by asking for them in German from the children who have them.
7. Turn on cassette of baroque music again, and present flags of the countries dramatically, laying them on the appropriate countries on the

floor map of Europe. Incorporate other information, in German, about size of countries, and so forth. Ask children to pick up, give the teacher or each other flags of each of the countries. Repeat until all flags have been practiced.

8. Point out how much German has been used thus far! Explain craft activity in German—each child will choose a flag and will claim that country as her or his home country (you can follow through with this activity for the entire duration of the course or for just a few days). Children will make flags of their countries using 4" × 6" cards, precut strips of construction paper, and precut symbols for *DDR* and *Schweiz*. Attach a 3" × 5" card with glue to bottom of flag and have each child write her or his name on the card.

9. Send children to tables to work, using German to direct them.

10. Have children complete craft activity. Be alert for children putting *DDR* and *BRD* stripes on in the wrong order.

11. Review what has been learned and place the following on the blank calendar outline: miniature flags, names that have been lettered on small construction-paper stars, and shapes with the five colors they have learned.

12. Clean up and model "Auf Wiedersehen!" Shake hands with each child on the way out, collect name tags.

Day 2
Objectives

Children will be able to do the following:

- Associate German names with the children in the class
- Successfully pronounce their own German names and the name of at least one other child
- Respond to previous commands, colors
- Respond to the following new commands:

English	Plural	Singular
(Raise your hands.)	Hebt die Hand!	Heb die Hand!
(Hand down.)	Hand 'runter!	Hand 'runter!
(Jump.)	Springt!	Springe!
(Touch ___.)	Faβt ___ an!	Faβ ___ an!
(Lay ___ on ___.)	Legt ___ auf ___!	Leg ___ auf ___!

- Identify and manipulate numbers 1 to 3 when directed to do so; be able to do things a certain number of times (*einmal, zweimal, dreimal*), on command.

- Respond to the following vocabulary:

  (head)   der Kopf
  (foot)   der Fuß
  (knee)   das Knie
  (dog)   der Hund
  (witch)   die Hexe
  (frog)   der Frosch

- Say the numbers *eins, zwei,* and *drei* clearly with the group and participate confidently in the game rhyme

Materials

- *Wundertüte* (magic-mystery box—see chapter 12)
- Jump rope
- Puppets: dog, witch, frog
- Large numbers 1 to 3
- Flags
- Aluminum pie plate
- Large colored circles: *rot, schwarz, gold, blau, weiß, gelb* (yellow), *grün* (green), *braun* (brown).
- Electronic keyboard or rhythm box
- Precut construction-paper heads, paper hair in all learned colors for clown or jumping jack (*Hampelmann*) craft activity
- Calendar symbols for information learned today

Activities

1. Exchange "Guten Morgen" greeting with class as a group.
2. Have entire group respond to commands such as: "Steht auf!" (Stand up.) "Setzt euch!" (Sit down.) "Dreht euch um!" (Turn around.) Add "Hebt die Hand!" (Raise your hand.) "Hand 'runter!" (Hand down.)
3. Call on individual children: "Steh auf! Komm her!" (Stand up. Come here.) Give a child another child's name tag and have her or him give it to the correct owner: "Gib __ den Namen!" Greet the child with the name tag and shake hands. Repeat until all names are distributed.
4. Take attendance using calendar—have each child remove name from the calendar in the square for Day 1 and place it on the square for Day 2: "Nimm den Namen von (Day 1) . Kleb' den Namen an (Day 2) ."

5. Play *Echospiel* (Echo Game). Say child's name; have the class say name in unison; have child say own name. Use electronic keyboard, swing rhythm, to establish rhythm for game after first few attempts.

6. Play *Tellerdrehen* (Spin the Plate). Begin by asking "Wollen wir spielen?" (Shall we play?). Spin the plate and call a child's name. Child tries to catch plate before it falls. Then the child spins the plate and calls another name. Repeat until all children have had a turn, or until just before enthusiasm for the game begins to wane.

7. Review colors from yesterday and add three new colors, using procedures of taking and giving colors on command. Add the following:

   Faβ ＿ an! (Touch ＿.)

   Leg ＿ auf Annas Fuβ! (Knie, Kopf) (Lay ＿ on Anna's foot, knee, head.)

   Heb gold! (Lift up gold, *rot, weiβ*, and so forth.)

   Heb braun und gelb! (Lift up brown and yellow.)

   Heb die Hand! (Raise your hand.) (Have child hold up hand and leave it up through several other commands, as if you have forgotten. Then release the hand!)

   All children should end up sitting on the floor, some with colors on various parts of their anatomy. Have one child collect all the colors and give them to the teacher.

8. Have all children stand up and go through group commands. Add: "Springt!" (Jump.)

9. Numbers 1 to 3. Follow same procedure as for colors: point, take, give, lay, touch, and so forth, using large numerals.

10. Model numbers 1 to 3; have children imitate them in a group. Use electronic keyboard or rhythm board to set rhythm; repeat numbers to rhythm.

11. Teach "Eins, zwei, drei und du bist frei!" (1-2-3 and you are out) game rhyme. Call up seven children. Give the first three in the row the large numerals 1, 2, and 3 in order. Teach the rhyme by pointing at individuals. The child who is "frei" (out) sits down each time, and the teacher shakes the child's hand dramatically, expressing regret ("Schade"), saying "Auf Wiedersehen!", and using the command "Setz dich!" (Sit down.) each time. Put the numerals 1, 2, and 3 in the hands of the first three children in line for the rhyme on each repetition. Have the entire class chant rhyme until only one child is still standing. This child also gets a handshake and applause, and the teacher says "Ich gratuliere!" (Congratulations.) Repeat with differing numbers of children, so they cannot immediately predict who will be "out."

12. Take a jump rope from the *Wundertüte* (magic-mystery box). Try to jump. Give rope to child who volunteers. ("Hebt die Hand!") (Raise your hand.) Direct the child to jump once—twice—three times. ("Springe einmal, zweimal, dreimal!") Give several children a chance to jump individually. Add *vorwärts* and *rückwärts*, and have individual children jump *forward* and *backward*, and then a specified number of times forward and a specified number of times backwards. Then call up two children and have them jump together, varying number of times they jump.

13. Take flags from the *Wundertüte*. Have children choose the flag being named from a group of several, give them to others, give them back to the teacher. Children raise hands to show which country they "live" in.

14. Take dog (*der Hund*) from the *Wundertüte*. Describe it by color; explain the difference between "bow-wow" in U.S. and "wau-wau" in German-speaking countries—*auf deutsch!* Next take the witch (*die Hexe*) from the *Wundertüte* and contrast with American witch in black hat and cloak. Finally take out the frog (*der Frosch*) from the box. Have the frog stick out its tongue the number of times you say: "Zeig die Zunge 3 mal!" Frog cooperates for the first few times, then refuses. Try to convince it by saying "bitte!" (please) and then prompt the children to beg frog with "bitte!" Pass out the creatures, request them back *auf deutsch*.

15. If there is time, play *Seven-up*. Have three children come to center or front of room. All other children put down their heads and close their eyes ("Legt den Kopf auf die Arme und macht die Augen zu!"). Children in the center move around the class and each touches another child's head ("Faβt einen Kopf an!"). Those touched stand up, on a signal from the teacher, and take turns guessing who touched them. If the child guesses, they trade places. If not, the child sits down ("Setz dich, ___!"). Then a new round begins. Use all learned commands. Children need only to be able to say one another's names in order to participate in the game.

16. Do calendar work. Talk about things that happened or were learned on each day, perhaps about who was absent, and so forth. Have children attach symbols for learned items to the calendar square for that day.

17. Give children construction paper precut in the shape of a head, to begin making a clown or a *Hampelmann* (German jumping-jack). They will add one part of the body each day during the course of the class, so that on the final day they will have a complete German toy. Show an example of the completed project, and demonstrate a real German *Hampelmann* made of wood. Have the children choose a hair color from the options provided and paste it on their figures.

18. Close class period with "Auf Wiedersehen!" and collect name tags.

Day 3
Objectives

Children will be able to do the following:

- Respond to previously learned commands in new situations and more complex combinations
- Respond to new body parts: *die Schulter* (shoulder), *der Po* (seat), *der Ellbogen* (elbow), *der Rücken* (back)
- Respond to new colors: *rosa* (pink), *grau* (gray)
- Use numbers 1 to 8
- Eat an open-faced sandwich with knife and fork in continental fashion, keeping the hands on the table when not in use for eating
- Accept the offer of food with "bitte" (please) and thank with "danke" (thank you)
- Understand that there are several ways to greet, depending on the time of day, and accept the handshake as part of the greeting

Materials

- Numbers 1 to 8
- Flags
- Clock
- Time-of-day flashcards
- *Wundertüte:* colored beanbags, adding *grau* (gray) and *rosa* (pink), apple, fork, knife, hat, dog, witch, frog, blindfold, Alpine hat
- Items for food activity: rye bread, cheese, wurst, unsalted butter or margarine, apple juice, paper plates, plastic forks and knives, napkins, plastic glasses or cups
- Precut Alpine hats, feathers in all learned colors for *Hampelmann*
- Electronic keyboard

Activities

1. Greet children individually and as a group with "Guten Morgen!" Lay name tags out on the floor. Point to a child and ask "Wer ist das?" (Who is that?) Children are prompted to respond "Das ist __." Find name tag from floor and give it to the child. Ask class for next child: "Wer ist das?" Class responds. Find name tag and say to the first child, "__, gib __ den Namen." Repeat until all name tags are passed out.

2. Do calendar work. Talk about who is absent; children move names from day 2 to day 3.

3. Have class respond to various combinations of these commands:

English	Plural	Singular
(Jump ___ times.)	Springt ___-mal!	Springe ___-mal!
(Stand up.)	Steht auf!	Steh auf!
(Sit down . . .	Setzt euch!	Setz dich!
. . . on the floor.	. . . auf den Fuß-boden!	
. . . on red.	. . . auf rot!	
. . . at your place.)	. . . auf den Platz!	
(Raise your hand.)	Hebt die Hand!	Heb die Hand!
(Raise your left/right hand.)	Hebt die linke/rechte Hand!	Heb die linke/rechte Hand!
(Raise your left/right foot.)	Hebt den linken/ rechten Fuß!	Heb den linken/ rechten Fuß!
(Lay your ___ on your ___.)	Legt ___ auf ___!	Leg ___ auf ___!

hand	die Hand
head	der Kopf
seat or bottom	der Po
back	der Rücken
knee	das Knie
elbow	der Ellbogen
shoulder	die Schulter

Variation 1: Direct children to touch the knee, elbow, back, shoulder, foot or head of another child, and leave the hand in place. Continue until all children are connected with each other—almost like creating a living sculpture. Then give the command to *jump!*

Variation 2: Direct children, one after another, to touch the back of the child ahead of them. When all are connected in a line, direct the children to sit down on the floor—and then to stand up again.

4. Use clock and flashcards to demonstrate greetings for different times of day:

(Good morning.)	Guten Morgen!
(Good day.)	Guten Tag!
(Good evening.)	Guten Abend!
(Good night.)	Gute Nacht!

Comment on use of handshake in greeting (*auf deutsch*). Then introduce game (adapted from New Games "People to People", Fluegelman 1976): Say four times in rhythm:

> Guten Morgen!　　　Guten Tag!　　　Guten Abend!　　　Gute Nacht!

With each greeting, children shake hands with their partner; when they say "Gute Nacht!" they change partners. (The teacher should participate only to make pairs come out evenly.) After two rounds of the greetings, change the words to "Hand zu Hand" four times, and children touch hands with their last partner to the rhythm, for four times. Return to the refrain, keeping a strong rhythm going. Then give two other parts of the body which have been learned, and children touch those parts with a new partner. Carry on until enthusiasm is just past its peak. Use rhythm on the electronic keyboard to maintain momentum.

5. Draw colored beanbags out of *Wundertüte*, two or three at a time, counting them and directing children to do things with them. Emphasize placing beanbags on various parts of the body and on each other. Add *grau, rosa* (gray, pink).

6. Review numbers 1 to 3; add 4 to 8, using commands as above, trying to use all parts of the body. At the end of review of new materials in 4 and 5, each child should have either a number or a color, or perhaps one of each.

7. Tell children to lay numbers and colors in front of them on the floor, so all the other children can see them. Practice with the children first: slap lap with hands, clap hands, snap fingers on the left hand, snap fingers on the right hand. Repeat. This should be done in slow, steady, even beat: slap, clap, snap left, snap right. Then ask, in rhythm:

> Wer　　　hat　　　eins?　　　　　　　　　　　　(Who has one?)
>
> (slap　　　clap　　　snap left　　　snap right)

Then the class responds:

> —　　　　—　　　　Pe–　　　　ter!　　　　(name of child with the *one*)
>
> (slap　　　clap　　　snap left　　　snap right)

If children cannot answer, ask the question again; if still no answer, you give the answer, always in rhythm. If the responses are too soft, say "lau-ter" (louder) in the constant, steady rhythm. The children answer only with names.

8. Direct one child to come to the center and sit on the floor. Direct other children to come and lay their numbers or colors on parts of the body: left foot, right foot, left/right hand, left/right knee, left/right shoulder, head, and so forth. After each child has placed a number or color, they

are directed to sit on the floor, where they may themselves become recipients of numbers or colors.

9. Use the *Wundertüte*. Take out creatures from Day 2. Pass them out and around in the class, and retrieve. Take out an Alpine hat. Give it to a child and have child set it on another child's head. Repeat several times, having individual children take the hat and place it on heads—their own and the heads of others. Blindfold the last child to be wearing the hat (better yet, begin with an assistant). Direct children to walk in a circle around the child and have one child steal the hat, holding it behind the back. All the children stand with their hands behind their backs. When the group counts to three (in German!) child in center removes blindfold and turns to one child at a time requesting the hat by saying only "bitte!" and holding a hand out to the child suspected of having the hat. If the IT is right, the children exchange places and the new IT is blindfolded. If IT is wrong, she or he has one more chance to guess (or more chances, depending on size of class).

10. Use the *Wundertüte* again. Take out apple, fork, knife. Cut apple and describe what you are doing.

11. Say, "Hast du Hunger?" (Are you hungry?) to assistant or puppet. Lay utensils and food for eating activity on a tray where all can see them. Direct assistant to take items one at a time.

    "Nimm ein Stück Brot!" (Take a piece of bread.)

    "Nimm das Messer!" (Take the knife.)

    "Schneide die Butter!" (Cut the butter.)

    "Schmiere die Butter auf das Brot!" (Spread butter on the bread.)

    Work the entire activity through with assistant, laying cheese and sausage on the buttered bread, taking knife in right hand and fork in left and eating continental style. Point out that this is how they eat in each of the five German-speaking countries, and also in many other parts of the world.

12. Send children to tables and repeat commands for them as they eat. Precede the mini-meal with "Guten Appetit!" Offer *Apfelsaft* (apple juice), showing the relationship to the apple from the earlier activity, and give it to them only if they say "bitte" rather than "danke" when the juice is offered.

13. Clear tables and give out hats and feathers for the *Hampelmann*. Children should choose the color of their feather as you name the colors; then they paste on the head and return to you or lay it in the center of the work table.

14. Discuss what has been learned and place symbols on the calendar: numbers 4 to 8, bread, glass, apple juice, cheese, wurst, butter, elbow, bottom, shoulder, back, hat, knife, fork, plate, and colors pink and gray.
15. Initiate farewell routine by saying "Auf Wiedersehen!" to individuals and the group.

Day 4
Objectives

Children will be able to do the following:

- Respond to previously learned commands, with addition of commands for use at chalkboard, opening and closing plastic eggs
- Give own name in a sentence: "Ich heiße ___." (My name is ___.)
- Use numbers 0 to 10 in math activities, game situation
- Identify and repeat names of months of the year in a group
- Sing the Spanish Counting Song (or another number song) with group
- Participate in guessing games, command game with confidence
- Use names of all class members accurately
- Respond to new body parts: *linkes/rechtes Ohr* (left/right ear)

Materials

- Numerals 0 to 9
- Chalkboard, chalk, eraser
- Magnetic numerals 0 to 9 (2 sets)
- Calendar and symbols
- Wheel of months (cardboard circle with a pie-shape for each month—initial and symbol indicate month)
- Floor cloth with map and number squares
- *Wundertüte:* dog, witch, hen, frog, ball, flags, small plastic eggs and beanbags in different colors—include colors *violett* (purple) and *orange* (orange)
- Electronic keyboard
- Number line
- Precut paper to make left ear for *Hampelmann*

Activities

(Note: at every opportunity work in asking pardon with "Verzeihung!")

1. Greet class with "Guten Morgen!" Put a child's name tag on and claim to be that child (begin with an assistant, if you have one). Assert *many* times: "Ich heiße *David!*" (with many dramatic voice variations). If there is no response from first child, put on a different name and keep claiming to be that child, until one of the children responds to the challenge and responds "Nein, *ich* heiße David!" "Argue" a bit, then give in and claim to be a different child until all children have practiced identifying themselves.

2. Play *Concentration* with names. Practice motions in rhythm first: two slaps on knees, two claps of hands, two left-hand snaps, two right-hand snaps. On left-hand snap say own name, on right-hand snap say name of someone else in the group. As a good beginning, have everyone in the group call the leader's name, whenever they are called on. When game seems secure, let them call anyone they like. Whenever rhythm is broken, turn goes back to leader (teacher).

3. Review and vary commands. Emphasize "Faßt *rot* an!" (Touch red, or other colors.) Add *linkes/rechtes Ohr* (left and right ear).

4. Review numerals. Teach 9, 10, 0. Do sums and subtraction, using number line on the floor. Practice with numerals in center of circle, using entire range of commands and adding "Leg *9* unter den Platz!" (Lay 9 under your seat).

5. Using an assistant or a puppet, or modeling yourself, direct children to do the following:

    "Geh an die Tafel!" (Go to the chalkboard.)

    "Nimm die Kreide in die Hand!" (Pick up the chalk.)

    "Schreibe ___!" (Write ___.)

    "Leg die Kreide hin!" (Lay the chalk down.)

    "Nimm den Wischer in die Hand!" (Pick up the eraser.)

    "Wische ___!" (Erase ___.)

    "Leg den Wischer hin!" (Lay down the eraser.)

    Repeat and vary.

6. Use the wheel of months. Talk through the months of the year in the target language, saying something about each month, making heavy use of cognates, where appropriate. Go through months and call for group imitation of months. For German class, explain (in German) about "April, April," the German equivalent of "April Fool," and have children repeat that month twice, every time it is cued.

7. Practice numbers 0 to 9. Choose one of the following activities: Place magnetic numerals on chalkboard (or magnet board), one set on each

side of the board. Send two children to the board, call out a number and have them locate it and move it to the center.

Variation 1: Give each child a different number and then have the class perform a math activity with the two numerals, within the limits of the numbers they have learned (add them or subtract them).

Variation 2: Place numerals on the chalkboard in random order, and then palm one (or more) of the numbers. Children try to figure out which one is missing.

8. Teach Spanish Counting Song (or another counting song): "1-tra-la-la, 2-tra-la-la, 3-4-5-6 tra-la-la, 7-tra-la-la, 8-tra-la-la, 9-10-tra-la-la." Sing it for the class. Then have class sing only *tra-la-la's*, then only the numbers; then divide class in half and have one group sing numbers, the other the *tra-la-la's*. Finally have whole class sing song. Give individual children numbers and have them stand up whenever their number occurs in the song. Later variation: sing the song loud, soft, like a bear (gruff), like a witch, and so forth.

9. Do floor map activities. Take colored beanbags from the *Wundertüte*, spreading out the floor map and directing: "Wirf grün auf die DDR!" (Throw green on the GDR.), and so forth. Have children sit, stand, touch body parts on different countries. Use assistant or puppet to demonstrate the North Sea, the Rhine, and so forth.

10. Draw other items from the *Wundertüte*. Pass out items, reviewing colors with each item. Direct children to give items to each other. Ask who would like an item, direct children to give it to her or him; ask for item yourself, invite children to ask for items they want. (If this is handled carefully, children will begin asking for items without prompting.) Relevant language:

"Gib mir die Hexe, bitte!" (Give me the witch, please.)

"Wer will die Henne haben?" (Who wants the hen?)

"Fritz, gib Anna die Henne, bitte!" (Fritz, please give Anna the hen.)

Make extensive use of *bitte!* (please, you're welcome) and *danke!* (thank you) throughout. Try to avoid having children address you directly, so they won't have to use the formal address.

11. Take a white egg from the *Wundertüte*. "Die Henne legt ein Ei!—ein weißes Ei!" (The hen lays an egg—a white egg.) Take out other eggs of various colors and comment on them: "ein grünes Ei! ein gelbes Ei!" (A green egg! A yellow egg!) Pass out colored eggs. Have children open them ("Mach das Ei auf!"). Direct other children to take numerals from the chalkboard and put them in eggs of various colors:

"Geh an die Tafel und nimm 9!" (Go to the board and take the 9.)

"Geh zu Fritz and leg 9 in das grüne Ei!" (Go to Fritz and lay 9 in the green egg.)

"Fritz, mach das Ei zu!" (Fritz, close the egg.)

Repeat with all the colored eggs. Then challenge the class to remember who has what number: "Wer hat 9?" To make it harder, have the children pass eggs around a few times and then ask the question!

12. Introduce show-and-tell activity. Give each child a paper ring for each item brought from home that reflects the target culture, except in the case of *many* objects, such as coins. As possible, make comments in German about the items brought, introduce vocabulary, and manipulate items that have potential for future use in class conversation.

13. Distribute *Hampelmann* heads; add left ear. During the craft time, children can also form paper rings into a chain. Direct them one by one: "Kleb deinen Ring an Davids Ring!" (Glue your ring to David's ring.)

14. Play the game *Touch Blue*. Demonstrate that children are to find the color *blue* (or other colors, as called) in the room or on one another's clothing, and to touch it when directed to do so. To make it more exciting, count to 10 as a way of adding urgency. You may expand to include touching the desk, the floor, the chalkboard, the ears, hair, and so forth.

15. Do calendar activity. You will need these calendar items: numbers 9, 10; chalk, eraser, egg, hen; colors violet and orange; ball; "ich heisse" picture; ear.

16. Close with "Auf Wiedersehen!"

Day 5
Objectives

Children will be able to do the following:
- Respond to previously learned commands in new combinations, with the addition of *Geht 3 Schritte vorwärts* (Go 3 steps forward.), *rückwärts* (backwards), *nach links* (to the left), *nach rechts* (to the right), *wirf*, as contrasted with *gib* (throw—give)
- Contrast *groß* and *klein* (large and small)
- Participate in skit situation
- Show time on clockface when given in German
- Sing two songs with the group, one review and one new

Materials
- Numerals 0 to 9
- Large and small color circles
- Circle of months

- Magnetic numbers
- Sponge balls in two sizes
- Packs of playing cards with A to 10 only in all four suits—suits should be separated
- Clock with movable hands
- Materials to make clocks during activity period: clock face circles, hands cut out of colored construction paper, punched with paper punch and reinforced with gummed rings (or laminated), 9" × 12" colored construction sheets; glue or paste, felt pens
- *Wundertüte:* dog, cat, hen, *Kasperle* (puppet), *Springseil* (jump rope), egg with 3 smaller eggs inside
- Floor map
- Precut paper to make right ear for *Hampelmann*

Activities

(Have color circles, both large and small, and flags lying in the center of the circle at the beginning of class.)

1. Open the class with individual and group commands such as the following:

    "Gib mir rot!" (Give me red.)

    "Springe auf rot!" (Jump onto red.)

    "Nimm rot und leg rot auf Annas Knie!" (Take red and lay red on Anna's knee.)

    "Nimm die Fahne von Österreich!" (Take the Austrian flag.)

    "Nimm die Farben von der Schweizer Fahne und leg sie neben die Fahne!" (Take the colors of the Swiss flag and lay them beside the flag.)

    Give variations of these commands, combined with other commands you have taught thus far.

2. Teach new commands:

    Geht 3 Schritte vorwärts! (Go 3 steps forward.)

    Geht 3 Schritte rückwärts! (Go 3 steps back.)

    Hebt den linken Fuss! (Lift your left foot.)

    Geht 3 Schritte nach links/rechts! (Go 3 steps left/right.)

3. Play *Challenge Game.* Have children turn name tags over. Then ask children to take turns pointing to a child they think you may not know

by (German) name. All the children together ask "Wer ist das?" Continue until all children have been named. (Or, in a small class, teacher or assistant closes eyes or is blindfolded. Child comes forward and IT touches *only* the shoe. Class asks "Wer ist das?" and IT tries to answer.)

4. Do a skit with the class. Call up two children and say:

   T: Ich bin in Hornbachers (a local supermarket known to all), und ich sehe Fritz und Anna. Ich kenne Fritz, aber ich kenne Anna nicht. (I am in Hornbachers, and I see Fritz and Anna. I know Fritz, but I don't know Anna.)

   T: Guten Morgen, Fritz! (shake hands)

   F: Guten Morgen, Frau/Fräulein/Herr _____.

   T: Fritz, wer ist das?

   F: Frau/Fräulein/Herr _____, das ist Anna.
   Anna, das ist Frau/Fräulein/Herr _____. (Will require prompting)

   T: Guten Morgen, Anna! (offers hand)

   A: Guten Morgen, Frau/Fräulein/Herr _____!

   T: Es ist spät;. Auf Wiedersehen, Fritz und Anna!

   F u. A: Auf Wiedersehen, Frau/Fräulein/Herr _____!
   (Handshaking all around)

   Do with several children who volunteer. Change location to other stores children are familiar with.

5. Review wheel of months, using the command "Zeig uns . . ." (Show us . . .).

6. Review numbers. Divide children into groups of three or four. Give each group one suit of the numbers 1 to 10 from a playing-card deck (or possibly two suits to each group for greater challenge). Direct them to lay the cards out face up in the center of the group. As you call numbers, the children try to be the first to lay their flat hand on the card. If two children are touching the card, neither of them gets to keep it. The children hold up the card for confirmation, and then you call another number. Continue until all numbers have been called at least once—call some numbers more than once. If the card is not there in the center (because it has been called before), all the children raise their hands above their heads. Clap for the person with the most cards at the end of the game.

7. Review counting song.

8. Practice numbers and add numbers 11 and 12, using magnetic numbers or large numbers.

9. Draw items from the *Wundertüte* and move them around the class. Have the *Kasperle* puppet first claim (as the teacher did in Day 4) to be one or more of the children. Then have *Kasperle* introduce himself properly and ask names of other children. Add the command *wirf!* (throw) and alternate with *gib* (give). Bring out a small sponge ball and set up a throwing pattern using commands—children should always throw to and receive from the same people. Then introduce a large sponge ball and introduce a different pattern with that ball. Try to keep both patterns going at once! Return all objects to center of circle and sit down.

10. Practice telling time. Bring out clock (*die Uhr*), move hands to different times and say what they are, making particular note of *ein Uhr*. Show how times relate to greetings:

> 9 a.m. Guten Morgen!
>
> 1 p.m. Guten Tag!
>
> 6 p.m. Guten Abend!
>
> 11 p.m. Gute Nacht!

Have child come up to clock and move the hands on the clock to show different times: "Zeig uns ein Uhr!" (Show us one o'clock), and so forth. Give several children this opportunity.

11. Sing a song: Guten Morgen, guten Tag, guten Abend, Kinder, eine gute Nacht!

12. Contrast *groß* and *klein*. Remove large white egg from the *Wundertüte*: say "ein weißes Ei, ein großes Ei! Was ist im Ei?" (a white egg, a big egg—what's in the egg?). Call up a child to open the egg ("Mach das Ei auf!"), in which there is a smaller egg. Contrast large and small, have child close the larger egg ("Mach das große Ei zu!") and pass each egg to a different child. Continue opening eggs until the smallest egg has been reached. Make other contrasts of large and small—numbers, circles, people, countries, and so forth.

12. Do craft activity. Introduce clock-making as an important activity in the Alps in Switzerland. Show examples of carefully decorated clocks. Give children precut pieces and have them decorate and assemble their own clocks. (Mosaic clocks work well for Spanish culture.)

14. Add right ear to puppet figure.

15. If there is time, have children show times on their own clocks when you call them out.

16. Do calendar activity. Include numbers 11 and 12, clock, large-small contrast, song, pointing hand (*zeig*), cat, dialog in supermarket.

17. Close class with *Auf Wiedersehen!* and hand-shaking with individuals and the entire group.

Day 6
Objectives

Children will be able to do the following:
- Respond to learned commands of increasing complexity and length
- Identify birthday month (perhaps pronounce it)
- Identify themselves with *ich heiße*
- Use numbers 0 to 19
- Recognize new animals in magic-mystery box; produce sounds the animals make
- Sing all songs learned to date
- Participate in playground dialog
- Respond to adverbs *schnell, langsam, hoch* (fast, slow, high) with commands
- Recognize components of German breakfast and use appropriate meal behavior

Materials

- Wheel of months, with names of children, teacher and assistant on small pieces of construction paper attached to center of wheel
- Electronic keyboard
- *Wundertüte:* dog, cat, rooster, donkey, eggs, flags, beanbags, bouncing ball
- Precut body sections for *Hampelmann*

Activities

1. Do a role-play—students introduce themselves to "visitor" in class. Visitor will be wearing a prop of some kind. (Or, use puppet character such as *Kasperle* to fill the role.)
2. Review TPR commands. Introduce some commands that will be used in fantasy activity (activity 12) and *klatschen* (clap). Use adverbs combined with verbs to have children doing actions fast, slow, high.
3. Take out the wheel of months. After you model, have each child take her or his own name and place it on the month in which they have a birthday. "Wann hast du Geburtstag?" or "In welchem Monat hast du Geburtstag? Ah, du hast im _____ Geburtstag! Klasse: im _____!" (When is your birthday? What month is your birthday? Oh, your birthday is in _____. Class, in _____.)
4. Play *Fruit-Basket Upset* with birthday months. Call out two months, and

children with birthdays in those months must all exchange chairs. While the exchange is going on, take one of the seats left empty. One child will be without a seat, and becomes the leader. This child calls two months, and the game continues.

5. Take large and small eggs from *Wundertüte*. Practice opening and closing eggs, eyes, mouth, door, hand, and so forth.

6. Present rhyme: Eins, zwei, drei, die Henne legt ein Ei.
   Die Henne legt ein weißes Ei, eins, zwei, drei.
   Use as a "count out" rhyme. Child counted out chooses color of egg to chant in the next round. (So the last line becomes, for example, "Die Henne legt ein *rotes* Ei, eins, zwei, drei.")

7. Practice numbers. Add 13 to 19, using formula "3 und 10 ist 13," and so forth.

8. Review countries, flags, colors with commands. Play "Wer hat gold—David!" with flags and colors. (See Day 3, Activity 7.)

9. Present a dialog. Model with assistant or puppets. Have two children playing, one jumping rope, the other bouncing a ball. Child 1 (with ball) bumps into child 2 and says:

1: O, Verzeihung!	(Excuse me)
2: Bitte, bitte!	(That's all right)
1: Wie heißt du?	(What's your name)
2: David. Und du?	(David. What's yours?)
1: Ich heiße Jette.	(My name is Jette.)
Wollen wir spielen?	(Do you want to play?)
2: Ja, gern.	(Yes)

   (alternative version)

1: Wollen wir Ball spielen?	(Do you want to play ball?)
2: Nein. Wollen wir springen?	(No, do you want to jump?)
1: Ja, gern! (Yes)	

10. Return to *Wundertüte* and take out animals, providing for each the sound they make in German: dog (*der Hund*), "wau-wau"; cat (*die Katze*), "miau"; rooster (*der Hahn*), "kikeriki"; donkey (*der Esel*), "i-a". Take out bouncing ball and have children bounce it a specified number of times.

11. Review time-telling. Have children use their bodies to make times on command, using one arm for the minute hand and the other for the hour hand. Talk about things we do at different times of the day; contrast with German-speaking countries.

12. Create a fantasy. Talk about getting sleepy at night, have children rest heads on arms (on desks), close eyes, sleep, with baroque music playing

in background. Talk them through waking up in the morning, giving and modeling the commands that follow. Then move them into place for the German breakfast that concludes the fantasy.

Legt die Arme auf den Platz. (Lay your arms on the desk.)

Legt den Kopf auf die Arme. (Lay your head on your arms.)

Macht die Augen zu. (Close your eyes.)

Schlaft! (Sleep.)

Nein, nicht schnarcht! (Don't snore!)

Est ist 11 Uhr (1 Uhr, 3 Uhr . . .) . . . schlaft, schlaft!

(It is 11 o'clock, and so forth . . . sleep, sleep.)

At this point ring a hand bell, alarm clock, or play tape of church bells.

Die Glocke läutet! Wacht auf! (The bell is ringing—wake up.)

Steht auf! (Get up.)

Streckt euch! (Stretch.)

Geht ins Badezimmer! (Go into the bathroom.)

Wascht euch! (Wash up.)

Kämmt euch! (Comb your hair.)

Geht ins Schlafzimmer! (Go into the bedroom.)

Macht das Bett! (Make the bed.)

Zieht euch an! (Get dressed.)

Geht ins Eβzimmer! (Go into the dining room—or kitchen.)

Setzt euch an den Tisch! (Sit down at the table.)

Eβt das Frühstück! (Eat breakfast.)

13. Eat a *deutsches Frühstück* (German breakfast) consisting of Brötchen (hard rolls), *Butter, Marmalade,* and *heiβe Schokolade* (hot chocolate).

"Macht das Brötchen auf!" (Open the roll.)

"Schmiert die Butter auf das Brötchen!" (Spread butter on the roll.)

"Schmiert die Marmalade auf das Brötchen!" (Spread marmalade . . .)

"Esst das Brötchen!" (Eat the roll.)

"Trinkt die heiβe Schokolade!" (Drink the hot chocolate.)

14. Have children add body (der Körper) to *Hampelmann* figure.

15. Work with calendar. Add numbers 13 to 19; cat, rooster, donkey; breakfast vocabulary.

Day 7
Objectives

Children will be able to do the following:

- Respond to learned commands in new combinations
- Choose games and songs to do as group
- Participate in rhyme with accuracy of actions, confidence in speaking
- Succeed in playing class games
- Understand the need to differentiate forms of request between children and teacher

Materials

- *Wundertüte:* witch, frog, donkey, dog, cat, bear, rooster, hen, egg, jumprope; ball
- Colored chalk for chalkboard
- Flashcards for rhyme
- Handkerchief for teaching rhyme
- Floormap and flags
- Blindfold
- Precut arms for *Hampelmann*

Activities

1. Review commands and add a new variation: "Alle Kinder mit rot an, geht 3 Schritte vorwärts." (All children with red on go 3 steps forward.) Add parts of face: *die Augen* (eyes), *die Nase* (nose), *der Mund* (mouth). Add *Hampelmann* (jumping-jack) calesthenics.

2. If appropriate, do a role reversal: invite children to be the teacher. Take off your name tag, hold it up and ask: "Wer ist Frau/Fräulein/Herr ____? or Wer will Frau/Fräulein/Herr ____ sein?" (Who is Ms./Mr. ____? Who wants to be Ms./Mr. ____?) If a child volunteers, take the child's nametag and allow the child to give several commands to the entire group. Give two or three children this opportunity, if they have an interest.

3. Give a variety of commands, having children go to the board (using colored chalk).

   "Nimm die *rote* Kreide in die Hand!"   (Pick up the *red* chalk.)

   "Schreib den Namen!"   (Write your name.)

"Schreibe ___ (numbers)"	(Write ___ (numbers).)
"Mache einen Kopf . . .	(Make a head.)
(1-2-3 . . .) Augen	(1-2-3 . . . eyes)
einen Mund	(a mouth)
(1-2-3 . . .) Ohren	(1-2-3 . . . ears)
"Mache einen Kreis um . . ."	(Make a circle around . . .)
"Wische . . ."	(Erase . . .)

4. Play a game: *Command Chairs*
Played like musical chairs, except the children follow your commands as a group until you call out, "Setzt euch auf den Platz!" (Sit down in your seat.) At that point all the children scramble to sit down on a chair—but there is always one fewer chair than children because you remove a chair after each round. Continue until all children are eliminated but one. Variation: children who are "out" can take turns giving the commands.

5. Take these items from *die Wundertüte:*

die Hexe (witch)	das Ei (egg)	der Hund (dog)
der Frosch (frog)	der Hahn (rooster)	die Katze (cat)
der Esel (donkey)	der Bär (bear)	

Practice asking and thanking each other for the objects. Set up the situation so the children want to ask you for a favorite object, and become "insulted" when they use "Gib mir ___," the familiar form. Explain in German that you are an adult addressed with a title and so they must request things using "Geben Sie mir ___." Give them several opportunities to practice this in the course of the activity.

6. Use flash cards and actions to teach this rhyme:

Eins, zwei Polizei	(policeman)
Drei, vier Offizier	(officer)
Fünf, sechs alte Hex'	(old witch)
Sieben, acht gute Nacht!	(good night)
Neun, zehn auf Wiedersehen!	(goodbye)

(Have handkerchief available for waving goodbye)

7. Ask, "Wollen wir spielen?" (Do you want to play?) As children respond to this question, go through several games the class likes to play.

Add this new game: A child is blindfolded (or closes eyes). Another child is chosen to come forward. They shake hands and say "Guten Morgen!" (or "Guten Tag!") Then the blindfolded child asks "Wie heißt du?" The other child replies "Ich heiße *Kasperle!* (or *Schnick-schnack, Lumpi, Mieze,* or another name that has been used in class for visiting puppets or other creatures). The blindfolded child responds, "Nein, du heißt ___!" (No, your name is ___.) If the blindfolded child is right, they change places. If wrong, another child tries to fool the blindfolded child.

8. Ask, "Wollen wir singen?" (Shall we sing?) Then ask, *"Was* wollen wir singen?" (What shall we sing?) Sing several songs the class likes. Add this new song:

   Singen, das wollen wir,

   Singen, das wollen wir,

   Singen, das wollen wir, wollen wir, ja!

   Substitute *spielen, springen,* and other learned verbs for *singen.*

9. Draw these items from the *Wundertüte: der Ball, das Springseil* (jumprope). Have children use *Springseil* to make a circle on the floor. Direct children to jump into circle, out of circle, beside circle, and so forth. ("Springe in den Kreis, aus dem Kreis, neben den Kreis, . . .)

10. Practice dialog with props. (*Du, wie heißt du denn?*)

11. If there is time, practice commands with floor map and flags.

12. Have children add a left arm and elbow to Hampelmann.

13. Add to calendar: vocabulary from rhyme "Eins, Zwei, Polizei"; creatures from *Wundertüte.*

Day 8
Objectives

Children will be able to do the following:
- Respond to all learned commands
- Respond to very familiar commands when delivered in writing rather than orally
- Participate in dialog, with some help
- Choose how they feel from pictures of faces
- Locate the Rhine River on the floor map
- Successfully differentiate between *groß* and *klein* in a variety of situations
- Sing all learned songs; perhaps learn one more

Materials

- *Struwelpeter* puppet
- Large and small ball

- Large and small colored circles
- Large numbers 0–9
- Magnetic numbers
- Pictures of faces showing feelings (fine, great, so-so, not so good, terrible)
- Large and small clocks and students' own clocks
- Packaged salt and sugar and grapes
- Sugared popcorn, white and red grape juice, plates, glasses, bowls for food activity
- *Wundertüte*: flags, donkey, rooster, raccoon, bear, dog, cat, ball, jumprope
- Cards with written commands on one side, numbers on the other, for use in pocket chart
- Taped circle, square, triangle, pentagon, hexagon on the floor
- Precut arms for *Hampelmann*

Activities

1. Introduce *Struwelpeter*: "Ich heiße ___," with children's names. Children ask his name; he keeps claiming to be one of them. Distribute the name tags in this way, finally give out his name.
2. Do a quick series of commands, including all basic commands.
3. Invite children to do a role reversal, becoming the teacher for a series of commands.
4. Take a jumprope from the *Wundertüte*. Have children make a circle and other figures. Jump into, beside, and over the circle. Have them find shapes on floor around room to go to, jump into, over, and so forth.
5. Take out the ball. Review dialog: "Du, wie heißt du, denn"?
6. Have a child lie down. Review *large* and *small* by having children place large and small circles, numbers, and clocks on and beside various parts of the body. Include *der Bauch* (stomach), *das Bein* (leg), *der Arm* (arm). Alternative activity: Have a child lie down on a piece of butcher paper. Trace child's shape. Then have class draw in facial features (or place them on the shape), place props on the shape. Oversized eyes, ears, nose, and mouth are effective props for this activity.
7. Take out creatures from *Wundertüte*. Have students practice asking for, giving. Make sure children differentiate forms of address between teacher and each other. Take out *die Trauben* (grapes). Using floor map, locate *der Rhein* (Rhine River). Explain in German about growing grapes on the banks of the Rhine. Use flags and grapes on floor map; also place hands and feet, and so forth, on map.

8. Do intensive commands (several commands in sequence) with group and with individuals.

9. Do a reading activity. Place reading cards, with very familiar commands on one side and familiar numbers on the other, in a pocket chart with the number side visible. Have a child choose card from number on back, then read the card silently and perform the activity. After the action has been performed, read the card aloud while showing it to the class, and place it in the center of the circle. At the end, have all children perform activities on all cards used.

10. Introduce "Wie geht's?" ("How are you?") "Und dir?" ("And you?")—or "Und Ihnen?" in the case of an adult. Work with puppets or an assistant to demonstrate greetings and how responses might sound. Use pantomime and pictures or flash card faces to show a variety of options for response. Go around class and let individual children choose the flash card that shows how they would respond. "Wie geht's?" (How are you?); "Danke, gut" (Fine, thanks); "Nicht so gut" (Not so good); "So-so" (so-so); "Schlecht" (Terrible).

11. Review songs. If there is time, begin learning one new song:

    Der Kopf, die Schulter, das Knie, der Fuß (repeat 3 times)

    Und wir klatschen in die Hände!

    (The head, the shoulder, the knee, the foot, and we clap our hands.) Sung to the camp song melody "My head, my shoulders, my knees, my feet . . . and we all clap hands together."

12. Tell the children, "Mund auf, Augen zu . . ." (Open your mouth and shut your eyes . . .) Give a grape to each child while the eyes are closed. Introduce the snack by contrasting sugar and salt—*Zucker und Salz.* "Zucker ist süß, Salz ist salzig!" (Sugar is sweet, salt is salty.)

13. Do a food activity with *Zuckerpopcorn* (sugared popcorn), *Traubensaft* (grape juice), *Trauben* (grapes). Have children take turns adding sugar to popcorn in the bag, and choosing white or red grape juice and/or green or red grapes.

14. Add to calendar for the day.

15. Add second arm to *Hampelmann.*

Appendix B

Sources for Professional Information and Support

Note: As of publication, this information is accurate to the best of the authors' knowledge.

International Organizations, Institutions, Conferences

AFS International/Intercultural Programs, Inc.
313 East 43d St.
New York, NY 10017
212-949-4242

Canadian Association of Immersion Teachers
1815 promenade Alta Vista, Suite 101
Ottawa, Ontario K1G 3Y6
Canada

Canadian Parents for French
309 Cooper Street, Suite 210
Ottawa, Ontario K2P 0G5
Canada

Council on International Educational Exchange
205 East 42d St.
New York, NY 10017
212-661-1414

The Experiment in International Living
Kipling Rd.
Brattleboro, VT 05301
802-257-7751

International Association for Learning Laboratories
Language Media Center
125 Schaeffer Hall
University of Iowa
Iowa City, Iowa 52242

International Association of Teachers of English as a Foreign Language
(IATEFL)
16 Alexandra Gardens
Hounslow
Middlesex TW3 4HU
England

Institute of International Education
809 United Nations Plaza
New York, NY 10017
212-883-8200

The Ontario Institute for Studies in Education (OISE)
252 Bloor St. West
Toronto, Ontario M5S 1V6
416-923-6641

National Organizations, Institutions, Conferences

Academic Alliances in Foreign Languages and Literatures
Marymount College
Tarrytown, NY 10591
914-332-4918

Advocates for Language Learning
Madeline Ehrlich
PO Box 4964
Culver City, CA 90230
213-398-4103

American Association for Applied Linguistics
Albert Valdman
Committee for Research and Development in Language Instruction
Ballantine Hall 602
Indiana University
Bloomington, IN 47405

American Association of Teachers of Arabic
Gerald E. Lampe, SAIS
Johns Hopkins University
1740 Massachusetts Ave. NW
Washington, DC 20036
202-785-6237

American Association of Teachers of French
Fred M. Jenkins, Dept. of French
University of Illinois
57 E. Armory Ave.
Champaign, IL 61820
217-333-2842

American Association of Teachers of German
523 Building, Suite 201
Route 38
Cherry Hill, NJ 08034
609-663-5264

American Association of Teachers of Italian
4 Oakmount Road
Welland, Ontario L3C 4X8
Canada
416-732-2149

American Association of Teachers of Slavic and East European Languages
M.L. 340
University of Arizona
Tuscon, AZ 85721
602-621-3702

American Association of Teachers of Spanish and Portuguese
Mississippi State University
PO Box 6349
Mississippi State, MS 39762-6349

American Classical League
Miami University
Oxford, OH 45056
513-529-4116

American Council of Teachers of Russian
815 New Gulph Road
Bryn Mawr, PA 19010
215-525-6559

American Council of Teachers of Uncommonly Taught Asian Languages
Dinh-Hoa Nguyen, Dept. of Linguistics
Southern Illinois University
Carbondale, IL 62901

American Council on the Teaching of Foreign Languages (ACTFL)
579 Broadway
Hastings-on-Hudson, NY 10706
914-478-2011

American Translators Association (ATA)
109 Croton Ave.
Ossining, NY 10562
914-941-1500

Amity Institute
PO Box 118
Del Mar, CA 92014
619-755-3582

Association of Departments of Foreign Languages (ADFL)
Cheryl Demharter, Coordinator
10 Astor Place
New York, NY 10003

Association of Teachers of Japanese
Department of East Asian Languages and Literature
Van Hise Hall
1220 Linden Drive
University of Wisconsin-Madison
Madison, WI 53706
608-262-1740

Center for Applied Linguistics (CAL)
1118 22d Street NW
Washington, DC 20037
202-429-9292

Chinese Language Teachers Association
161 South Orange Avenue
South Orange, NJ 07079
201-761-9447

Computer Assisted Language Learning and Instruction Consortium
  (CALICO)
3078 JKHB
Brigham Young University
Provo, UT 84602
801-378-7079

Concordia Language Villages
Concordia College
Moorhead, MN 56560
218-299-4544

ERIC Clearinghouse on Languages and Linguistics (ERIC/CLL)
Center for Applied Linguistics
1118 22d Street NW
Washington, DC 20037
202-429-9551

ERIC Document Reproduction Service (EDRS)
Computer Microfilm International Corp.
3900 Wheeler Avenue
Alexandria, VA 22304

Foreign Language Education Forum on CompuServe (FLEFO)
CompuServe Information Services
PO Box 20212
Columbus, OH 43220
800-848-8199 (outside Ohio)

Global Perspectives in Education (GPE)
45 John Street
Suite 1200
New York, NY 10038
212-732-8606

Joint National Committee for Languages and Council for Languages and
    Other International Studies
20 F St. NW, 4th Floor
Washington, D.C. 20001
202-783-2211

Kraus Curriculum Development Library
One Water Street
White Plains, NY 10601
914-761-9600

Linguistic Society of America
1325 18th St. NW, Suite 21
Washington, DC 20036-6501
202-835-1714

The Modern Language Association of America (MLA)
62 5th Ave.
New York, NY 10011
212-741-5588

National Association for Foreign Student Affairs (NAFSA)
1860 19th St. NW
Washington, DC 20009
202-462-4811

National Clearinghouse for Bilingual Education (NCBE)
11501 Georgia Avenue, Suite 102
Wheaton, MD 20902
301-933-9448
800-647-0123

National Committee for Latin and Greek
Division of Curriculum and Development
Texas Education Agency
1701 North Congress Avenue
Austin, TX 78701-1492
512-463-9585

National Council of State Supervisors of Foreign Languages
Bobby LaBouve, Director of Languages
Division of Curriculum Development
Texas Education Agency
1701 N. Congress Ave.
Austin, TX 78701

National Council on Foreign Language and International Studies (NCFLIS)
45 John St., Suite 1200
New York, NY 10038
212-732-8606

National Foreign Language Center
11 Dupont Circle
Suite 802
Washington, DC 20036
202-667-8100

National Network for Early Language Learning (NNELL)
Chair: Nancy Rhodes
1118 22d Street NW
Washington, DC 20037
202-429-9292

Second Language Acquisition by Children Conference (SLAC)
Rosemarie Benya
East Central Oklahoma University
Ada, OK 74820

Societes des Professerus de Francais en Amerique
Micheline Herz, Dept. of French
Rutgers University
R.D.1, 192 Canal Rd.
Princeton, NJ 08540

Society for the Advancement of Scandinavian Study
Department of Germanic Languages
University of Illinois
707 South Mathews
Urbana, IL 61801
217-333-4852

Teachers of English to Speakers of Other Languages (TESOL)
1118 22d St. NW
Washington, DC 20037
202-625-4569

Regional Conferences Associated with ACTFL
(American Council on the Teaching of Foreign Languages)

Note: Each state has a foreign language association and most have state
    chapters of language-specific organizations. For help in locating these
    organizations, contact ACTFL or your state foreign language super-
    visor.

Central States Conference on the Teaching of Foreign Languages
Ohio State University Foreign Language Center
155 Cunz Hall
Columbus, OH 43210-1229
614-457-9741

Northeast Conference on the Teaching of Foreign Languages
Box 623
Middlebury, VT 05753
802-388-4017

Pacific Northwest Council of Foreign Languages
Department of Foreign Languages and Literatures
Oregon State University
Corvallis, OR 97331-2289
503-754-2478

Southern Conference on Language Teaching
Box 20
Spelman College
Atlanta, GA 30314
404-681-3643

Southwest Conference on Language Teaching
3005 Heatheridge Lane
Reno, NV 89509
702-348-6611

Other Regional Organizations, Institutions, Conferences

Classical Association of the Atlantic States
Joanna Glazewski, Chair, Dept. of Classics
Faulkner House 14
Drew University
Madison, NJ 07940

Classical Association of the Middle West and South
Furman University
Greenville, SC 29613
803-294-3056

Classical Association of New England
71 Sand Hill Road
Amherst, MA 01002
413-549-0390

Classical Association of the Pacific Northwest
Department of Classics
University of Washington
Seattle, WA 98195
406-243-2401

Middle States Association of Modern Language Teachers
Michael Halbig
Language Area Studies
U.S. Naval Academy
Annapolis, MD 21401

Rocky Mountain Modern Language Association
Victor Castelli, Dept. of Foreign Languages
University of Denver
Denver, CO 80210

South Atlantic Modern Language Association
Sofus E. Simonsen
Foreign Language and Literatures
North Carolina State University
P.O. Box 8106
Raleigh, NC 27695-8106

International Journals, Newsletters

Canadian Modern Language Review
La Revue canadienne des langues vivantes
237 Hellems Avenue
Welland, Ontario L3B 3B8
Canada

CONTACT (Canadian Review for French Teachers)
Simon Fraser University
Faculty of Education
Burnaby, BC V5A 1S6
Canada

Practical English Teaching
Mary Glasgow Publications, Ltd.
Avenue House
131-133 Holland Park Avenue
London W11 4UT
England

National Journals, Newsletters

AATF National Bulletin
American Association of Teachers of French
57 East Armory Ave.
Champaign, IL 61820

ATJ Newsletter
Association of Teachers of Japanese
Dept. of East Asian Languages and Literature
University of Wisconsin
Madison, WI 53706

The Classical Bulletin
Michael Harstad
Asbury College
Wilmore, KY 40390

The Classical Outlook
Richard A. La Fleur, Classics Dept.
Park Hall
University of Georgia
Athens, GA 30602

Die Unterrichtspraxis
American Association of Teachers of German
523 Building, Suite 201
Route 38
Cherry Hill, NJ 08034

FLES News
Marcia Rosenbusch, Editor
300 Pearson Hall
Iowa State University
Ames, IA 50011

Foreign Language Annals
American Council on the Teaching of Foreign Language
579 Broadway
Hastings-on-Hudson, NY 10706
914-478-2011

French Review
Ronald W. Tobin, Dept. of French
University of California
Santa Barbara, CA 93106

German Quarterly
American Association of Teachers of German
523 Building, Suite 201
Route 38
Cherry Hill, NJ 08034

Hispania
Donald W. Bleznick, Dept. of Romance Languages
University of Cincinnati
Cincinnati, OH 45221

Italica
Robert Rodini, Dept. of Italian
University of Wisconsin
Madison, WI 53706

Journal of the Association of Teachers of Japanese
Naomi Hanaoka McGloin
Association of Teachers of Japanese
Dept. of East Asian Languages and Literature
University of Wisconsin
Madison, WI 53706

Journal of the Chinese Language Teachers Association
F.S. Hsueh
162 S. Orange Ave.
Institute of Far East Studies
Seton Hall University
South Orange, NJ 07079

Journal Français d'Amérique
Anne Prah-Pérochon
1051 Divisadero St.
San Francisco, CA 94115

Language in Society
32 East 57th Street
New York, NY 10022

The Modern Language Journal
Journal Division
The University of Wisconsin Press
114 North Murray Street
Madison, WI 53715
608-262-4952

NABE Journal
National Association for Bilingual Education
Reynaldo Macias
Rm. 405
1201 16th St. NW
Washington, DC 20036
202-822-7870

NABE Newsletter
Nancy F. Zelasko
Rm. 405
1201 16th St. NW
Washington, DC 20036

Russian Studies Newsletter
Susan M. Biddle
P.O. Box 262
Holden, MA 01520

TESOL Quarterly
Teachers of English to Speakers of Other Languages
1118 22d St. NW
Washington, DC 20037

Appendix C

Sources for Classroom Materials and Supplies

The lists below include suppliers of materials and resources known to the authors at this time through their own work. The addresses given were believed to be accurate at the time of printing.

The authors do not pretend to have produced a balanced or a definitive list of resources, nor to have noted all possible useful materials available from each source listed. The list is intended to give teachers a starting point for exploring the wealth of materials available to them, but the best information can be obtained from the companies themselves. Teachers are encouraged to go beyond the list offered here, by visiting exhibits at foreign language and elementary school teacher conferences, and by writing for catalogs and other information from companies that advertise in professional journals. The authors welcome suggestions from readers for sources to add to the list.

Textbook Publishers

Addison-Wesley Publishing Co.
World Language Division
Reading, MA 01867

Alemany Press
PO Box 5265
San Francisco, CA 94101

Allyn and Bacon
7 Wells Ave. Dept. 25
Newton, MA 02159

Amsco
315 Hudson St.
New York, NY 10013

Cambridge Book Co.
888 7th Ave.
New York, NY 10019

EMC Corporation
180 East Sixth St.
St. Paul, MN 55101

Encyclopedia Britannica
  Educational Corp.
425 N. Michigan Ave.
Chicago, IL 60611

Follett Publishing Co.
1010 W. Washington Blvd.
Chicago, IL 60607

Harcourt Brace Jovanovich
6277 Sea Harbor Drive
Orlando, FL 32821

Harper & Row/Newbury House
10 East 53d St.
New York, NY 10022

D.C. Heath and Co.
125 Spring St.
Lexington, MA 02173

Heinle and Heinle Publishers, Inc.
20 Park Plaza
Boston, MA 02116

Holt, Rinehart and Winston
CBS Ed + Prof. Bldg.
383 Madison Ave.
New York, NY 10017

Houghton Mifflin Company
1 Beacon St.
Boston, MA 02108

Laidlaw Brothers
Thatcher and Madison
River Forest, IL 60305

Langenscheidt Publishers
46-35 54th Rd.
Maspeth, NY 11378

Longman Inc.
95 Church St.
White Plains, NY 10601

McGraw-Hill Book Co.
1221 Avenue of the Americas
New York, NY 10020

Macmillan Publishing Co.
Front and Brown Streets
Riverside, NJ 08370

Merrill Publishing Co.
1300 Alum Creek Dr.
PO Box 508
Columbus, OH 43216-0508

National Textbook Co.
4255 West Touhy Ave.
Lincolnwood, IL 60646-1975

Oxford University Press
200 Madison Ave.
New York, NY 10016

Prentice-Hall/Regents
Educational Book Division
Englewood Cliffs, NJ 07632

Random House School Division
400 Hahn Rd.
Westminster, MD 21157

Santillana Publishing Co.
257 Union St.
Northvale, NJ 07647

Scholastic Book Services
904 Sylvan Ave.
Englewood Cliffs, NJ 07632

Scott, Foresman and Co.
1900 E. Lake Ave.
Glenview, IL 60025

Scribner Educational Publishers
Front and Brown Sts.
Riverside, NJ 08075

Silver Burdett Co.
250 James St.
Morristown, NJ 07960

Importers and Distributors

Continental Book Company
11-03 46th Ave.
Long Island City, NY 11101

Flame Co.
1476 Pleasantville Rd.
Briarcliff Manor, NY 10510

French and Spanish Book Corp.
115 5th Ave.
New York, NY 10003

Iaconi
300 Pennsylvania Ave.
San Francisco, CA 94107

Imported Books
PO Box 4414
Dallas, TX 75208

Interstate Periodical Distributors, Inc.
Box 2237, 201 E. Badger Rd.
Madison, WI 53701

Kiosk
19223 De Havilland Dr.
Saratoga, CA 95070

Kurtzman Book Sales, Inc.
1887 Chippingway
Bloomfield, MI 48013

Libros Españoles
1898 SW 8th Street
Miami, FL 33135

Midwest European Publications/
    Adler's
915 Foster Street
Evanston, IL 60201

Pan-American Book Co.
4362 Melrose Ave.
Los Angeles, CA 90029

Rizzoli International Publications
712 5th Avenue
New York, NY 10019

Mary S. Rosenberg
100 West 72d St.
New York, NY 10023

Western Continental Book Co.
625 E. 70th Ave. Unit #5
Denver, CO 80229

Sources for Visuals, Realia, and Manipulatives

ABC School Supply Inc.
6500 Peachtree Industrial Blvd.
PO Box 4750
Norcrosse, GA 30091

American Guidance Service (AGS)
Publisher's Building
Circle Pines, MN 55014

Cole Supply
PO Box 1717
Pasadena, TX 77501

Constructive Playthings
5314 W. Lincoln Ave.
Skokie, IL 60007

Cuisinaire Co. of America, Inc.
12 Church Street
Box D
New Rochelle, NY 10802

Delta Education
Box M
Nashua, NH 03061-6012

Discovery Toys
400 Ellingwood Way, Suite 300
Pleasant Hill, CA 94523

DLM Teaching Resources
PO Box 4000
One DLM Park
Allen, TX 75002

Easy Aids
256 S. Robertson Blvd.
Beverly Hills, CA 90211

Good Apple, Inc.
Box 299
Carthage, IL 62321

Ideal School Supply Co.
11000 S. Lavergne Ave.
Oak Lawn, IL 60453

Lakeshore Curriculum Materials Co.
2695 E. Dominguez Street
PO Box 6261
Carton, CA 90749

Magnetic Way
2495 N. Forest Rd.
Amherst, NY 14068

Milliken Publishing Co.
1100 Research Blvd.
PO Box 21579
St. Louis, MO 63132-0579

MPI-Michigan Products, Inc.
1200 Keystone Ave.
PO Box 24155
Lansing, MI 48909-4155

Nasco
901 Janesville Ave.
Fort Atkinson, WI 53538

National Dairy Council
6300 N. River Rd.
Rosemont, IL 60018-4233

N.C.T.M. Educational Materials
1906 Association Dr.
Reston, VA 22091

Society for Visual Education, Inc.
1345 S. Diversey Pkwy.
Chicago, IL 60614-1299

Language–Specific Materials in Several Languages

Alpha Plus Foreign Language
Systems
PO Box 3323
Edmond, OK 73083

Applause Learning Resources
85 Longview Rd.
Port Washington, NY 11050

B.B.C. (The British Council)
65 Davies St.
London WIY 2AA

Berty Segal, Inc.
1749 Eucalyptus Street
Brea, CA 92621

Board of Education of the City of
New York
Curriculum Production Unit
131 Livingston Street, Room 167
Brooklyn, NY 11201

Creative Learning Center
2518 Allen Blvd.
Middleton, WI 53562

European Publishers
Representatives, Inc.
1103 46th Street
Long Island City, NY 11101

Foreign Language Press
R.R. 1 Box 37A
Hull, IA 51239-9799

Gessler Publishing Company
131 East 23rd St.
New York, NY 10010

International Film Bureau, Inc.
332 South Michigan Ave.
Chicago, IL 60604

International Learning Systems, Inc.
1715 Connecticut Ave. NW
Washington, DC 20009

Lingo Fun
PO Box 486
Westerville, OH 43081

Sky Oaks Productions, Inc.
PO Box 1102
Los Gatos, CA 95031

Smile Press
PO Box 5451
Madison, WI 53705

Sumo Publishers
1005 Debra Ln.
Madison, WI 53704

Teacher's Discovery
1130 E. Big Beaver
Troy, MI 48083-1997

UNICEF
331 E. 38th St.
New York, NY 10016

J. Weston Walch, Publisher
PO Box 658
Portland, ME 04104

Wible Language Institute
24 South Eighth St.
Allentown, PA 18105

World Press
135 West 29th St.
New York, NY 10001

Language Specific Materials— Spanish

Alan Company
Box 16250
Clayton, MO 63105

American Dental Association
Marketing Services Dept.
211 E. Chicago Ave.
Chicago, IL 60611

Amidon Publications
1966 Benson Ave.
St. Paul, MN 55014

Ballard and Tighe Co.
480 Atlas St.
Brea, CA 92621

Bilingual Educational Services
2514 S. Grand Ave.
Los Angeles, CA 90007

Bilingual Media Productions
PO Box 9337
North Berkeley Station
Berkeley, CA 94709

Bilingual Publications Co.
1966 Broadway
New York, NY 10023

Borg Warner Spanish Systems 80
600 W. University Dr.
Arlington Heights, IL 60004-1889

CEEDE (Center for Educational
    Experimentation, Development,
    and Evaluation)
N345 Oakdale Hall
University of Iowa
Oakdale, Iowa 52319

Children's Book and Music Center
5373 W. Pico Blvd.
Los Angeles, CA 90019

Children's Press
1224 West Van Buren St.
Chicago, IL 60607

Communication Skill Builders
3130 N. Dodge Blvd.
Tucson, AZ 85733

Continental Press
PO Box 554
Elgin, IL 60120

George F. Cram Co.
PO Box 426
Indianapolis, IN 46206

Donars Spanish Books
PO Box 24
Loveland, CO 80539-0024

Dormac, Inc.
PO Box 1699
Beaverton, OR 97075-1699

Economics Press, Inc.
12 Daniel Rd.
Fairfield, NJ 07006

Editorial Juventud
Provenza 101
Barcelona-15
Spain

Educational Activities
PO Box 392
Freeport, NY 11520

Eye Gate Media
3333 Elston Ave.
Chicago, IL 60618

Fiesta International, Inc.
1026 Meadow Lark Lane
Darien, IL 60559

Fiesta Publishing Co., Inc.
1123 Moreno Blvd.
San Diego, CA 92110

Fiesta Publishing Corp.
6360 N.E. 4th Court
Miami, FL 33138

Flame Co.
1476 Pleasantville Rd.
Briarcliff Manor, NY 10510

Follett Library Book Co.
4506 Northwest Hwy.
Crystal Lake, IL 60014

Graphic Learning
PO Box 13829
Tallahassee, FL 32317

Grolier Educational Corp.
845 3d Ave.
New York, NY 10022

Hammond, Inc.
515 Valley St.
Maplewood, NJ 07040

Heffernan School Supply Co.
2111 W. Ave.
PO Box 5309
San Antonio, TX 78201

Incentives for Learning
600 W. Van Buren St.
Chicago, IL 60607

Jamestown Publishers
PO Box 9168
Providence, RI 02940

Joe Kelly Film Productions
4806 Ave. C
Corpus Christi, TX 78410

Lectorum Publications
137 W. 14th St.
New York, NY 10011

Linguametrics Group
PO Box 3495
San Rafael, CA 94912-3495

Listening Library, Inc.
PO Box L
Old Greenwich, CT 06870

Marshfilm
PO Box 8082
Shawnee Mission, KS 66208

Media Marketing, Inc.
PO box 564
Fairfax, VA 22030

Melton Peninsula, Inc.
1949 Stemmons Freeway, Suite 690
Dallas, TX 75207

Miami-Dade Community College
11011 S.W. 104th St.
Miami, FL 33176

Milliken Publishing Co.
1100 Research Blvd.
PO Box 21579
St. Louis, MO 63132-0579

National Clearinghouse on Bilingual
    Education
11501 Georgia Ave.
Wheaton, MD 20902

National Dairy Council
6300 N. River Rd.
Rosemont, IL 60018-4233

National Foundation for
    Improvement of Education
1201 16th Street NW #803E
Washington, DC 20036

National Health Information
    Clearinghouse
PO Box 1133
Washington, DC 20013-1133

Network Publications
ETR Associates
1700 Mission St., Suite 203
PO Box 1830
Santa Cruz, CA 95061-1830

Nienhuis Montessori
320 Pioneer Way
Mt. View, CA 94041

Notas Latinas
PO Box 8122
St. Paul, MN 55113

Nystrom
333 Elston Ave.
Chicago, IL 60618

Organization of American States
20006 Technical Music Unit
Washington, DC 20013

Pan-American Book Co.
4362 Melrose Ave.
Los Angeles, CA 90029

Rand McNally and Co.
Box 7600
Chicago, IL 60680

Rio Grande Book Co.
PO Box 2795-1101
McAllen, TX 78501

Santillana Publishing Co.
257 Union St.
Northvale, NJ 07647

Spanish Book Corporation of
America
115 5th Ave.
New York, NY 10003

Troll Associates
320 Ft. 17
Manwah, NJ 07430

United Learning
6633 W. Howard St.
Niles, IL 60648

United States Government Printing
Office
Superintendent of Documents
Washington, DC 20402

Yuquiyu Publishers
2546 W. Division St.
Chicago, IL 60622

**Language Specific Materials—
French**

Centre Franco-Ontarien des
Ressources Pédagogiques
339, rue Wilbrod
Ottawa (Ontario) K1N 6M4
Canada

Editions Etudes Vivantes
6700, chemin Côte de Liesse
Saint-Laurent (Quebec) H4T 1E3
Canada

Hachette
79, boulevard Saint-Germain
75288 Paris CEDEX 06
France

Hatier-Didier USA
220 East 95th St.
New York, NY 10028

Independent School Press
51 River Street
Wellesley Hills, MA 02181

Larousse (Continental Book Co.)
Div. of Eurobooks, Inc.
80-00 Cooper Ave. Bldg. #29
Glendale, NY 11385

Nathan, Inc. (USA)
200 5th Ave.
New York, NY 10101

Ontario Institute for Studies in
Education (OISE)
252 Bloor St. West
Toronto, Ontario
Canada M5S 1V6

Open Court Publishing Co.
Box 599
Peru, IL 61354-0599

Pergamon Press, Inc.
Fairview Park
Elmsford, NY 10523

Swiss National Tourist Office
608 5th Ave.
New York, NY 10020

Language Specific Materials—
German

American Association of
Teachers of German
Materials Center
Suite 201, Route 38
Cherry Hill, NJ 08034

German-American Chamber of
Commerce
666 5th Ave.
New York, NY 10019

German Federal Railroads
11 West 42d St.
New York, NY 10036

German Information Center
410 Park Ave.
New York, NY 10022

German Language Publications, Inc.
560 Sylvan Ave.
Englewood Cliffs, NJ 07632

German National Tourist Office
747 3d Avenue, 33d Floor
New York, NY 10017

German News Company, Inc.
218 East 86th St.
New York, NY 10028

Inter Nationes
Kennedyallee 91–103
5300 Bonn 2
Federal Republic of Germany

Langenscheidt Publishers
6-35 54th Rd.
Maspeth, NY 11378

Mail Order House "Quelle"
6050 Kennedy Boulevard East
West New York, NJ 07093

Swiss National Tourist Office
608 5th Ave.
New York, NY 10020

Language Specific Materials—
Asian Languages

Asian–American Bilingual Center
(Berkeley Schools)
2168 Shattuck Ave. 3d Floor
Berkeley, CA 94704

Bay Area Bilingual Education
League
2168 Shattuck Ave. Rm. 217
Berkeley, CA 94704

J.A.C.P. Inc.
414 E. 3d Ave.
San Mateo, CA 94401

Kodansha Int./USA
10 E. 53d St.
New York, NY 10022

Appendix D

Sample Objectives for Subject-Content Areas

Source: From *Milwaukee Public Schools Outcome-Based Education, Grades One and Four, for Mathematics, Science, and Social Studies.* 1987. Reprinted with the permission of the Milwaukee Public Schools.

GRADE ONE
LEARNER EXPECTATIONS
MATHEMATICS

A. Arithmetic

read, write, and say numbers (0 to 99)
identify place value for numbers to 99
identify halves, thirds, and fourths of a region or set
name or write the number that comes before or after any given number up
   to 100
compare numbers through 99
join and separate sets and write the appropriate equation
recall sums and differences to 10
solve addition and subtraction equations through 18 using concrete objects

B. Geometry

recognize when two figures appear to be the same shape

C. Measurement

measure in centimeters or inches a line segment that is a whole unit in length
identify penny, nickel, dime, and quarter and name the values
read, write, and tell time to the hour

D. Problem Solving

tell and solve simple story problems involving addition and subtraction using pictures

GRADE ONE
LEARNER EXPECTATIONS
SCIENCE

A. Problem-Solving

see relationships among objects and/or events
see exceptions to patterns
make accurate observations using the senses
order or group objects in terms of common properties
use characteristics of objects to group them

B. Knowledge

Properties of Objects
identify size, shape, and color as properties of objects
classify objects by size, shape, and color
identify the sources of different kinds of textures
identify the eyes, ears, nose, tongue, and skin as parts of the body that are able to detect particular sensations

Living Things
state that living things eat, move, grow, and change
observe, describe, and compare characteristics of living things and nonliving things
observe and describe different animals
describe ways that animals move, obtain food, protect themselves, and find shelter
observe that new plants can be produced from seeds and other parts of plants
observe and describe the roots, stems, and leaves of plants
group leaves and seeds by their properties
observe and describe ways that plants are different from each other
identify foods obtained from plants

Air and Water
observe air directly with the sense of touch and indirectly with the senses of sight, hearing, and smell
demonstrate that air occupies space and takes the shape of the container
demonstrate that water can change form
show that liquid water does not have its own shape

tell ways that people use water
identify and describe ways that water can be wasted and conserved
predict what would happen if plants and animals went without air and water
tell ways that people have polluted the air and water and how we can help
   to reduce this pollution

The Weather
describe different kinds of weather
observe and record appropriate changes in the weather
describe appropriate activities for different kinds of weather
describe appropriate clothing for different weather conditions

Rocks
observe and describe physical properties of rocks and soil
describe places where rocks may be found
list some ways that people use rocks and minerals
state some ways that plants and animals use soil

C. Nature of Science

show an awareness of some of the different ways that scientists make
   observations
become familiar with occupations in the field of science

D. Science, Technology, and Society

understand that developments in science and technology can improve or
   change the food we eat

GRADE ONE
LEARNER EXPECTATIONS
SOCIAL STUDIES

A. American Studies

locate and identify the United States on a map of North America
explain what a capital is and name our national capital
recognize symbols of our country and that Independence Day is our nation's
   birthday
recognize that the United States is made up of people from all over the world
recognize that the lifestyle of the pilgrims was different from the Native
   Americans they came to know

B. Social Sciences

recognize that every individual is both similar to and different from other
   people

recognize that families living near one another make up a neighborhood
recognize that most families live in neighborhoods and that several neighborhoods make up a large community
name and locate Milwaukee and Wisconsin on map
give examples of wants and needs
demonstrate how money is used
explain that families need food, clothing, and shelter
explain that families today depend on many workers to supply their basic
   needs
name special days that families celebrate
recognize that everyone has feelings and should be respected
discuss selected news events and media sources
use photographs, drawings, and charts to make observations about social
   happenings

C. World Studies

give examples of how people are alike and how they are different
recognize that people dress differently around the world
recognize that certain types of weather require special kinds of clothing
recognize that certain shelters are suitable for certain climatic conditions
illustrate some ways family members work together
compare a picture and a map

GRADE FOUR
LEARNER EXPECTATIONS
MATHEMATICS

A. Arithmetic

read, write, and say numbers 0 to 100 million
list factors for numbers through 50
read and write mixed numbers
identify the decimal number for a region or set (100ths)
order a group of numbers (0 to 100,000) from least to greatest
write any whole number in expanded notation
compare two fractions with like denominators
multiply mentally by 10, 100, or 1000
find products (a one-digit factor and a two-digit factor)
find quotients with one-digit divisors
estimate quotients and products
add and subtract fractions with like denominators

B. Geometry

identify pentagon, hexagon, and octagon

identify congruent figures including segments and angles
identify points, lines, and rays
find perimeter of polygon given the lengths of its sides

C. Measurement

estimate common lengths using standard units
measure length (km and mm)
measure capacity and volume (ml, l)
tell, read, and write time to the nearest minute

D. Statistics

construct bar graphs

E. Problem Solving

choose the correct operation in solving word problems
use the guess-and-test strategy in solving word problems

GRADE FOUR
LEARNER EXPECTATIONS
SCIENCE

A. Problem-Solving

note similarities and differences among objects and events
describe exceptions to patterns
use a variety of resources in seeking information about objects and events
observe objects and describe their chracteristics
use balances, scales, and other standard measuring devices to collect data
use observations and known information to predict events
use observations to make inferences
observe a variety of characteristics of an object and be able to place it in a
    given group

B. Knowledge

Insects
observe and describe the parts of an insect
describe and discuss how the specific features of insects help them survive
    in other habitats
name and describe a variety of habitats where insects live
explain why poisonous powders and sprays may affect people, animals and
    plants
discuss how insects grow and change (life cycle)

Machines and Force
use and identify force as a push or pull
identify parts of five simple machines and describe how each simple machine
    makes work easier
tell what friction is
discuss ways that the development of machines have changed certain aspects
    of human life

Bones and Muscles
identify various bones in the body and describe their function
identify different kinds of joints and demonstrate their actions
identify cartilage and ligaments and describe their function
observe and describe the actions of muscles and tendons

Matter
identify properties common to all matter
measure changes in temperature when heat is added or taken away from
    matter
observe and describe physical changes that take place in matter when heat
    is added or taken away
classify matter as solid, liquid, or gas based on its physical properties
explain some of the benefits of being able to change matter from one form
    to another

The Earth's Atmosphere
state that air is matter, has mass, and takes up space
name several gases in the atmosphere and state the importance of each
define air pressure as the force that is caused by air molecules pressing
    against objects
compare the mass of equal volumes of cold and warm air
describe the movements of air as it is heated and cooled
state three ways to keep the air from becoming polluted

The Solar System
identify the three major types of objects that make up the solar system
explain the action of the force that holds the members of the solar system
    together
use models to demonstrate a revolution and describe a year as the time
    required for one revolution
use models to demonstrate rotation and explain how it causes night and day
demonstrate the relationship between the slant of the sun's rays and the
    temperature of the air
explain the reason for the apparent movement of planets in the sky
identify and describe some features and characteristics of the planets in our
    solar system
discuss ways that space travel and exploration can affect certain aspects of
    our lives

Rocks and Fossils
observe various rocks and group them by their properties
observe crystals and describe how they are formed
describe the conditions necessary for the formation of igneous, sedimentary, and metamorphic rocks
explain how fossils have helped us learn more about the history of our Earth
name and describe two varieties of sedimentary, igneous, and metamorphic rock

Sunlight and Green Plants
observe and describe the process of photosynthesis and explain its importance
describe chlorophyll and its function
describe the structure and function of roots, stems, and leaves
observe and label the parts of green plants
describe the process of pollination and explain its importance

C. Nature of Science

understand that science can be practiced by many kinds of people at different levels of complexity
know that there is no single "scientific method" that is used by all scientists

D. Science, Technology, and Society

appreciate that the proper management of natural resources greatly affects the quality of life on Earth now and in future generations
understand that technological developments affect the way students and members of their families live and work
understand that technological developments affect the way people use their leisure time
understand that medical science and technology improve chances of good health and longer life

GRADE FOUR
LEARNER EXPECTATIONS
SOCIAL STUDIES

A. American Studies

locate Wisconsin on a map of the United States
name the four states adjacent to Wisconsin
identify Madison as the capitol of Wisconsin
locate Lake Michigan, the Mississippi River, and the Wisconsin River on a map of Wisconsin

recognize that Native Americans were the first people to populate the United States

recognize that Wisconsin is populated with humans from all over the world

recognize that all of the people who populated Wisconsin contributed to our culture

recognize that Wisconsin moved from a basically agricultural economy to an industrial economy

B. Social Sciences

describe the lifestyles of the Native Americans found in Wisconsin

explain how European explorers and missionaries came to the area that was to become Wisconsin

recognize how permanent settlers led to statehood for Wisconsin

recognize the impact permanent settlers had on Native Americans

discuss the impact of lumbering, farming, and manufacturing on the history of Wisconsin

explain the legislative, executive, and judicial branches of Wisconsin state government

identify the two basic types of local governments found in Wisconsin (city and county)

explain how citizens of Wisconsin may participate in the national government

recognize how Wisconsin was a pioneer in the area of women's rights

explain how urban areas such as Milwaukee are important to the state of Wisconsin

identify the key elements of Wisconsin economy today (manufacturing, farming, tourism, services)

C. World Studies

describe the climate of Wisconsin

explain how glaciers affected Wisconsin's topography.

define and illustrate physical features of the earth (plateau, canyon, delta, harbor, etc.)

define the term *hemisphere*

recognize key lines of latitude and longitude (equator, prime meridian, arctic circle)

use contour lines to determine elevation

describe and locate examples of forest regions

describe and locate examples of desert regions

describe and locate examples of the two types of plains

describe and locate examples of mountain regions

analyze how different regions affect lifestyles of people around the world

illustrate that regions are interdependent because of the uneven geographical distribution of resources

Appendix E

A Core Library for the Elementary School Foreign Language Teacher

The following references have been particularly useful to the authors, both in their own classroom work and in the preparation of this book. At the time of publication they represent, in our opinion, the key resources for a professional library on elementary school foreign languages. (The numbers in parentheses indicate the chapters to which these references apply.)

Asher, James J. *Learning Another Language Through Actions: The Complete Teacher's Guidebook.* 3d Edition. Los Gatos, CA: Sky Oaks Publications, 1986.

The definitive description of Total Physical Response; includes an extended day-by-day plan. (8)

California State Department of Education, Bilingual Education Office. *Studies on Immersion Education: A Collection for United States Educators.* Los Angeles: California State University; Evaluation, Dissemination, and Assessment Center, 1984.

Summarizes immersion research and its implications for programs in the United States. (3, 6)

Cantoni-Harvey, Gina. *Content-Area Language Instruction: Approaches and Strategies.* Reading, MA: Addison-Wesley, 1987.

A practical set of applications of content-based teaching to the language classroom. (7, 8)

Damen, Louise. *Culture Learning: The Fifth Dimension in the Language Classroom.* Reading, MA: Addison-Wesley, 1987.

A thorough guide to the concept of culture and its role in the language classroom. (9)

Dixon, Carol, and Denise Nessel. *Language Experience Approach to Reading (and Writing): Language Experience Reading for Second Language Learners.* Hayward, CA: Alemany Press, 1983.

Provides information about the Language Experience Approach and activities for various stages of second language development. (8)

Dulay, Heidi, Marina Burt, and Stephen Krashen. *Language Two*. New York, NY: Oxford University Press, 1982.
An informative and practical discussion of second language acquisition in theory and practice. (5)

Johnson, David W., and Robert T. Johnson. *Learning Together and Alone*. Englewood Cliffs, NJ: Prentice-Hall, 1987.
Background and strategies for developing cooperative learning structures in the classroom. (10)

Klippel, Friederike. *Keep Talking: Communicative Fluency Activities for Language Teaching*. New York: Cambridge University Press, 1984.
Group and pair activities, with guidelines for using them. (8, 10, 13)

Krashen, Stephen D., and Tracy Terrell. *The Natural Approach. Language Acquisition in the Classroom*. Hayward, CA: Alemany Press, 1983.
Discussion of second language acquisition theory and its implications for the language classroom. Contains guidelines for a communicative, action-based approach to language teaching. (5, 8)

Lipton, Gladys. *Practical Handbook to Elementary Foreign Language Programs*. Lincolnwood, IL: National Textbook Company, 1988.
Compendium of information regarding establishing and maintaining FLES, FLEX and Immersion programs. (1-14)

Rhodes, Nancy, and Audrey Schreibstein. *Foreign Language in the Elementary School: A Practical Guide*. Washington, DC: Center for Applied Linguistics, 1983. ED 225 403.
A concise description of models and summary of techniques for elementary school language programs. (3, 4)

Savignon, Sandra J. *Communicative Competence: Theory and Classroom Practice: Texts and Contexts in Second Language Learning*. Reading, MA: Addison-Wesley, 1983.
Discusses the communicative competence movement and provides practical guidelines for curriculum and materials. A basic resource for the communicative syllabus. (5, 11)

Schinke-Llano, Linda. *Foreign Language in the Elementary School: State of the Art*. Washington, DC: Center for Applied Linguistics, 1985.
Explores theoretical and practical aspects of elementary second language programs. Contains an extensive bibliography. ED 264 715. (2, 3, 4)

Wright, Andrew, D. Betteridge, and M. Buckby. *Games for Language Learning* (2d ed.). New York: Cambridge University Press, 1984.
A resource book of games, with emphasis on communication and cooperation. (13)

Yunus, Noor Azlina. *Preparing and Using Aids for English Language Teachers*. Kuala Lumpur, Maylaysia: Oxford University Press, 1981.
Presents techniques for making and using a variety of teaching aids, such as flannel boards, pocket charts, pictures, and so forth. (12)

Works Cited

This list includes the works that have been cited within the chapters of this book. *For Further Reading*, at the end of each chapter, lists additional reference books and articles which may be of interest for specific topics.

Some of the resources listed are identified by an ERIC (Educational Resources Information Center) Document number (e.g., ED 208 653). These documents can be read on microfiche at libraries with an ERIC collection, or ordered in paper copy from the ERIC Document Reproduction Service (EDRS), 3900 Wheeler Avenue, Alexandria, VA 22304. For the location of an ERIC collection nearest you, write to ERIC Clearinghouse on Languages and Linguistics, Center for Applied Linguistics, 1118 22d Street NW, Washington D.C. 20037.

Academic Preparation for College: What Students Need to Know and Be Able to Do. New York: The College Board, 1983.

ACTFL. *Second Languages and the Basics.* Hastings-on-Hudson, NY: American Council on the Teaching of Foreign Languages, 1984.

Ada, Alma Flor, and María Pilar de Olave. *Hagamos Caminos.* Reading, MA: Addison-Wesley, 1986.

Alkonis, Nancy V., and Mary A. Brophy. "A Survey of FLES Practices." *Reports of Surveys and Studies in the Teaching of Modern Foreign Languages, 1959–1961.* New York: The Modern Language Association of America, 1961.

Anderson, Helena. Personal communication, Milwaukee, 1980 and 1982.

Andersson, Theodore. *Foreign Languages in the Elementary School: A Struggle Against Mediocrity.* Austin, TX: University of Texas Press, 1969.

Asher, James J. *Learning Another Language Through Actions: The Complete Teacher's Guidebook.* 3d ed. Los Gatos, CA: Sky Oaks Publications, 1986.

Bassano, Sharron, and Mary Ann Christison. *Look Who's Talking.* Hayward, CA: Alemany Press, 1987.

Becoming a Nation of Readers: The Report of the Commission on Reading. Washington, DC: National Institute of Education, 1985.

Byrne, Donn. *Materials for Language Teaching 1 and 2, Interaction Packages A and B.* Oxford, England: Modern English Publications, 1980.

Byrnes, Heidi, and Michael Canale, eds. *Defining and Developing Proficiency Guidelines, Implementations, and Concepts.* Lincolnwood, IL: National Textbook Company, 1987.

California State Department of Education, Bilingual Education Office. *Studies on Immersion Education: A Collection for United States Educators.* Los Angeles: California State University; Evaluation, Dissemination, and Assessment Center, 1984.

Campbell, Russell N. "The Immersion Approach to Foreign Language Teaching." *Studies on Immersion Education: A Collection for United States Educators.* Sacramento: California State Department of Education, 1984: 114–143.

Campbell, Russell N., Tracy C. Gray, Nancy C. Rhodes, and Marguerite Ann Snow. "Foreign Language Learning in the Elementary Schools: A Comparison of Three Language Programs." *The Modern Language Journal* 69 no. 1 (Spring 1985):44–54.

Canale, Michael, and Merrill Swain. *Communicative Approaches to Second Language Teaching and Testing.* Toronto: The Minister of Education, 1979.

Cantoni-Harvey, Gina. *Content-Area Language Instruction: Approaches and Strategies.* Reading, MA: Addison-Wesley, 1987.

Carpenter, John A., and Judith V. Torney. "Beyond the Melting Pot." In Patricia Maloney Markun, ed., *Childhood and Intercultural Education: Overview and Research.* Washington, DC: Association for Childhood Education International, 1974: 14–23.

Center for Applied Linguistics. "Total and Partial Immersion Language Programs in U.S. Elementary Schools." Unpublished list. 1987.

Chamot, Anna Uhl, and J. Michael O'Malley. *A Cognitive Academic Language Learning Approach: An ESL Content-Based Curriculum.* Rosslyn, VA: National Clearinghouse for Bilingual Education, 1986.

Cohen, Andrew D. "The Culver City Spanish Immersion Program: The First Two Years." *The Modern Language Journal* 58 no. 3, 95–103.

College Board. *Academic Preparation for College. What Students Need to Know and Be Able To Do.* New York: The College Board, 1983.

Cook, Doris M., ed. *A Guide to Curriculum Planning in Reading.* Madison, WI: Wisconsin Department of Public Instruction, 1986.

Crandall, JoAnn, ed. *ESL through Content-Area Instruction: Math, Science, Social Studies.* Englewood Cliffs, NJ: Prentice Hall, 1987.

Cummins, James. "The Role of Primary Language Development in Promoting Educational Success for Language Minority Students." *Schooling and Language Minority Students: A Theoretical Framework.* Los Angeles: California State University; Evaluation, Dissemination, and Assessment Center, 1981.

Curtain, Helena Anderson. "Integrating Language and Content Instruction," *ERIC/CLL News Bulletin* 9 no. 2 (March 1986).

Curtain, Helena Anderson, ed. *The Milwaukee Public Schools Immersion Programs: A Teacher's Guide.* Milwaukee: Milwaukee Public Schools, 1987.

Dixon, Carol, and Denise Nessel. *Language Experience Approach to Reading (and Writing): Language Experience Reading for Second Language Learners.* Hayward, CA: Alemany Press, 1983.

Dolson, David P. *The Application of Immersion Education in the United States.* Rosslyn, VA: National Clearinghouse for Bilingual Education, 1985.

Donoghue, Mildred R. *Foreign Languages and the Elementary School Child.* Dubuque, IA: William C. Brown, 1968.

Dreke, Michael, and Wolfgang Lind. *Wechselspiel.* New York: Langenscheidt, 1986.

Dulay, Heidi, Marina Burt, and Stephen Krashen. *Language Two.* New York: Oxford University Press, 1982.

Estelle, Emelda. Personal communication, Chicago, 1985.

Fluegelman, Andrew, ed. *The New Games Book.* Garden City, NY: Dolphin Books, Doubleday, 1976.

Gardner, David P., ed. *A Nation at Risk: The Imperative for Educational Reform.* Washington, DC: U.S. Department of Education, 1983.

Genesee, Fred. "Historical and Theoretical Foundations of Immersion Education." In *Studies on Immersion Education: A Collection for United States Educators.* Sacramento: California State Department of Education, 1984: 32–57.

Global Perspectives in Education. *Intercom: Moving Toward a Global Perspective: Social Studies and Second Languages.* New York, NY: Global Perspectives in Education, 1983.

Glover, John A., and Roger H. Bruning. *Educational Psychology: Principles and Applications.* 2d ed. Boston: Little, Brown, and Company, 1987.

Grittner, Frank. *Teaching Foreign Languages.* New York: Harper and Row, 1977.

Grittner, Frank, ed. *A Guide to Curriculum Planning in Foreign Language.* Madison, WI: Wisconsin Department of Public Instruction, 1985.

Gunderson, Barbara, and David Johnson. "Building Positive Attitudes by Using Cooperative Learning Groups," *Foreign Language Annals* 13 (1980):39–43.

Hansen-Krening, Nancy. *Language Experiences for All Students.* Menlo Park, CA: Addison-Wesley, 1982.

Holdzkom, D., L. Reed, E. Porter, and D. Rubin. *Research Within Reach: Oral and Written Communication.* Washington, DC: The National Institute of Education, 1982.

Holobow, N., F. Genesee, W. E. Lambert, M. Met, and J. Gasright. "Effectiveness of Partial French Immersion for Children from Different Social Class and Ethnic Backgrounds.": *Applied Sociolinguistics,* 1987.

Johnson, David W., and Robert T. Johnson. *Learning Together and Alone.* Englewood Cliffs, NJ: Prentice-Hall, 1987.

Jonas, Sister Ruth Adelaide. "The Twinned Classroom Approach to FLES," *Modern Language Journal* 53 no. 5 (May 1969):342–46.

Kalivoda, Theodore B., Genelle Morain, and Robert J. Elkins. "The Audio-Motor Unit: A Listening Comprehension Strategy That Works," *Foreign Language Annals* 4 no. 4 (May 1971):392–400.

Kennedy, Dora F., and William De Lorenzo. *Complete Guide to Exploratory Foreign Language Programs.* Lincolnwood, IL: National Textbook Company, 1985.

Klippel, Friederike. *Keep Talking: Communicative Fluency Activities for Language Teaching.* New York: Cambridge University Press, 1984.

Knop, Constance K. Workshop handout. Concordia College, Moorhead, MN, 1986. Also in Frank Grittner, ed. *A Guide to Curriculum Planning in Foreign Language.* Madison: Wisconsin Department of Public Instruction, 1985: 55.

Krashen, Stephen D. "Bilingual Education and Second Language Acquisition Theory," in *Schooling and Language Minority Students: A Theoretical Framework.* Los Angeles, CA: California State University; Evaluation, Dissemination, and Assessment Center, 1981(a).

Krashen, Stephen D. *Second Language Acquisition and Second Language Learning.* Oxford, England: Pergamon Press, 1981(b).

Krashen, Stephen D., Robin C. Scarcella, and Michael H. Long, eds. *Child-Adult Differences in Second Language Acquisition.* Rowley, MA: Newbury House, 1982.

Krashen, Stephen D., and Tracy Terrell. *The Natural Approach. Language Acquisition in the Classroom.* Hayward, CA: Alemany Press, 1983.

Lambert, Wallace E., and Otto Klineberg. *Children's Views of Foreign People.* New York: Appleton-Century-Crofts, 1967.

Lambert, Wallace E., and G. Richard Tucker. *Bilingual Education of Children: The St. Lambert Experiment.* Rowley, MA: Newbury House, 1972.

Lambert, Wallace E. "An Overview of Issues in Immersion Education." In *Studies on Immersion Education: A Collection for United States Educators.* Sacramento: California State Department of Education, 1984:8–30.

Landry, Richard G. "The Enhancement of Figural Creativity Through Second Language Learning at the Elementary School Level," *Foreign Language Annals* 7 no. 1 (October 1973): 111–115.

Linse, Caroline. *The Children's Response. TPR and Beyond Toward Writing.* Hayward, CA: Alemany Press, 1983.

Lipton, Gladys, Nancy C. Rhodes, and Helena Anderson Curtain, eds. *The Many Faces of Foreign Language in the Elementary School: FLES, FLEX and Immersion.* Champaign, IL: American Association of Teachers of French, 1986. ED 264 727.

Long, Michael. "Native Speaker/Non-native Speaker: Conversation in the Second Language Classroom." In M. Clarke and J. Handscomb, eds., *On TESOL '82: Pacific Perspectives on Language Learning and Teaching.* Washington, DC: TESOL, 1983.

Los Angeles County Office of Education. *Sheltered English: Content Area Instruction for Limited English Proficient Students—Training Guide.* Los Angeles, CA: Los Angeles County Office of Education, 1983.

Masciantonio, Rudolph. "Tangible Benefits of the Study of Latin: A Review of Research." *Foreign Language Annals* 10 no. 4 (September 1977): 375–382.

McGillivray, W. Russ, ed. *More French, S'il vous plaît!* Ottawa: Canadian Parents for French, 1985.

Met, Myriam. Personal communication, Cincinnati, 1982.

Met, Myriam, and Eileen Lorenz. "What It Means to Be an Immersion Teacher." In preparation.

Milwaukee Public Schools. *Outcome-Based Education Curriculum*. Milwaukee, WI: Milwaukee Public Schools, 1987.

Mohan, Bernard. *Language and Content*. Reading, MA: Addison-Wesley, 1986.

Morrow, Keith. "Principles of Communicative Methodology." In Keith Johnson and Keith Morrow, eds., *Communication in the Classroom*. Burnt Mill, Harlow, Essex, UK: Longman, 1981.

NABIEP. "Critical Needs in International Education: Recommendations for Action." *A Report to the Secretary of Education by the National Advisory Board on International Education Programs*. Washington, DC: U.S. Government Printing Office, 1983.

Nerenz, Ann and Constance Knop. "The Effect of Group Size on Student's Opportunity to Learn in the Second Language," In Alan Garfinkel, ed., *ESL and the Foreign Language Teacher*, Skokie, IL: National Textbook Company, 1982.

New York State Association of Foreign Language Teachers. *Foreign Languages in Careers: A Handbook for Teachers and Supervisors*. New York: New York State Association of Foreign Language Teachers, 1982.

New York State Education Department. *Modern Languages for Communication. New York State Syllabus*. Albany, NY: The State Education Department, 1987.

Omaggio, Alice C. *Games and Simulations in the Foreign Language Classroom*. Arlington, VA: Center for Applied Linguistics, 1978.

Penalosa, Fernando. *Introduction to the Sociology of Language*. Rowley, MA: Newbury House, 1981.

President's Commission on Foreign Language and International Studies. *Strength through Wisdom: A Critique of U.S. Capability*. Washington, DC: United States Government Printing Office, 1979.

Rafferty, Eileen A. *Second Language Study and Basic Skills in Louisiana*. Baton Rouge: Louisiana Department of Education, 1986.

Rathmell, George. *Benchmarks in Reading*. Hayward, CA: The Alemany Press, 1984.

Ratte, E. H. "Foreign Language and the Elementary School Language Arts Program." *The French Review* 42 (1968): 80–85.

Rigg, Pat. "Reading in ESL: Learning From Kids." In Rigg, Pat and D. Scott Enright, eds., *Children and ESL: Integrating Perspectives*. Washington, DC: TESOL, 1986.

Rigg, Pat, and D. Scott Enright, eds. *Children and ESL: Integrating Perspectives.* Washington, DC: TESOL, 1986.

Rivers, Wilga M. "Comprehension and Production in Interactive Language Teaching." *The Modern Language Journal* 70 no. 1 (1986):1–7.

Romijn, E., and C. Seely. *Live Action English.* Elmsford, NY: Pergamon Press, 1983.

Savignon, Sandra J. *Communicative Competence: Theory and Classroom Practice: Texts and Contexts in Second Language Learning.* Reading, MA: Addison-Wesley, 1983.

Schinke-Llano, Linda. *"Programmatic and Instructional Aspects of Language Immersion Programs."* Unpublished manuscript, 1984. Available from SRA Technologies, 2570 W. El Camino Real, Suite 402, Mountain View, CA 94040.

Schinke-Llano, Linda. *Foreign Language in the Elementary School: State of the Art.* Washington, DC: Center for Applied Linguistics, 1985. ED 264 715.

Schnitzler, Wolfgang. Personal communication, New York, 1986.

Seelye, H. Ned. *Teaching Culture.* Lincolnwood, IL: National Textbook Company, 1984.

Segal, Berty. *Teaching English Through Actions.* Brea, CA: Berty Segal, Inc., n.d. Available from Berty Segal, Inc., 1749 Eucalyptus St., Brea, CA. 92621

Simon, Paul. *The Tongue-Tied American. Confronting the Foreign Language Crisis.* New York: Continuum Publishing Corporation, 1980.

Snow, Marguerite Ann. *Immersion Teacher Handbook.* Los Angeles: UCLA, Center for Language Education and Research (CLEAR), 1987.

Strasheim, Lorraine A., and Walter H. Bartz. *Modern Foreign Language Generic Competencies Levels I–IV.* Advance copy. Indianapolis, Indiana: Indiana Department of Education, 1984.

Swain, Merrill. "What Does Research Say About Immersion Education?" In Beth Mlacak and Elaine Isabelle, eds., *So You Want Your Child to Learn French.* Ottawa, Canada: Canadian Parents for French, 1979.

Swain, Merrill. "A Review of Immersion Education in Canada: Research and Evaluation Studies." In *Studies on Immersion: A Collection for United States Educators.* Sacramento, CA: California State Department of Education, 1984:87–112.

Swain, Merrill. "Communicative Competence: Some Roles of Comprehensible Input and Comprehensible Output in Its Development." In Susan M. Gass and Carolyn G. Madden, eds., *Input in Second Language Acquisition.* Series in Second Language Research. Rowley, MA: Newbury House, 1985, 235–253.

Swain, Merrill, and Sharon Lapkin. *Bilingual Education in Ontario: A Decade of Research.* Toronto: Ontario Institute for Studies in Education, 1981. Available from Ontario Institute for Studies in Education, 252 Bloor St. West, Toronto, Ontario M5S 1V6.

Thonis, Eleanor Wall. *Teaching Reading to Non-English Speakers.* New York: The Macmillan Company, 1970.

Van Ek, J. A. *The Threshold Level for Modern Language Learning in Schools.* The Council of Europe. London: Longman, 1977.

Vygotsky, Lev. *Thought and Language.* Cambridge, MA: MIT Press, 1986.

Wadsworth, Barry J. *Piaget's Theory of Cognitive and Affective Development.* 3d ed. New York: Longman, 1984.

Winocur, S. Lee. "Developing Lesson Plans with Cognitive Objectives." In Arthur S. Costa, ed., *Developing Minds: A Resource Book for Teaching Thinking.* Alexandria, VA: Association for Supervision and Curriculum Development, 1985.

Wollstein, John D. Personal communication. Atlanta, 1987. (For information about TELEclass he may be contacted at Hawaii Dept. of Education, 189 Lunalilo Home Rd., Honolulu, Hawaii 96825.)

Wong-Fillmore, Lily. "The Language Learner as an Individual: Implications of Research on Individual Differences for the ESL Teacher." In M.A. Clark and J. Handscombe eds., *On TESOL '82: Pacific Perspectives on Language Learning and Teaching.* Washington, DC: TESOL, 1983.

Wong-Fillmore, Lily. "When Does Teacher Talk Work as Input?" In Susan M. Gass and Carolyn G. Madden, eds., *Input in Second Language Acquisition.* Series in Second Language Research. Rowley, MA: Newbury House, 1985: 17–50.

Wright, Andrew, D. Betteridge, and M. Buckby. *Games for Language Learning* (Second edition). New York: Cambridge University Press, 1984.

Yorkey, Richard. *Talk-A-Tivities.* Reading, MA: Addison-Wesley, 1985.

Yunus, Noor Azlina. *Preparing and Using Aids for English Language Teachers.* Kuala Lumpur, Malaysia: Oxford University Press, 1981.

Zamora, Gloria Rodriguez, and Rebecca Maria Barrera. *Nuevo Amanecer: Teacher's Reference Book.* Lincolnwood, IL: National Textbook Company, 1985.

Zeydel, Edwin H. "The Teaching of German in the United States from Colonial Times to the Present." *Reports of Surveys and Studies in the Teaching of Modern Foreign Languages, 1959–1961.* New York: The Modern Language Association of America, 1961.

Index